THE
MAGNIFICENT
SEASONS

THE MAGNIFICENT SEASONS

ART SHAMSKY

WITH
BARRY ZEMAN

INTRODUCTION BY
BOB COSTAS

FOREWORDS BY
JOE NAMATH, TOM SEAVER,
AND **BILL BRADLEY**

THOMAS DUNNE BOOKS
ST. MARTIN'S PRESS NEW YORK

www.stmartins.com

Design by The Book Design Group

Library of Congress Cataloging-in-Publication Data

Shamsky, Art.
  The magnificent seasons / Art Shamsky with Barry Zeman; introduction by Bob Costas; forewords by Joe Namath, Tom Seaver, and Bill Bradley.
    p. cm.
  ISBN 0-312-33358-7
  EAN 978-0312-33358-4
  1. Sports—New York (State)—New York—History—20th century. 2. Football—New York (State)—New York—History—20th century. 3. Baseball—New York (State)—New York—History—20th century. 4. Basketball—New York (State)—New York—History—20th century. I. Zeman, Barry. II. Title.
  GV584.5.N4S53 2004
  796'.09747—dc22

                                                                                    2004052781

First Edition: November 2004

10 9 8 7 6 5 4 3 2 1

This book is dedicated to every player, coach, and manager who was part of these three teams that are etched in history. Quite simply, they are the reasons there are magnificent seasons to write about. It is their significance and importance that made this incredible period of time the best in New York City sports history. At the same time, against the backdrop of tremendously trying times in the city and a country constantly in turmoil, these teams not only honored themselves, but raised the spirits of everyone who followed them. All of the members of these teams are forever entrenched in the memories of people who were actually there and even those who weren't, but have had the legacy passed on to them.

In memorium:

Jets	Mets	Knicks
Weeb Ewbank	Gil Hodges	Red Holzman
Clive Rush	Rube Walker	Dave DeBusschere
Joe Spencer	Cal Koonce	Nate Bowman
Verlon Biggs	Tommie Agee	Danny Whelan
	Tug McGraw	
	Gus Mauch	

Contents

Acknowledgments

I cannot begin to thank all of the people who helped in this book's endeavor. Without them the end result would not have been possible. No doubt I will forget to mention someone. If that happens, please forgive me. First, I would like to thank Barry Zeman for his knowledge and valuable help. He was able to make sense out of many of my words and sentences and was able to help me turn them into much better results. My personal thanks go out to Joe Namath, Tom Seaver, Bill Bradley, and Bob Costas for their confidence in me and their graciousness in writing down their thoughts. I would also like to thank LeRoy Neiman, an incredible talent who has allowed me to use his artwork for the cover. Thanks to Peter Wolverton and John Parsley from St. Martin's Press, whose steady guidance helped me through this process. Additional thanks go to Tony Seidl for his belief in the book from the beginning.

To all the wonderful people I conducted interviews with, thank you for your time, your insight, your patience and most importantly, your memories. Without all of you, quite simply, there would be no book.

Other people who have contributed include John Cirilla, Margeret Adams, Lee Stacey, Danielle Clyne, Drew Nieporent, Jim Martin, Dennis D'Agostino, Jonathan Supranowitz, Dick Gordon, John Campi, Ira Berkow, Melody Wright, Pam Davis, Cabot Marks, Ed Schauder, Patrick Barragan, John J. Tormey III, Mary Dattner, and Maury Allen. And, special thanks to Angela Zeman for her encouragement, patience, and expert writing advice. My sincerest thanks to all of you.

Finally, I would like to thank my wife Kim, who kicked me in the rear to pursue this project. She is the reason it finally came to fruition.

Foreword
by Joe Namath

My most vivid and cherished memories, as you would imagine, are of the Jets' 1968 season culminating in winning the AFL–NFL Championship on January 12, 1969. Now called the Super Bowl, our championship changed the face of professional football. It was a happy and enthusiastic time for the Jets, Jets fans, and AFL fans, amid a dark and troublesome time in the annals of our country and New York City.

The rewards and great memories for me come not only from being part of a team and a league that were overwhelming underdogs and winning it all, but equally because we lifted people's spirits in a very difficult time. The political climate, lack of trust and confidence in many of our leaders, and unresolved social issues, all combined to put citizens of our country and New York City in a continual state of turmoil. I have been told many times over the years that the Jets, and then the Mets and Knicks, helped people emotionally deal with all this adversity. As sports figures, we were important to our society as a whole, not only for what we did, but how we did it. The Jets of that season were known as underdogs, the working man's team; an unselfish and cohesive unit that never gave up. Our fans have never forgotten. That has been as great an honor as the championship itself.

The Jets, Mets, and Knicks struggled for many years to get to the pinnacle. They had to overcome big odds and fight hard to get there. Anyone who has been an underdog will appreciate what happened during that time when these three teams rose to the top to capture their sport's ultimate prize. Along the way they also captured the hearts and minds of the people as well.

While I personally may have won many accolades in that championship season, my fondest memory comes back to a season shared with incredible teammates who made it all happen. While the New York Jets were the first to win a world championship in that period, the Mets and Knicks followed in a way that most likely will never happen again. It was a time of unparalleled darkness, and yet, all of our teams brought light into that darkness. All of us who were on those teams are very proud to have been part of that.

This book will give an unusual insider's look into what happened in that remarkable sixteen-month period when three unlikely New York City teams all won their first world championships. For the fan, or indeed anyone who wants to read a rousing story of heart, courage, and perseverance, *The Magnificent Seasons* is for you. Much of what you read will appear as if it took place in another world. In many ways it did. This book will take you back in time, but only to learn more about what it was really like. Three teams—three world champions. Never before have I seen so many insights from so many individuals involved in such unique events. I believe you will enjoy it.

Foreword
by Tom Seaver

Time seemed to stand still in 1969 as the world rolled forward. Men walked on the moon. The Vietnam War raged on as campuses and city streets erupted in protest over our involvement in Southeast Asia. President Richard Nixon was in the Oval Office, and Clay Shaw was acquitted of conspiracy charges in the murder of John F. Kennedy. James Earl Ray was sentenced to ninety-nine years in prison for the murder of Dr. Martin Luther King, and the Charles Manson murders took place in southern California.

The *Saturday Evening Post* ceased publication, *Bonanza* was the top-rated show on TV, and *Midnight Cowboy* walked away with the Academy Award for Best Picture. Over half a million people flocked to upstate New York for a music festival we all remember as Woodstock.

Joe Namath and the New York Jets brashly stunned the world of professional football by defeating the Baltimore Colts in the Super Bowl. The New York Knicks became world champions as well in professional basketball. And, amazingly, the New York Mets defeated the powerhouse Baltimore Orioles in five games to win the World Series and cap off baseball's 100th anniversary.

I vividly recall some of the events of 1969, such as "The Eagle has landed . . . that's one small step for man, one giant leap for mankind," as Neil Armstrong stepped off Apollo XI and onto the surface of the moon. It was arguably one of the proudest days in American history.

Some of my memories are vague with the passage of time and some very vivid, such as the men on the moon. I do not remember the longest dock strike in New York history ending after fifty-seven days or Governor Nelson Rockefeller traveling to South America selling the merits of New York State or the passing of former President Dwight D. Eisenhower.

But, I certainly remember very vividly the steely strength and leadership of Gil Hodges as he directed with precision a group of young men through the course of a 162-game season.

Among the most vivid memories of that 1969 season was the solid rock behind our pitching staff: Jerry Grote. As we gathered for spring training in St. Petersburg, Florida, Jerry would boast in the locker room or on the practice field to anybody who would listen that the Mets could and would win the "whole shootin' match." (Don't forget, he's a Texan.) I must say most of us on the team thought he was crazy, as we had finished ninth the previous year, but he had seen glimpses of our promise. In hindsight, with Jerry being on the receiving end of a pitching staff with the fine young arms of Jerry Koosman, Gary Gentry, Nolan Ryan, Tug Mc-Graw, Jim McAndrew, and myself, he had firsthand recognition that we could potentially be good enough to do the same thing Joe Namath and the young franchise of the New York Jets had done just a month earlier.

When the Jets won the Super Bowl I was probably in the middle of final exams at USC, and I'm sure the thought of the 1969 Mets accomplishing the same thing was light-years from my mind.

Gil Hodges was on the same page as his catcher when he stated, "I think we can win eighty-five games. Imagine that. If I think we are capable of winning eighty-five games, then why can't I figure out a way to win ten more games and the division?"

Gil, of course, was right on the money. We clinched the N.L. East on September 24th with a 6–0 victory over St. Louis at Shea Stadium. It was our ninety-sixth win of the year. We ended up with a record of 100–62.

Our longest losing streak of that magical '69 season was five, way back at the end of May, and was followed by a season high of eleven straight victories. In the middle of August, we were nine games behind the

Chicago Cubs. It was the farthest out of first place we had been since being nine back at the end of May. At that point, I'm not sure I believed
Grote's prediction.

Starting August 15th, we won twelve of thirteen to go from nine back
to just two games behind the Cubs. In our last forty-nine games, we had a
record of 38–11, including a doubleheader sweep of the Pirates in Pittsburgh by identical 1–0 scores on shutouts by Jerry Koosman and Don
Cardwell. If there were any doubters left, that had to be the moment they
thought Grote just might be right with his prediction. Ironically, both of
the pitchers drove in the winning runs in their games. As they say, the rest
is history.

We scored 27 runs in a three-game sweep of the Atlanta Braves to
win the N.L. Pennant, and the only bump in the road on the march
through the World Series was my losing the first game to the Orioles in
Baltimore.

My most vivid images of that World Series are like those of most
fans: the spectacular catches in the outfield by Tommie Agee and Ron
Swoboda. The most vivid verbal memory was Don Clendenon, in a way
trying to raise my spirits after pitching poorly in Game One, saying
"We're going to beat these guys. They didn't get the real you, and they get
Koosman tomorrow."

On October 16, 1969, the New York Mets were crowned World
Champions and the darlings of New York, following in the footsteps of
the New York Jets.

During the course of that season, the one off-the-field visual that
stands out in my mind more than any other occurred in Montreal, Canada.
At the end of a seven-game road trip that began in Chicago by winning
two out of three from the Cubs, Jack DiLauro got the win in the tenth inning of the second game of a Sunday doubleheader against the Expos.

At the Montreal airport, as we waited for our plane back to New
York, the entire team was huddled around a television, along with virtually
all the other travelers in the area. We watched, unbelievably, as a man
stepped onto the surface of the moon. Thoughts of it being impossible
and that it must be science fiction read on everyone's face. Someone on
our team said if they can get a man on the moon, we can win the World
Series. At that time we were four and a half games behind the Chicago
Cubs.

Winning as a team brings back some of the fondest memories of that
championship season. There were contributions from every corner, like

Al Weis slugging a three-run homer to beat the Cubs in a 5–4 win. Bobby Pfeil putting down a perfect squeeze bunt in the tenth inning of that second game at Montreal. Garrett, Agee, Harrelson, Jones, Clendenon, and all the rest bring back the memories of the greatest highlight of any young professional athlete's career: a World Championship.

One of the most telling photographs of the '69 World Series for me is a shot of Gary Gentry and me, in a vacant Shea Stadium, standing on the mound of a playing field littered with remnants of the turf ripped apart by the celebrating Met fans.

It was a moment for me that offered one of life's magic lessons. All our youth we dream of the post-victory celebration. The spraying of champagne, revelry, and hugs with your teammates. That is all a wonderful part of winning, but I think Gary and I both realized what can easily be read in that photograph. The real joy of the '69 championship season was on the field and the year-long process of the march toward victory. The excellence of applying one's trade, the competition, communication, and teamwork were, and are, what is most important and memorable from any season, and the 1969 championship was the crowning jewel for everyone on that team.

Foreword
by Bill Bradley

Sports fans love to argue about who is the greatest. You'll never hear any person who was part of the 1970 Knicks championship team participate in the debate on whether one of us was the greatest player ever. At different times and in different games, each of us was the greatest. But you will hear us talk about a team that shared the basketball and the glory and meshed into one beautiful unit. My relationship with my former teammates will never die. I see and talk to most of the guys on a pretty regular basis. Whenever we see each other, we are reminded of how close we were on the court.

Of course, there is no single sport that is perfect, but for me basketball comes the closest. It is about as pure and unblemished a team sport as one could find. I can lose myself in its nuances, subtleties, and its competitiveness. And the epitome of that competition is the professional ranks. For me, that's where it was in 1969–70.

When I played, going out on the court transformed me, put me at another level of awareness—and enjoyment. One must think, have physical stamina, possess prowess and agility, but most of all, be unselfish—if the team is to achieve true success. These ingredients typified the 1969–70 NBA Champion New York Knicks.

The Knicks of that season were a team in every sense of the word, and that is what made us successful. However, we could not do it alone. A great coach and leader like Red Holzman was essential, and loyal fans, an absolute necessity, too. Without the combination of all of these things, the heights we achieved could not have been reached. The fans supported, enlivened, focused, and inspired the team. To know these fans are counting on you is tantamount to relying on your teammates on a day-in and day-out basis. It was elemental to our achievements. The fans in New York embraced and supported our team in a very special way. I think they saw a lot of themselves in our efforts. They are the greatest basketball fans in the world, and they appreciated our unselfishness and determination. That magnificent season was one of the most memorable times of my life. It cannot be duplicated. I would not want it to be.

Our team was the epitome of how people can work together for a common goal. It wasn't solely the fact that we won an NBA championship for the first time—it's how we won. With a bond between the players and our coach, we were able to achieve the ultimate prize an athlete can earn. Not only a championship, but also the knowledge that we were part of a team that gave its all, its heart and soul, whenever we were on the court.

In a time when New York City needed something to lift its spirits, the Jets, Mets, and Knicks were able to do just that. All three teams found common ground as they captured the hearts and minds of their fans. The exploits of these three remarkable teams had an important and positive impact on the sport of the city when people needed it most. Their legacy endures today.

The 1969–70 New York Knicks are just one part of the story. An important part, no doubt, but only one of three. The parts as a whole make for an incredible story that lives forever in the minds of those who were part of it. For those who were there as fans, this book will take you back to the thrill of those accomplishments. For those who heard about it from the myriad fans still talking about it today, sit back and learn about history. This book tells the story of those "magnificent seasons."

Introduction
by Bob Costas

1969 . . . Nixon inaugurated. Eisenhower dies. Men walk on the moon. Chappaquiddick. My Lai. Woodstock. The Beatles are still together. *60 Minutes* is just beginning. *The Godfather* and *Portnoy's Complaint* are best-sellers. Gas is thirty-five cents a gallon. Tiny Tim gets married on Johnny Carson's *Tonight* show. *Midnight Cowboy* wins best picture.

And in sports, three truly unforgettable New York teams win championships (okay, the Knicks actually won theirs in 1970 but the season *started* in 1969, so go with us here and don't mess up the story line).

The pages that follow lay out the particulars about these remarkable squads. But in a general sense, here's what I think ties them together:

1. They overcame huge odds. The Mets, after all, had never even come close to having a winning season. Their very name was synonymous with comic baseball futility. Then, seemingly overnight, they not only got good, they got good enough to upset a truly great Baltimore Oriole team in the World Series. It wasn't just surprising; it was preposterous.

In January of that year, another Baltimore team, the NFL's Colts, were viewed as invincible. They'd gone through the season with only one loss. They had crushed the Browns in Cleveland 34–0 in the NFL title game. Their superiority over the Jets and the NFL's superiority over the upstart AFL were so taken for granted the Colts were a nearly three-touchdown favorite in Super Bowl III.

Well, we know what happened that day and early evening in Miami; and what Joe Namath and the Jets pulled off still ranks among the handful of greatest upsets in American sports history.

Even the Knicks, who were already certified as a legitimate title contender, found the deck stacked against them in the NBA finals. When Willis Reed went down in Game Five against the Lakers of Chamberlain, Baylor, and West, the odds shifted heavily against New York—which of course only made what happened next all the more dramatic and everlasting.

2. In their own way, each team became a unifying force in a contentious time in a beleaguered city. Some say the Mets even helped reelect a mayor. The Amazins' October exploits came so close to the November election that John Lindsay got a feel-good bounce.

3. They each represented something fresh and new, while at the same time embodying old virtues.

The Jets, of course, were symbolized by Broadway Joe Namath. He seemed the personification of the new sports star. Long hair, flashy clothes, brash persona, and lots of cash ($400,000 was a lot of money in the sports world of the sixties). But stylish and charismatic as he was, there was something decidedly old school about Namath. He earned the respect of crew-cut teammates and opponents by being a genuine team player and displaying on-field courage and grit in the face of debilitating injuries. By shocking the Colts and the NFL, Namath and the Jets raised the banner of a new league and a new time in sports, although much of what they were about would have rung true anytime.

As lovable losers, the Mets had already won the hearts of a good portion of New York, but they won their first championship at a pivotal point in New York and baseball history. It was the year after Mickey Mantle's retirement, so the last vestige of the now crumbled Yankee dynasty was gone. The city was there for the taking, and the Mets took it. In the first season of divisional play the Mets became the first team to win the N.L. League Championship Series and then the World Series. They did it with an irresistible combination of young stars like Seaver, Koosman, and Jones, along with well-traveled veterans making their last baseball stands—Clendenon, Charles, and Weis. Their high-spirited style won over a new generation of fans, but also reminded older fans of New York's Dodgers and Giants of the forties and fifties, rekindling that National League following.

The Knicks oozed style, glamour, and personality. Like Namath, Walt Frazier owned the boulevards of New York. Frazier, Reed, DeBusschere, Bradley, and Barnett were all stars, but the whole was infinitely greater than the sum of its impressive individual parts. Their team chemistry, intelligence, and unselfishness illuminated basketball's larger beauty and truth and seemed to invest this team and its games with a meaning that went beyond the scoreboard. Hip and cutting edge as they may have seemed, the Knicks of 1969–70 are one of the enduringly great teams because they exemplified what should be their sport's enduring values.

4. While all championships bring excitement, sometimes even joy, each of these teams had something more. They each had a kind of soulfulness and authenticity of spirit not often seen—then or now.

That's how those teams seemed to me as a teenager growing up in New York and that's how I see them now, some three and a half decades later. Now let's turn the story of that remarkable time over to those who lived it.

PART I

THE MAGNIFICENT SEASONS

1. The Magnificent Seasons

Many professional teams have won championships in their sport. Many times their victories have become storied events. Those victories have even galvanized their home cities in some real way. However, what happened from January 1969 through May of 1970 in New York City will go down in sports history as a unique happening and the most phenomenal consecutive seasons of sporting events in this country's history. They are remarkable not only for the victories themselves, but also for the circumstances under which they occurred, the blending of individual players into well-rounded and cohesive teams, and, most important, what each one of these teams did for a city and a country torn apart by strife and despair.

While sports by their very nature of competition can be very unpredictable, no one could have imagined in the fall of 1968 that three teams from New York City, two of which were first-order underdogs, would win consecutive world championships. Add to this the fact that all three championships were the first in each team's history and you have the makings of a season in sports that has remained in people's minds forever.

What I've tried to do here is reflect on a time when the good did over-come the bad. Maybe that might be taking it to extremes, but for many it became the truth. When successes on the field and court gave us all a sense of hope and a feeling of accomplishment. The three championships are indeed one remarkable story, yet each one of these teams has its own unique and wonderful story full of grit, passion, charm, camaraderie, and obsessively loyal fans. History was also made in other ways. By winning Super Bowl III in January 1969, the New York Jets, who were seventeen point underdogs to the Baltimore Colts, changed the face of professional football forever. That victory led to a merger of the upstart American Football League with the long established National Football League on almost equal terms, creating a power that is the most dominant profes-sional sports organization operating today. The New York Mets, who were known as the "lovable losers," overcame 100–1 odds at the beginning of the 1969 baseball season to become World Series winners, defeating the powerful Baltimore Orioles, one of the best teams ever put together. And, to finish off this wonderful "threesome," the New York Knicks, with their classic style combined with unselfish, intelligent, and disciplined play, stunned the favored Los Angeles Lakers in May of 1970, to win the National Basketball Championship.

Arguably, there will never be another fabled championship run like this—one after another in one city. To paraphrase Dickens, in America during this period it was the worst of times, but yet, if you were a sports fan, particularly in New York City, it was the best of times. Countless books have been written about these three unusual teams, and they have achieved legendary status that has grown stronger over the years. But, make no mistake about it; whatever has been written or said is well de-served. Not only because the players who were part of it have become leg-endary heroes, but because these three teams all related to the underdog in all of us—the downtrodden, the guy who was knocked down and then got back up to fight and, more important, win. What they did was simply make people believe again.

While this book is about three teams, one might notice that I've given the Mets a little more than the other two, but, hey, I was there and have some firsthand knowledge. It certainly doesn't lessen the importance of the Jets and Knicks. All three teams are equally important and they all have their place in history.

In a world that yearned for heroes there is no doubt that 1969–70 in New York City gave people what they needed. The real heroes should have been the people who served in Vietnam, but by the time 1969 rolled around many people in this country were so disheartened by the deaths and injuries to American fighting forces, and disillusioned with the military, that returning soldiers faced rebuke from many and apathy from others. So the players on these underdog teams became America's surrogate heroes instead. And it wasn't just the stars. All the players who were part of it were idolized then, and still remembered and loved today, for just that—being part of it. Ask any former Jet, Met, or Knick from that season how fans regard them today. Each will tell you that reactions range from thanks to adoration. All of us who were part of this incredible time have felt the undeniable affection from the untold number of people who still fervently hold memories from that championship season, and will continue to, seemingly forever.

In the sixteen months from January 12, 1969, through May 8, 1970, the exploits of three underdog New York City professional sports teams lifted the spirits of people and made them believe again. This book will explore what it meant then and still means today—to the players, the city, and the people who lived through it. We will also discover the legacy of the three teams and how it has grown to near mythical proportions.

At the time it was said that the triumph of the Jets in Super Bowl III was the greatest single-game victory in the history of American sports. That may be debatable, but there is no doubt that from that moment on the Super Bowl became the mega event it is now, and for New York City it was the beginning of the "Championship Trifecta." Besides Joe Namath, names like Don Maynard, Matt Snell, Emerson Boozer, Gerry Philbin, John Schmitt, Larry Grantham, George Sauer, Pete Lammons, Dave Herman, Winston Hill, and Coach Weeb Ewbank are etched in New York City sports forever. How did it come together? How was it possible to beat the almost "invincible" Baltimore Colts? Those and other questions will be explored.

Soon after the Jet victory, the New York Mets opened spring training, and no one thought that they would follow the Jets with a championship of their own. How can a team lose 120 games their first year, six years later matching their best season ever—finishing one game out of last place—then win a World Series the next? You will hear the thoughts of these unlikely heroes about that year and how that victory changed each of their lives. Names like Hodges, Seaver, Koosman, Kranepool, Swoboda, Grote, Boswell, Charles, Jones, Clendenon, Weis, Martin, Harrelson, and even Shamsky have been passed on to later generations.

And yet there was another team of destiny. The New York Knicks beat a favored Los Angeles Lakers team, with three all-time superstars—Wilt Chamberlain, Jerry West, and Elgin Baylor—to win the National Basketball Championship in May of 1970. Willis Reed, Walt "Clyde" Frazier, Dave DeBusschere, Dick Barnett, Bill Bradley, Cazzie Russell, Phil Jackson, and of course, Red Holzman are names engraved in the memory of everyone. Their style of play has actually become folklore. How were they able to conquer the mighty Lakers? Why have so many of the championship Knicks gone on to tremendous careers after their playing days were over?

Finally, this book will not only relive those days with the players and coaches on the winning and losing teams, but also get the thoughts and comments of sportswriters, sportscasters, news announcers, authors, celebrities, and politicians.

The players and the teams are forever linked together in a unique way. There have been countless events over the intervening years attended by individual players from each team, and on many occasions members of all three teams appeared together. A universal theme voiced by most of the players is that they miss the camaraderie of the clubhouse, and always look forward to getting together with their former teammates. And all the players know that the three teams share a common bond of being part of a special time for sports in New York history. Any team can win a championship, it happens every year, in each sport, but these seasons were special. These three teams, the era, and the fans made it that way. They still do today. This book is about their legacy.

2. The USA and New York City in Conflict and Turmoil

"Under our feet the ground was giving way."
—Governor Mario Cuomo

While this book is about championships and the good times they brought, all of that has to be put in the proper perspective. To do so, one has to go back and look at events in the years when these three teams conquered the world. Part of the legacy of the Jets, Mets, and Knicks of that time is that each team, through its success, had a part in giving people a sense of relief from a bleak point in their lives and, more importantly, giving many hope of good things to come.

The years 1968, 1969, and 1970 were so notable in our history that one would need volumes to write about all the things that affected us in some way. Mark Kurlansky, a well-known author, wrote a book entitled *1968*, published early in 2004. The year had so many dramatic moments (almost all bad) that Mark thought it worthy of this undertaking. I cannot fathom the amount of time and research he put into writing this important book, but can only say that our lives were all touched by those events.

The year 1968 was filled with some of the most traumatic events in American history. In Southeast Asia, in a place called Vietnam, thousands of miles from the United States, soldiers were being killed every day in a conflict that many Americans didn't want any part of. Daily protests and demonstrations were evident across the country, particularly in New York City. The government was determined to silence protesters' voices and was arresting its citizens. Many young men were fleeing to Canada to avoid the draft while some just decided to burn their draft cards. Newspapers and magazines were constantly filled with stories of conflict in every part of the country, and television showed the horrors of war in graphic detail on a daily basis. The country was in turmoil.

Looking back at that period of time in my own mind, I tried to think of some good things that happened in the country and the city. The only thing I could remember was "the walk on the moon" by astronaut Neil Armstrong and Edwin "Buzz" Aldrin in June of 1969. It was a great event and it did make Americans proud. But that was the only thing I could think of. It was not a great time for the country.

The Vietnam War, of course, was a major concern for many of us at this time, but there were other events or "happenings" in the United States that were coming to the forefront and beginning to change the face of the country. The civil rights movement was in full force and taking shape under the leadership of Dr. Martin Luther King Jr. who had the admiration of many people, black and white alike. Women's liberation groups were growing and making their presence known. They would soon unite their efforts with a group known as NOW, the National Organization of Women.

The year 1968 started auspiciously on January 10th with the United States reporting the 10,000th airplane lost over Vietnam. Thirteen days later North Korean patrol boats captured the USS *Pueblo*, a Navy intelligence-gathering vessel with eighty-three crewmembers on board. North Korea claimed the *Pueblo* was violating their twelve-mile territorial limit. This crisis would go on for eleven months, with the *Pueblo* crew not gaining their freedom until December.

January 31st saw the North Vietnamese launch the Tet Offensive with 70,000 regular troops supplemented by Viet Cong irregulars attacking all over South Vietnam. The offensive went on for weeks, and it would be stated that allied forces won a decisive victory, but all that our citizens saw on television was death and destruction. There are many who think this was the turning point for the American public's attitude toward the war. Noted author David Halberstam had this to say; "I think the Tet Offensive punctured the optimism of the country in 1968. Up until then most people still trusted the president and the generals, but Tet damaged that. And, soon you could see the growing political protests in 1968 as more and more middle class kids joined the dissenters and some even brought their parents with them. All the contradictions in American life came to the forefront in 1968. It was a year of great social conflict and great tragedy."

Martin Luther King Jr. delivered a prophetic sermon at a church in Atlanta on February 4th. He says that after his death, "I'd like somebody to mention that day that Martin Luther King, Jr. tried to give his life serving others. I'd like for somebody to say that day that Martin Luther King Jr. tried to love somebody, and that I tried to love and serve humanity. Yes, if you want to, say that I was a drum major for peace and for righteousness." Only a few days later, a civil rights protest at a "white only" bowling alley in Orangeburg, South Carolina became a tragedy. Efforts to break up the protest by highway patrolmen led to the deaths of three college students.

Two weeks later, on February 18th, the U.S. State Department announced the highest U.S. casualty toll of the Vietnam War. The previous week 543 Americans were killed in action and 2,547 were wounded.

March 16th marked a particularly startling event. Even though it wouldn't become public knowledge for more than a year, U.S. ground troops stormed through the Vietnamese hamlet of My Lai, killing more than five hundred Vietnamese civilians including infants and the elderly.

At around 6 P.M. on April 4, 1968, a single shot from a 30.06 rifle paralyzed the country. Martin Luther King Jr. while at a motel in Memphis for meetings to discuss a march on Washington, was shot by an assassin. He was pronounced dead about one hour later. Word of the assassination sparked rioting in Boston, Chicago, Detroit, Kansas City, Baltimore, Washington, D.C., Newark, and other cities. Across the country forty-six deaths were attributed to the riots. An international manhunt began for James Earl Ray, the man suspected of killing Dr. King. Arrested in June in England, he was convicted of murder and later died in prison in 1998.

On the night of June 4th, Robert Kennedy, campaigning for the Democratic nomination for president following victories in California and South Dakota primaries, addressed a large crowd of supporters at the Ambassador Hotel in Los Angeles. He was confident that his campaign would go on to unite the many factions that divided our country. Leaving the stage at 12:13 A.M. (the morning of the 5th) he was shot by Sirhan Sirhan, a twenty-four-year old Jordanian living in Los Angeles. His motive was said to be anger at pro-Israeli speeches Kennedy made during his campaign. Robert Kennedy died early in the morning of June 6th. The country wept again following another assassination.

In July, the "Yippie" movement formed by activists Abbie Hoffman, Jerry Rubin, and Paul Krassner, started their activities with disruptions at the New York Stock Exchange and Grand Central Station in New York City. Six weeks later we would hear more about these activists at the Democratic Convention in Chicago.

Early in August, Republicans gathered in Miami Beach and nominated Richard Nixon to be their candidate for the Presidency. The next day Nixon selected Spiro Agnew as his running mate. With President Lyndon Johnson not seeking re-election, the Democrats held their convention the week of August 26th, and Hubert Humphrey would be nominated to run against Nixon. Chicago police attempted to enforce an eleven o'clock curfew as major demonstrations led by Abbie Hoffman and others were widespread in the city. On Wednesday the 28th, police took action against demonstrators. One hundred people were sent to emergency rooms and 175 arrested. Demonstrators and witnesses claimed there was no provocation.

In early September, women's liberation groups and NOW joined together to target the Miss America Pageant in Atlantic City. "Bra burning" would become a common phrase when talking about "Women's Lib."

At the summer Olympics, thirty-two countries boycotted due to the participation of South Africa, but the most notable action occurred when two United States athletes, Tommie Smith and John Carlos, both medalists, gave the black power salute during the 200-meter dash medal ceremony while the U.S. national anthem was played.

Former New York Governor Mario Cuomo summed up this period of our history in elegantly simple terms: "The country had been so dominant after World War II, but then in the sixties we slipped into a slew of problems starting with Vietnam. It was a very unsettling time with social and cultural changes. Under our feet the ground was giving way."

The city of New York did not lack in antiwar protests, social unrest, and political upheaval. David Halberstam put it succinctly when he said, "I think New York City always felt things more quickly. There was a feeling by the administration in Washington that whatever happened in New York wasn't happening in the rest of the country. But, in New York City in 1968 . . . there was an acute sense of anti-war and a country in conflict with itself."

New York in the late 1960s was a city changing. It was coming into an era where things that had worked socially and economically for a long time simply weren't going to continue the same way. For many years the city had been the center of manufacturing, but it was becoming a service city, a tourist city, and of course there was Wall Street. The economy was changing and the city was in a transition. On top of that civil rights was starting to play a big part politically. It just wasn't the civil rights of Dr. Martin Luther King Jr., but the radical civil rights of H. Rap Brown, Sonny Carson, and the Black Panthers.

The mayor of New York City was John Lindsay, an upper-class liberal politician who tried to govern a working-class, ethnically diverse city. He won the mayoral election in 1965, defeating Conservative William Buckley and Democrat Abe Beame, then the city's controller. Lindsay inherited a city with many complicated fiscal and economic problems. As manufacturing was disappearing, many middle-class residents were fleeing the city and public sector workers were starting to unionize. Union militancy would turn out to be the curse of Lindsay's administration. On his first day as mayor, the Transportation Workers Union shut down the city with a complete halt of subway and bus service. The strike lasted twelve days and badly hurt the city. Because of subsequent strikes, welfare costs, and general economic decline, New Yorkers by 1970 would be paying over $350 per person in taxes, the highest in the nation.

The same year also saw a nine-day sanitation strike. Lindsay was blamed for letting the strike happen without making a counteroffer to a pre-strike proposal by the union. During the strike, quality of life for New Yorkers reached its lowest point as mounds of garbage accumulated on the city's sidewalks. When it was over, the strikers received a retroactive pay raise, setting a bad precedent for labor negotiations and contributing to the worsening financial situation. As David Garth, former political advisor to John Lindsay and many other politicians related, "Things were difficult in the city for a long time during this period. Unemployment and jobs were tough. There were a lot of tensions in the schools. The city was very shaky. The nervousness, the black-white tensions, it was something everyone talked about but did nothing about. We had lots of problems." As far as all the strikes that were occurring in New York City, Garth said, "The strikes happened because the unions tried to pick up the momentum they had lost. That's when I developed the slogan 'It's the second toughest job in America' for John Lindsay."

During this time the city was becoming a major home for the counterculture. Thousands of hippies found their way to Greenwich Village, making life unpleasant for those who lived there. Bizarre as it now sounds, the Lindsay administration, in hopes of finding someone to control the hippies, put Abbie Hoffman and Jerry Rubin on the city's payroll at $100 a week.

During John Lindsay's term as mayor crime soared in New York City. Unfortunately, even though whites committed the majority of crimes, many white New Yorkers associated crime exclusively with minorities. David Garth added, "You were really talking about two New Yorks. To some, crime didn't exist in our section (of town). But the black and Spanish communities were having real trouble. The confrontation between the whites and blacks and Spanish grew tremendously in that period and that's when you had the riots."

On March 22, 1968, Abbie Hoffman brought over 3,000 people to Grand Central Terminal at midnight to create havoc. The police went into the crowd with clubs sending dozens to hospitals.

April 4th, the day that Martin Luther King Jr. was assassinated, over 400 people were arrested in Harlem after the news was announced. "When Martin Luther King was shot," says David Garth, "I was called and went down to the theatre and got John Lindsay to take him to Gracie Mansion. He was shocked to hear about the assassination. We left shortly and went up to 125th Street. The one thing about Lindsay was when there was a problem he went right to it. When we got to 125th Street there were only a few cops. The place was seething with people who were upset. And Lindsay, instead of walking away, walked right into the crowd and told them how terrible the assassination was and sorry he was." Jeff Greenfield, now a senior analyst for CNN, who came to work for John Lindsay after working for Robert Kennedy said, "I came to work for John Lindsay because, basically, there were two white politicians who could talk to black Americans. One was Robert Kennedy and the other was John Lindsay."

On April 23rd, a rally on the campus of Columbia University led by Students for a Democratic Society protested the university's participation in the Institute for Defense Analysis, which led to the occupation of an administrative office building. It was quickly cut short by conservative students and university security officers. The demonstrators, however, marched to the site of a proposed new gymnasium in Morningside Heights to stage a protest in support of neighbors who used the site for recreation. This led to protester occupation of five university buildings and shut down the university. It ended seven days later when police stormed the buildings and forcibly removed the protesters at the university's request. A few days later on April 26th, over 200,000 high school and college students marched in a protest against the Vietnam War.

On June 3, 1968, pop-artist Andy Warhol was shot in his New York City loft by a struggling actress and writer. The next day Robert Kennedy was shot and killed. Later in the month Abbie Hoffman went back to Grand Central with Rubin and Krassner to demonstrate with his Yippie movement and added disruptions at the New York Stock Exchange for good measure.

After thirteen teachers in a school in the Brownsville section of Brooklyn were fired, the United Federation of Teachers, the teacher's union, went on strike. It delayed the start of the school year in September for fifty-five days, creating a rift in the relationship between blacks and Jews. This became a symbol of the chaos of New York City.

Former New York State governor Mario Cuomo noted, "It was a time of tremendous social unrest and poverty in the city. We were in a corroding period, and the city bore the brunt of all the problems and the real use of major drugs started around this time." Spike Lee recalled, "I was definitely aware of things. My parents made sure we all knew what was happening. The civil rights movement, the assassinations, everything. The whole country was in turmoil."

Former New York City mayor Rudy Giuliani, a law clerk around this time, recalled the general atmosphere very clearly: "In 1968 . . . the country was not feeling very good about itself and the city was not feeling good about itself. They both needed some things to feel good about." And, as fate would have it, three unlikely sports teams did just that.

3. New York City Sports—Disappointment and Despair

"People expect a championship every year. When it doesn't happen disaster has struck."
—Ira Berkow

New York City has always been known as a championship city. After all, haven't the Yankees won more World Series than any other team? In the early 1960s the Yankees did win two world championships—in 1960 and 1962. In 1963 the Los Angeles Dodgers beat them in four straight in the World Series and in 1964 they lost the Series in seven games to the St. Louis Cardinals. But from 1965 until the later part of the seventies, the Yankees struggled. The Mets, of course, were the Mets, finishing last every year from their inception in 1962 through 1967. However, they did improve in 1968, finishing ninth in the ten-team National League. The expansion Houston Astros had the dubious distinction of finishing in last place below the Mets that year—but by only one game. The New York Giants football team had some sound teams around that time, but they hadn't won a National Football League Championship since 1956. The American Football League New York Jets, formerly the Titans, played second fiddle to the Giants throughout this period, although there was some excitement in 1965 when they drafted and signed a brash quarterback out of the University of Alabama by the name of Joe Namath.

The New York Rangers hockey team was the real culprit here. They were one of the original six National Hockey League teams, but the Rangers hadn't won a Stanley Cup since 1941. So, to put it bluntly, world championships in professional sports in New York City from 1963 through 1968 were nonexistent. *New York Times* sportswriter Ira Berkow said, "In New York, because of the Yankees, people expect a championship every year. When it doesn't happen, disaster has struck."

For a city that had a history of championship teams (granted it was mostly the Yankees) this was—and all of us who have ever played professional sports know the term—"a real slump." However, starting around July 10, 1968, when the New York Jets started training camp for the 1968 season, this was about to change.

PART II

THE JETS

4. The Jets—Coming of Age

"It still needed some lightbulbs and there were a few leaks."
—Don Maynard

The American Football League was the brainchild of Lamar Hunt, a wealthy Dallas businessman, who in the late 1950s was unsuccessful in acquiring a National Football League team. Rebuffed by the NFL owners, he decided to form his own league. In August of 1959, he was able to get other wealthy men to join his league, which would consist of eight teams. Each owner only had to initially put up approximately $125,000. The franchises included Boston, Buffalo, Houston, and New York in the Eastern Division and Dallas, Denver, Los Angeles, and Oakland in the Western Division. Joe Foss, a World War II Marine fighter ace, winner of the Congressional Medal of Honor, and former governor of South Dakota, became the first commissioner of the American Football League. The New York franchise was purchased by Harry Wismer and would be called the New York Titans. It was rumored that Wismer liked the name Titans because he thought a Titan was bigger than a Giant.

At the time the National Football League only had twelve teams and, in retrospect, the new AFL would broaden the scope of professional football in the United States. And, as it turned out, three of the original owners in the AFL—Lamar Hunt, Bud Adams, and Ralph Wilson—all have teams in the NFL that are now worth hundreds of millions each.

On November 22, 1959, the AFL held its first draft. The New York Titans first pick was George Izo, a quarterback out of Notre Dame, who decided not to sign with the team. Of all the players drafted in the 1960 draft, only one, Larry Grantham, was in the starting lineup on opening day that first season.

On December 18, 1959, the Titans hired their first coach, the legendary Sammy Baugh, and in 1960 Don Maynard became the first player to sign a Titans' contract. Maynard came to the Titans from Texas Western University by way of Canada. Maynard told me "The AFL was a great opportunity for guys like me and guys who were trying to hang on in professional football. Plus, it gave jobs not only to players, but coaches, front office people, and stadium folk. Besides, it kept you playing. I wanted to play even though I was a licensed plumber for five years in the off-season."

Harry Wismer was able to work out a deal for the Titans' home games to be played at the Polo Grounds, the former home of the baseball Giants before they moved to San Francisco. It was located across the Harlem River from Yankee Stadium, where the football Giants played their home games. The team colors would be blue and gold. "We played all five of our exhibition games on the road that first year. When we got to the Polo Grounds a day or so before our first home game, nobody had done anything. It needed mowing and cleaning up. There were weeds all over and the dressing rooms needed work. It had just been sitting there a couple of years. But, when we played our first game everything was cleaned up. It still needed some lightbulbs and there were a few leaks, but that was okay," Maynard said.

When I asked Larry Grantham about the Polo Grounds and those early years he said, "It was awfully tough and not many fans would come to the games. One day our equipment manager was in the locker room and he had this tin can and a stick and he was beating on the can and someone asked him what he was doing and he said, 'I'm running the rats out.' But, it wasn't all bad because I was a big baseball fan and for me to be in the Polo Grounds and playing on the same field where Willie Mays made that over-the-head catch in the World Series was a thrill. And, we were in the big city playing pro football and everything was okay until our checks started to bounce."

Needless to say, the National Football League was not happy to see the AFL in business. Things started to heat up when the NFL decided to put their own franchise in Dallas. In June of 1960, the AFL filed a lawsuit against the NFL for the Dallas incursion and for interfering with the AFL's ability to get a television contract. The lawsuit finally went to trial in 1962, and a judge ruled against the AFL. However, that didn't deter the new league and the owners' determination. Their perseverance and staying power would prevail.

Many people felt the major problem the AFL would have would be the ability of the league to compete against the NFL for the top college talent. However, the AFL started with a bang in 1960 when the Houston Oilers signed Heisman Trophy winner Billy Cannon, who already had agreed to a contract with the Los Angeles Rams. This too went to court with the Oilers winning the case. The war for talent between the two leagues had started.

The Titans played their first home game of the 1960 season at the Polo Grounds, beating Buffalo 27–3 in front of 10,200 fans, only 5,727 of which paid for their admission. The rest were freebies. The starting quarterback in that first game for the Titans was Al Dorow from Michigan State. He had some pro football experience having previously been with the Washington Redskins. The Titans finished in second place in their division with a record of 7–7. Attendance for the fourteen games they played during the season, home and away, was 221,285 or an average of 15,806 per game.

One of the problems the league was having was that sportswriters were generally putting the new league down. "Maybe they were set in their ways. I could never figure out why they blasted us back then," said Maynard.

The first two years of the AFL the Houston Oilers won the league championship. In 1962, the Dallas Texans beat the Oilers in what turned out to be the longest game in professional football history. It lasted two overtimes for a total of seventy-seven minutes and fifty-four seconds.

The same year the New York Titans started to have some problems. Harry Wismer decided to make a coaching change and hired Clyde "Bulldog" Turner to be the new Titans coach. They signed highly regarded Lee Grosscup as their new quarterback and beat Oakland 27-17 in their opening game. Wismer admitted that he was having financial troubles and the AFL took over the costs of running the team until the end of the season. "I think he just didn't have the funds," said Grantham. "When he didn't pay or bounced checks we decided not to practice and things got a little rough then." The total attendance for all seven home games that year was only 36,161 and the team finished with a record of 5–9.

In 1963, a syndicate that included Sonny Werblin, Leon Hess, and Philip Iselin, purchased the Titans franchise for $1 million. They hired a new coach and general manager, Weeb Ewbank, who had been the coach of the Baltimore Colts. That same day they decided to change the Titans' name to the Jets. "The name didn't matter to me. It was all right. I think it was a smart marketing deal. A short name with one syllable," said Maynard. As for the new ownership, Maynard related, "The fact that Mr. Werblin was a big time promoter was good. I just said to myself, 'Gee whiz, this is going to be a blessing and I won't have to worry about certain things.'" Larry Grantham added, "When Weeb Ewbank came in things got better. We didn't have any more bounced paychecks. As a matter of fact, Sonny Werblin asked us if we had lost any money with Wismer, and if we did, he was going to make it up to us. We knew right away that he was going to take care of us." Also, that year the Jets and Oakland were part of a dispersal draft where other teams provided players because they were the two worst franchises in the league's short history.

That same year, the Jets drafted Matt Snell, a fullback out of Ohio State, as their number-one draft choice. In later rounds they drafted Dave Herman, Gerry Philbin, and Ralph Baker. All of them would become key members of the Jets' Super Bowl team. The Jets would finish the 1963 season with a record of 5–8–1, but would draw over 100,000 people for their seven home games, a remarkable turnaround. Things were starting to change, as Don Maynard reflected, "The first thing Mr. Werblin did was to have press parties all the time. He treated the press nice so in that way they couldn't keep from writing something nice about him. Also, we were starting to get some Giant fans who couldn't get tickets to Giant games."

When discussing playing in that era, Dave Herman reflected, "If you go back to that era you weren't playing for the money. Most of us weren't anyway, even though some people may have thought so. You played because you had a love for the game."

There was also a funny thing or two that happened in the early years. Billy Hampton, the longtime caretaker of the Jet locker room told me, "One time we were up in Boston playing at Fenway Park and Weeb was doing the usual pregame talk. He was pretty fired up this day and he was ranting a little and finally when he was through he yelled out, 'All right, let's go out and win this goddamn baseball game.' The players just cracked up." Hampton also remembered, "Back then we had only one type of helmet. We had a big tackle by the name of Sherman Plunkett and he couldn't fit into his helmet. We had to pound it onto his head and stretch the shit out of it. He was finally able to get it off and on his head."

Even though the league had been viable for a few years there were still some problems. "It was tough," Matt Snell said. "A lot of players who made up the Jets were older and who were rejects from the NFL. The conditions in the league were not too good. A lot of times we played in college stadiums, even semi-pro stadiums. The only good thing was Sonny Werblin and Weeb Ewbank did try to do things first-class as much as possible. When we went into the South to play there was still segregation going on. I used to see a lot of 'No Colored Allowed' signs all over the South."

Snell was also drafted by the Giants and told me he chose the Jets because "the thing I didn't like about the Giants was that they had Frank Gifford and Alex Webster as running backs and they had just drafted Joe Don Looney, another running back. I knew I would be sitting on the bench with them for a while. I don't believe that I would have learned much doing that so I decided to sign with the Jets."

In 1964, even though the Jets record was the same as the year before, the New York franchise and the AFL were starting to really establish themselves. NBC and the league announced a five-year television contract worth $36 million starting with the 1965 season. The year also marked the Jets move to Shea Stadium, the home of the New York Mets. In their first game at Shea the Jets beat Denver 30–6, in front of more than 45,000 fans and they had their first sellout that year at Shea in November with more than 60,000 people watching when they lost to Buffalo 20–7. Things were starting to look significantly brighter.

Not forgotten in all of this was the National Football League. As the AFL was becoming a viable option for many players, both leagues were throwing around money. As early as 1965 though, there were some people like Dallas president and general manager Tex Schramm, already looking to forge a merger between the two leagues. However, there were others who had different ideas. When Joe Foss stepped down as commissioner of the AFL in 1966, Al Davis, the general manager and coach of the Oakland Raiders, replaced him. Davis, a former New Yorker who had his first coaching job at Adelphi University, was a hard-liner who believed in stepping up the bidding war and raiding the NFL for players. Instead of only drafting players, Davis felt stealing players away from the other league would weaken the NFL. Davis was able to talk other AFL owners into doing just that. Davis was quoted in an interview at the time as saying, "I guess the AFL owners thought I would be a catalyst. It was a situation that called for some constant pressure to be put on the other side." Having the tough-minded Al Davis leading the way paid off. Two months after Davis took over as commissioner, the AFL and NFL agreed to a common draft, a championship game, and a complete merger by 1970. The agreement included an $18 million indemnity to be paid by the AFL to the NFL over the course of twenty years. And, under the agreement, Pete Rozelle would become the commissioner over both leagues. The AFL became a force in 1965.

The real beginning for the New York Jets, and certainly one of the most credible moments for the AFL, happened the day after the Orange Bowl in 1965. On that day the Jets signed a brash young quarterback out of the University of Alabama by the name of Joe Namath to a reported contract of $427,000. Namath not only had ability but he had charisma. He brought instant attention to both the Jets and the American Football League. Joe was from Beaver Falls, a small town in Pennsylvania where he was a terrific high school athlete. But he knew that quarterback was the position and football was the sport he wanted to pursue. An All-American at Alabama under Bear Bryant, Joe was the perfect choice for the Jets and the new league. New York needed a superstar of Namath's capabilities and the league needed the publicity that Namath could muster, on and off the field. Joe lived up to all the expectations and if it had not been for injuries, particularly bad knees, Namath would have put up even better numbers than he eventually did. Ironically, twenty-three days after signing with the Jets, Namath was operated on for cartilage and ligament damage to his right knee. Nagging knee problems would shorten Joe's playing career, but his signing was the beginning of a new era for the Jets. Four years later, Jet fans would have something very big to celebrate.

"We knew Joe was a high-priced quarterback," recalled Larry Grantham. "But he always took that hit. If he got knocked down he just got up off the ground and dusted himself off. Then he would call the next play. That helped the defense because our rallying cry on defense was, Let's get the ball back for Joe. Joe was worth whatever money he made."

"I got involved with the Jets when Namath first came to the team," recalled artist LeRoy Neiman. "Sonny Werblin got me interested. He started buying my paintings and he took a fancy to what I did. I did a number of things of Namath because right away you knew he had charisma.

All of a sudden I became the New York Jets' 'artist-in-residence.' " When asked how many paintings of Joe Namath he has done over the years LeRoy said, "Probably fifty to seventy-five."

In 1965, shortly after obtaining Joe Namath, the Jets signed Heisman Trophy winner John Huarte from Notre Dame. Also, in what was then called "the Red Shirt Draft," the Jets drafted George Sauer. Red shirting was originally started for players who were injured early in a college season, were unable to play the remainder of that year, and, as a result, were given an extra year of eligibility. However, it changed when colleges decided to "red shirt" a player if they were strong at that player's position. In essence they kept him from playing a particular year so he would still have four years of college eligibility remaining. Sauer fit into that "red shirt" category and would eventually become one of Namath's favorite targets over the years. Namath made his first appearance in the regular season in the second quarter of the second game. He made his first professional start in the third game of the season, throwing two touchdowns, in a 33–21 loss to the Buffalo Bills. For the third year in a row the Jets record was 5–8–1. However, Namath would pass for over 2,000 yards with 18 TDs, and be named the AFL's Rookie of the Year. An auspicious start for the guy they were now calling Broadway Joe.

In 1966, the Jets would end up drafting and signing Emerson Boozer and Pete Lammons, two key members of their future championship team. They started the season winning four out of five games, but four consecutive losses in the middle of the season led to a 6–6–2 record for the year. Still, Namath did pass for over 3,000 yards as the Jets began drawing larger and larger crowds both at home and on the road. In a recent interview, I asked George Sauer why the Jets didn't fare better in both 1965 and 1966. He told me, "I think there was just too much pressure on Joe."

In 1967, the Jets finished the season at 8–5–1, the best record in their history. This was the first year of the common draft between the two leagues and the Jets were able to draft John Elliott and Randy Rasmussen, who became mainstays on the team. That year also saw Joe Namath continue his maturing process, passing for over 4,000 yards. Joe was the only passer to go over the 4,000-yard mark in a fourteen-game season. George Sauer led the league in receptions with 75 and his teammate Don Maynard was second with 71. "How often do you see that?" Sauer remarked. During the 1967 season the Jets lost both of their outstanding running backs, Matt Snell and Emerson Boozer, to knee injuries. This cost the Jets dearly. Even though they didn't win a title that year the team set an AFL attendance record with 437,036 fans for seven home games. Every home game was sold out. The AFL had matured, and the Jets possessed a solid fan base.

Joe Namath was now the marquee name in the American Football League. He was the league's biggest star playing in the biggest city. Whenever there was any television footage about the league, it would start with Joe. He was a marketer's dream. Living in New York, the advertising and public relations world was able to capitalize on Joe, and he did just as an effective job capitalizing on them. Of course, being single, Joe was photographed around New York in the company of beautiful women. Namath felt that his off-the-field exploits never hurt him on the field. "He told me one time before a game," recalled *New York Times* sportswriter Ira Berkow, "that he had relaxed the night before a game with a blonde and a bottle of Johnnie Walker Red." But even with all that was written about him, the common denominator was that Joe Namath was a great quarterback, and many Jets felt he was the best teammate they ever had.

In May of 1968, the other Jets partners bought Sonny Werblin out of his ownership and the team relocated their training camp to Hofstra University on Long Island. Having come off their best record the year before, the Jets decided to make some subtle changes to a team that was shaping up to be one of the very best in the AFL. While the 1968 draft didn't yield any great names for the Jets, the team had gained confidence from the season before, and knew that with a change here and there they would definitely be contenders. "One key move Weeb made," said Matt Snell, "was he brought in Bob Talamini to solidify an offensive line that was already very good. With Namath, Maynard, Sauer, and Lammons, we definitely had the pass offense, and with myself and Boozer, and a very good offensive line, we knew we could run the ball. We knew our defense was going to be good, also."

By this time, Weeb Ewbank had established himself as a players' coach and a tough general manager. Some of the players reflected on their relationship with him. "Our relationship was like father and son," Larry Grantham said. "He originally told me I was too small to play for him, but then, when I did play, he treated me like a son. But most times he was really tight with money."

"Weeb was a great organizer," Gerry Philbin remembered. "But he was a cheap bastard. If he weren't so cheap we would have won three Super Bowls because he let some great players like Verlon Biggs go."

Almost every player had a positive experience with Coach Ewbank.

"He was a great guy," Dave Herman said. "He was my dad away from home. What Coach Ewbank did was put you through certain points in practice and wanted you to feel good about yourself. He wanted you to work hard, do the preparation, be successful, and feel good about yourself and the team. That was his way of coaching. He wasn't the dictator that's out there now. That doesn't make it right or wrong, it's just the way all sports have gone. Not only football, but all sports. With Weeb, he helped you and encouraged your preparation. Then he put the game plan together and we went out and executed it."

Linebacker Mike Stromberg also recalled his feelings about Coach Ewbank. "He wasn't the Knute Rockne type of motivator, but he was a great coach mainly because he surrounded himself with great people. He wasn't an imposing person but nobody wins a championship in two leagues with out having ability to coach."

"Weeb was just an easygoing guy," said Walt Michaels, the defensive coach on the Jets' Super Bowl team. "It was hard to get him upset. He was very detailed in the things he wanted to do and he was convinced that Joe could call his own plays and Weeb always listened to suggestions. He would always let the player play to his strength and never tried to get someone to do something they couldn't. He allowed the players to get involved in decisions."

Even artist LeRoy Neiman had his moments with Coach Ewbank. "Weeb was old school," said LeRoy. "He didn't have the greatest sense of humor, but he could say some funny things. I remember one play during the championship season when running back Billy Mathis came charging toward me on the sideline. He got tackled and slid right into me. I was covered in mud. Weeb came running over to holler at one of the officials and he stepped on my drawing. He looked down and said, 'You're getting better,' and walked away. He always thought I was in the way. He was probably right."

So when training camp opened for the Jets in July of 1968 the team had been pretty well shaped. The players and fans were filled with revived optimism. Still, things had to fall into place; the team had to hope there was no key injury, particularly to their star quarterback.

5. The Splendid Season

"Right then, I knew this team was going to be special."
—Joe Namath

A few weeks after training camp began in 1968, Don Lillis, who was president of the Jets, passed away, and the team named Phil Iselin as his replacement. At the beginning of the preseason the country was also going through continuing turmoil. On July 23rd a sniper attack on police in Cleveland, Ohio, initiated four days of rioting during which four civilians and three policemen were killed. It was a long, hot summer of civil disturbances all over the country.

By September 15th the Jets had played five preseason games, winning three and losing two, and were ready to open the season on the road in Kansas City.

"There was a high confidence level on our team at the start of the season in 1968," said guard Randy Rasmussen. "We felt we could win every time we went on the field. It was because we had good coaching, a good system, and two important ingredients for success. First, good athletes and second, people who could think out there."

"We knew in training camp it was going to be different that season," said former defensive back Johnny Sample. "To a man, everyone said it was time for us to go on and make a name for ourselves with a championship in the American Football League. And prove to the National Football League that we were as good as they were."

As far as the defense was concerned, assistant coach Walt Michaels had this to say about his Jet defense coming into the 1968 season. "In 1967 we were right near the top of the league defensively. We had a nucleus of a strong defense. But we had to stay healthy. We had two very strong defensive ends in Gerry Philbin and Verlon Biggs."

Before the first game of the season Joe Namath was named captain of the offense and Johnny Sample defensive captain. Looking back, the opening game in 1968 was a microcosm for the whole season. While they beat Kansas City on the road 20–19 in front of 48,871 fans and controlled the ball for the final 5:56 of the game, Al Atkinson, the Jets middle linebacker, was hurt and unable to play. In his place, the Jets started Mike Stromberg, who was a late-round draft choice earlier that year out of Temple University. Stromberg, who now owns a graphics design company in Long Island, New York, called The Great American Art Company remembered, "As a rookie in 1968, that first game of the season when I was thrust into that position was unbelievable. I ended up Defensive Player of the Week and was on the *Kyle Rote Show*. I also got a nice double-breasted suit from Barneys." Joe Namath analyzed it astutely, "The opening game in Kansas City, when we beat them with Mike Stromberg playing middle linebacker in place of Al Atkinson, was actually a defining moment for us. Mike played a hell of a game. Everyone rallied around him and it was wonderful. Right then, I knew this team was going to be special."

"I was happy for Mike Stromberg after that first game," said Walt Michaels. "I had scouted him in college and knew he could play. He was thrown into a very tough situation in that first game in 1968 against Kansas City. But he played extremely well."

Matt Snell felt the first game in Kansas City in 1968 was a good indication the Jets could compete against anyone in the AFL that year. "I remember that in the fourth quarter of the first game in Kansas City we were backed up on our 4-yard line. We then controlled the ball all the way to the end of the game. I think that drive sort of set the stage about how we felt the year would go. It helped our confidence and we knew then we could play with anybody."

The Jets had gone into the Kansas City game as six and one half point underdogs. They played very well initially, actually leading by 17–0 at one point, but ended up having to struggle to get the victory. The last drive of the game was a classic; fourteen plays that took almost six minutes off the clock. Kansas City's coach Hank Stram couldn't believe an opposing team could control the ball like that. In an interview after the game Stram said, "That last drive by Namath was fabulous. There was no way in the world I thought the Jets could go from their 4-yard line and maintain possession until the end of the game."

"That opening game in Kansas City was a great game," said place kicker Jim Turner. Jan Stenerud and I had a bunch of kicks. Holding the ball for the final six minutes of the game was something to see. Kansas City had a powerful team and it was a great start to our season."

"Even though it was the first game of the season for us," recalled Gerry Philbin, "it was a big win. The offense holding onto the ball the last six minutes of the game took the pressure off our defense. Kansas City had a very good team."

Johnny Sample explained further, "The Kansas City game proved the Jet coaches knew the players and picked the right people to play in their positions. I thought we dominated the game even though the score didn't indicate that. Kansas City had Len Dawson and Buck Buchanan and a lot of great football players. Riding back on the plane everyone was saying things like, 'if we play like this the rest of the year, who knows what can happen.'"

The second game of the season the Jets won by a big score against Boston, 47–31. The game was considered a road game for the Jets and was played in Birmingham, Alabama. Because of the unavailability of Fenway Park in Boston, the Patriots decided to move the game to another location. The Patriots chose Birmingham hoping to capitalize on Joe Namath's name and the fact he went to the University of Alabama. Additionally, according to the merger that was supposed to take place in 1970 between the NFL and the AFL, all teams had to play their games in stadiums having at least 50,000 seats. Fenway Park only had a little more than 37,000 seats and a new stadium proposal had been disapproved. The Patriots were thinking about leaving Boston after the season and this game was supposed to give the organization an opportunity to see how the fan reaction would be in Birmingham. They had to be disappointed, only 29,192 people showed up. Other cities the Patriots considered viable as a future home included Seattle, Memphis, and Montreal. They eventually settled on Foxboro, a Boston suburb where a new stadium would be built.

The 47 points the Jets scored against Boston were the second highest total in team history. Highlights of the game included a 68-yard interception return for a touchdown by Randy Beverly and a touchdown by Emerson Boozer, who was coming back after an injured knee. "I went four for four in field goals that game," said Jim Turner. "I think my field goals got lost in all the points."

The third game was also on the road but the Jets were heavily favored to beat Buffalo. With a crowd of 38,000 looking on, the Jets played poorly and lost a close one, 37–35. Namath was intercepted five times and three of those interceptions were run back for touchdowns. He also threw four touchdown passes. Buffalo lost three straight games prior to upsetting the Green and White. In an after-game interview Namath told the New York *Daily News*, "Of course, I blame myself. I was the one who threw the damn ball. I'm the dumb guy sitting right here." In his postgame interview Weeb Ewbank blamed the whole team. "We took them too lightly, they're professionals."

"I always tell people that Namath had a great game in Buffalo that year," said Don Maynard. "He threw a lot of touchdown passes; some to the Bills and some to us."

"That Buffalo game might have been Namath's worst game as a professional," recalled Johnny Sample. "I remember Curly Johnson asking Joe if he had rose-colored glasses on during the game because he threw a lot of balls to the guys in the wrong jerseys. On a serious note, even though we lost that game to a bad Buffalo team it made our offense work harder every week to be as good as they could be no matter who we were playing."

George Sauer also remembered that game. "The ironic thing about losing in Buffalo in 1968," said George, "was that Buffalo was one of the worst teams in football that year. They ended up getting the number-one draft choice the next year and picked O. J. Simpson. It turned out pretty good for them."

The first home game in the 1968 season, on October 5th, was another close contest. This one was against the San Diego Chargers. With a record crowd of 63,786 at Shea Stadium, the Jets pulled it out 23–20, as Emerson Boozer scored a touchdown on fourth and one with little time left in the game. The Chargers did come down the field with time running out, but defensive end Gerry Philbin hit Charger quarterback John Hadl just as he was throwing the ball and Johnny Sample intercepted.

"I was covering Lance Alworth," Johnny Sample recalled. "In my opinion he was the greatest wide receiver to ever play professional football. He could catch and run with the ball; he ran great pass patterns and was tough. When Philbin hit Hadl's arm the ball kind of fluttered, and I had a chance to get under it. I was lucky Lance didn't see the ball. He was still running his pattern. I saw what had happened and broke off and made the interception."

"We got a little lucky against San Diego," said Matt Snell. "They and Kansas City were the two most athletic teams in the AFL."

The next game was also at home against Denver. With another near capacity crowd of over 63,000 at Shea the Jets lost 21–13. The Jets were twenty-point favorites, but it turned out to be another bad day for Joe Namath. This time he threw five interceptions and was on pace to surpass his previous year's total of twenty-eight. Joe recalled, "That Denver game I just stunk." In a postgame interview Coach Ewbank again defended Joe. "It wasn't all Joe's fault. He was rushed pretty good." George Sauer recently said, "Denver was another bad team in 1968. We lost two games during the 1968 season to two of the worst teams in all of football." Randy Rasmussen remembered after the loss to Denver, "We're walking into our locker room and Curly Johnson yelled out, 'What's this bullshit, lose one, win one, lose one! Boys, that's not the way it's supposed to be.'"

Gerry Philbin remembered the Denver game for another reason. "I got thrown out of the Denver game and was fined $500 by the league. One of the officials made a stupid call in the second half, and I was yelling and screaming and pointing at him. I got pretty close to the official and when I pointed at him my finger got caught in his shirt by one of his buttons and the shirt tore. I had to go in front of Commissioner Pete Rozelle, and he read a letter the official had sent to the league office. I didn't realize I said all the expletives I supposedly said. I told the commissioner that $500 was a lot of money and he told me he would give the money back to me if I didn't get into any more trouble during the season. I ended up getting my money back."

"Looking back at that season," remarked Johnny Sample, "I was surprised we lost to both Buffalo and Denver. Actually, I am surprised we lost to anyone that season."

"We lost two games to Buffalo and Denver in 1968," said Walt Michaels. "They were both bad teams back then. Sometimes those things happen. Your players get a little complacent no matter what you say."

Five games into what would yet become a remarkable season, the Jets record was 3–2. While the season was about ready to really take off for the Jets, the real world outside the confines of the stadium was impossible to put aside. Some of the players shared their feelings with me. Joe Namath explained, "Turmoil was all around you. You were living it. That political era added to the lack of confidence in the honesty all people were dealing with, and the social and racial issues were out there, too."

Running back Emerson Boozer remarked, "Snell and I were in the National Guard. If anyone was reminded about certain things it was us."

Defensive tackle John Elliott told me, "Being from Warren, Texas, my world was a little sheltered and when I came to New York it was totally different. Unless you didn't read the newspapers, watch television, or talk to your teammates, you had to be aware of the problems around."

George Sauer added, "It was impossible not to be aware of what was going on. The country and New York City each had their own problems and it just wasn't the war, although I was probably on the side of the pro-testers regarding the war. I found it counterproductive the way the protests were going. Cumulatively over the years the protests have had some effect on policy, but any single protest seemed chaotic."

Offensive tackle Winston Hill offered an important perspective. "We had our own problems, but they were small compared to the problems in the city and the nation at the time. At times it was tough just to concen-trate on football." To illustrate what Winston was talking about, the day after the Denver game three policemen assigned to the troubled Ocean Hill-Brownsville school district due to the ongoing teachers' strike were wounded by rooftop snipers. At the same time city officials were hoping sanitation workers would ratify a tentative settlement before the strike deadline at midnight. The Patrolman's Benevolent Association was threat-ening a sick-out in the next few weeks to pressure the city to reopen their contract and the firemen's union instituted a work slowdown to force their wage negotiations. As if this weren't bad enough, peace talks held in Paris between the North Vietnamese and the U.S. were totally deadlocked after five months of fruitless discussion. All this happened within the span of a week! The fireman's slowdown ended on October 27th as did the police sick-out, however the teachers' strike, which started in September and was the largest and longest involving American educators, did not end until November 17th.

While it was a very difficult time for many people in the real world, the Jets were becoming a cohesive team on the football field that had its own personality and its own cast of characters. One of them was John "Curly" Johnson, the Jets' punter. He was, as everyone has told me, the craziest guy on the team. One of the many Texans on the Jet team that year, I asked him if it were true that everyone said he was the real character on the team? He said, "Yeah, I guess I was. I was the back-up tight end, the fifth running back, the punter, and kicked off sometimes. I had to keep my mind busy with things." Curly had played for Weeb Ewbank when Weeb was coaching in Baltimore and when he came to the Jets he gave Curly an opportunity to play. "We became good friends, but that didn't stop me from spoofing on him," Curly said. "I used to go out with the guys to clubs sometimes and get on stage and make fun of Coach Ewbank. One time, a couple of days after training camp started, it was hot and everyone was tired. I went and got a pillow, stuck it in my belly, put a baseball cap on and turned it sideways, and then I walked around to all the guys talking to them and giving them a lecture. They made a big circle around me and Weeb walked out. The guys spread out and I was on my knees. Coach Ewbank thought that was funny. Sometimes he would go in early at practice and set up a chalkboard with all of the X's and O's and then he would leave. I would sneak in and move the X's and O's around or erase one here and there. Then he'd start the meeting and look at the board and start talking about a play and scratch his head and say, "Well, goddamn, this ain't gonna work."

I finally asked Curly why he spoofed on Coach Ewbank so much and he just said, "We were friends because we went back to the days in Baltimore. Actually, nobody knows this but during some of the games I would go up to Coach Ewbank on the sidelines and make a suggestion to him and he listened. He never gave me credit when something worked though." Then Curly related that Ewbank, who was also the general manager, was a tough negotiator. "One year he asked me to kick off because our kicker couldn't put the ball in the end zone. He said, 'I'll give you a bonus for it.' So I kicked off for five years and he gave me a $1,500 bonus spread over five years."

"I loved to get Namath, too," Curly said. "You know he was a ladies' man and all that, and one time in training camp I got on the telephone and disguised my voice as a girl and told him that I had come up from New York and wanted to see him. The next thing I know, I see Joe running toward the front of the hotel to find her. I never told Joe I did it."

In 1968 the Jets had eleven players from the state of Texas. John Dockery, a defensive back and wide receiver with the Jets that year, grew up in Brooklyn and graduated from Harvard. John and I worked together for many years when we were both at WNEW-TV in the city, and John now works for CBS as a sports broadcaster and also owns his own facilities management company in New York. John told me, "I just remember all of the guys from Texas and to me they were like speaking another language from another planet. I was out of the Ivy League and hanging on the team by my fingernails. I remembered saying to myself, this is a very strange place to be. I would walk around just shaking my head." He remembered another occasion: "One day I came into the locker room and there was a big sign inside my locker that read 'Ivy League practice today.' So I went over to Namath, who was in the middle of a conversation with George Sauer, Bake Turner, and Don Maynard, and I said, 'OK, what's Ivy League practice?' The guys smiled and Joe said, 'Oh, that's touch football with pads.' So my only response was 'Well, that's the only place you couldn't have played football because you couldn't get in.'"

When asked who was craziest player on the team, Larry Grantham didn't hesitate a second. "Curly Johnson was at the top of the list," Larry said. "He is the funniest guy I ever met." On players who acted a little strange at times, Grantham said, "George Sauer. He was way out there. He wanted to be a writer. It seemed like sometimes he was in another world. But Maynard, man, he was the weirdest of all. Not funny weird, just weird. He was always selling things like ties and boots, and other things. He wanted me to sell some cleaning fluid for him called Swipe that would take paint off anything. It was so strong it would take your hide off. I didn't do it. I knew better."

Billy Hampton related in his interview with me, "Curly used to drive Weeb crazy. One time we were flying to Buffalo on a charter and Weeb asked the pilot to fly over Niagara Falls. And Curly yelled out, 'What the hell are we doing that for? You're taking time away from the bars.'"

Hampton also recalled, "Curly got all the players to bust Weeb's balls. Before the games you would have to raise your hand depending on which special team you were on. Curly would get one player on each to purposely not raise his hand and Weeb would yell out, 'Goddamn it, that's only ten guys.'"

"Curly was good for the team," said Walt Michaels. "He was versatile and could play a bunch of positions. And he was a comedian. When he did imitations of Coach Ewbank it was hilarious. He could say anything and if it was somebody else, Weeb might get upset. If Curly said it, it was fine. I guess Weeb felt that Curly was Curly and he was good for the team."

Larry Grantham also remembered the shenanigans Curly would pull on the coach. "Curly really got to Weeb when he finally let the players decide on what they wanted for a pregame meal. Weeb would say, 'How many people want a rare steak?' And then Weeb would count hands. Then he would ask, 'How many want their steaks medium,' then well done, etc. He would get through and add them up and say, 'Goddamn it, somebody voted too much or somebody didn't vote.' You see," Grantham said, "Curly would vote three or four times or not at all. He was always jerkin' Weeb around."

"Curly was like the jokester on the team," commented Johnny Sample. "Whenever Coach Ewbank thought something was fishy, he knew Curly was involved in it. He would always start something going when things were kind of solemn. He made things interesting, the team meals, the meetings, and everything else too. Curly, besides being a great punter, was very important by his presence on that Jet team."

John Schmitt, the Jets' offensive center, confirmed Curly Johnson's antics. "When I was a rookie I had to stand up in front of everyone at training camp and announce my position and my college. So, I told them I was a tackle from Hofstra University. Curly in his Texas drawl yelled out, 'Isn't Hofstra a girls' school? He was the absolute funniest guy," Schmitt said. "He had a way about him where he could say shit to someone and they would think it was sugar."

John also told me a couple of things relating to playing center in front of Joe Namath. After a practice one day a woman reporter came up to him and asked what was the difference between Joe Namath and Babe Parilli, the second-string quarterback. Schmitt said, "I told her there was a big difference. 'Joe's got a very soft touch.' She stopped writing and walked away. I thought she would just laugh, but she didn't."

As the season went on he got so many questions about Joe Namath, John just decided to tell this story to anyone who would listen. "My name is John Schmitt. I have the one position that every girl in the country wishes they had. I bend over in front of Joe Namath every Sunday, and Joe puts his hands between my legs."

"It was a good group of guys," John Elliott said. On Coach Ewbank, John recalled, "Weeb was a great coach. His philosophy was, 'I'm going to treat you like men as long as you act and play as men.' We didn't have many rules. Of course, if we'd had a lot Namath would have broken them."

That's how it was in the locker room for the Jets in 1968. It was a team of fun-loving characters, but also a team that could play football.

The Jets played the Oilers in Houston on October 20, 1968, and won 20–14. It was the start of a four-game winning streak. The game didn't start out great for the Jets or Namath, as Joe missed his first ten passes.

However, by halftime the Jets managed a 10–0 lead. They won the game when Matt Snell scored a touchdown in the final minute. The good news was that Namath didn't throw an interception and ended up twelve out of twenty-seven in passing. "The victory in Houston was really sort of an eye-opener for me," Grantham said. "Houston had a real good football team and when we beat them down there I knew we were going to have a good season."

The next game was on October 27th against the Boston Patriots. It turned into a rout for the Jets, as they defeated the Patriots 48–14. However, Namath suffered a jammed thumb and did throw another interception. Babe Parilli, Namath's backup, came on in the fourth quarter to lead the Jets to three touchdowns. Billy Joe, a backup to Matt Snell and Emerson Boozer, had a terrific game. The Jet defense showed what it could do and came up big with five interceptions.

The Buffalo Bills came into Shea Stadium on November 3rd. In the real world two days earlier, after three-and-a-half years, the largest bombing campaign since WWII came to an end in Vietnam. Called Operation Rolling Thunder, the campaign cost more than 900 American aircraft and 818 pilots were dead or missing. Amid this grim reminder of the ever-present war, the Jets had to perform.

Again the Jets were heavily favored and again they had trouble with this poor team. Although they pulled out a victory, 25–21, it wasn't easy. They had to rely on placekicker Jim Turner, who tied an AFL record with six field goals. The only Jet touchdown came on an interception by Johnny Sample run back for a touchdown. For the fifth game in a row Joe Namath failed to throw a touchdown pass. When asked about it in an interview after the game Namath replied, "This will be a win in the standings no matter how we did it." Jim Turner recalled his accomplishment. "I'm so proud of that Buffalo game at Shea in 1968," said Jim. "To be such a big part of that victory and able to tie the AFL record of field goals is obviously, a very special memory."

The Oilers followed the Bills into Shea the next weekend. It was another big crowd at the stadium. All three of the games in the three-week home stand drew over 60,000 fans. On a muddy field at Shea, the Jets won 26–7 as George Sauer had a great game. Although George only caught a total of four passes, they were good for 128 yards. Jim Turner also kicked four more field goals. And, it was the sixth game in a row Namath failed to complete a touchdown pass. "We had some games where we didn't score many touchdowns, so the kicking game had to come through," recalled

Turner. "As I looked back at that season over the years, I realized how well-balanced we were as a team. We were good in every aspect of play." Not everyone in the city was thinking of the Jets win that night though. In Queens, a firebomb was thrown into a police car that evening, and later a bomb exploded near a Harlem station house.

The Jets winning ways, however, were providing a weary populace with a reason for some joy. With a record of 7–2 they were on a roll. The next game, against the hated Oakland Raiders in Oakland, would turn out to be one of the most controversial games ever played in professional football.

The game was played on November 17, 1968, and was being watched by a national television audience. In a wild, high-scoring game with 1:05 left in the fourth quarter, NBC decided to cut away from the game so that the movie *Heidi* could start on time. With millions of viewers cut off, the Raiders scored twice in the last forty-two seconds to defeat the Jets, 43–32. The Jets had been leading 32–29 with 1:05 to play. The only bright spots for the Jets were Jim Turner kicking four more field goals that tied the AFL record set by Pete Gogolak of Buffalo in 1965, and Joe Namath throwing his first touchdown pass in seven weeks to Don Maynard. Joe's overall performance was stellar; he finished with 345 yards passing. The "Heidi" game, which is the name it was given, is still remembered by millions of football fans. Because of all the complaints from football fans I think NBC is still haunted by its programming decision back in 1968.

On the touchdown pass from Namath in the game, Don Maynard said, "It was wet in this area of the field and I ran my route and caught the ball and slipped and went down to one knee. The defensive guy came over and he also slipped. I just got up quicker and got into the end zone." As for Namath's not throwing touchdown passes in seven weeks, Maynard said, "We did whatever we needed to do to advance the ball and win games. We won games with our offense, defense, and special teams. Nobody had any pressure on them to score on touchdown passes."

Although the Jets would look back at the "Heidi" game as a blown opportunity and at the time a devastating defeat, their record was 7–3, and with four more regular season games left, could still have the makings of a very good season. "That game was a real tough loss for us and we were all down because of it," said John Schmitt. "We stayed on the west coast after the game because we were playing at San Diego the following week. We had a couple of days off so some of us decided to go out and have some drinks and try to forget the game. There was a lounge at the hotel where we were staying and Curly got up on stage and started telling jokes and imitating Coach Ewbank. He did it for a couple of nights in a row and it really helped us get over the Oakland loss. He really brought the team together and we started to concentrate on the San Diego game." After hearing this story I was starting to think that Curly Johnson missed a career as a stand-up comic.

"The game in Oakland was devastating, the way we blew it in the last minute," said Matt Snell. "But we got together as a team and decided to hang out as a team more. We put our heads together and decided to go forward and move on."

On the loss at Oakland defensive coach Walt Michaels had this to say. "It was terrible the way we lost in Oakland. But, on the other hand it solidified our team. Everybody got together. We went down to San Diego and stayed on the west coast and everybody picked up their game the next week." On getting fined by the league because he went down to the officials' dressing room after the Oakland game Michaels said, "We were getting penalized a lot on defense. There was a penalty called on Jim Hudson and he got mad, said something, and was thrown out of the game. I was upstairs in the coaches' booth. I really felt we were getting shortchanged by the officials. Our whole secondary had to be moved around. After Earl Christy fumbled the kickoff and the Raiders scored I was really mad. Everything started to compound. After the game, I wanted to confront the officials. One thing led to another and I went down to the officials' room and banged on the door. They opened it and I let them have mouthful. Sometime later I got a call and was told the league fined me $4,000. That was a lot of money back then. It paid a lot of bills. Phil Iselin told me later that he would help me with the fine and he did. I was always thankful for that."

Curly's actions must have done something because the Jets bounced back and won big in San Diego. They swamped the Chargers 37–15 to bring their season record to 8–3. The Jets defense intercepted Charger quarterback John Hadl four times. Placekicker Jim Turner added another thirteen points to his season total to give him 124 points. That broke George Blanda's record of 118 for a season. Also, Namath and Maynard hooked up for an 87-yard touchdown that set an AFL record for a New York team.

When the Jets arrived home from the California trip they were pleasantly surprised to realize that many sportswriters and fans were starting to look at them as not only a playoff team but also possibly getting to the 'Championship' game, as it was being called then.

The Jets clinched the eastern division title while they weren't even playing because Houston lost on Thanksgiving Day. There was no letdown as the Jets came home to Shea Stadium on December 1st and beat the Miami Dolphins 35–17. Another crowd of over 61,000 fans showed up to see the rout even though Emerson Boozer and Verlon Biggs didn't play because of injuries. Namath only played the first half and Babe Parilli ended up throwing three second half touchdown passes for the Jets. Don Maynard was in great form catching seven passes, three for touchdowns. Two of Maynard's TD passes came within forty-two seconds. That day Don broke former Baltimore Colt star Raymond Berry's total career yardage record of 9,275 yards. Maynard ended the game with 9,332 and was still going to play a lot more games. "The Miami game was just one of those days for me where everything went right," recalled Don. "As far as breaking the yardage record, it was great, because yardage is something I always thought was more important than the number of catches."

After the win, and with a record of 9–3, the Jets would have one more home game and then play their final regular season game in Miami. At worst, they would finish the season at 9–5.

Up to this point in the season, Joe Namath had some great games and a couple of bad ones. However, he was still a huge threat every game. "I remember asking Vince Lombardi about Namath," noted *New York Times* sportswriter and author Dave Anderson said. "He told me, 'Joe Namath is almost the perfect passer.' And Paul Brown said, 'With Joe Namath, the Jets can beat anybody.'"

In December, Shea Stadium can be a nightmare for football. Not only is it a chilly, dank place at that time of year, the wind can make it feel twice as cold when it's coming off the water near LaGuardia Airport. Most of the time, three or four layers of clothing don't do the job.

The next game, against the Cincinnati Bengals, drew another near capacity crowd. Each of the seven games the Jets played at home during the regular season in 1968 drew more than 60,000 fans. It was a tribute to the loyalty of the fans the Jets had attracted, and also the way the team played during the season. They didn't disappoint their faithful followers as they finished their home schedule by beating the Bengals 27–14. Namath threw two touchdown passes in the game. Afterward, Bengals coach Paul Brown said in an interview, "Namath was simply magnificent." Jim Turner kicked two more field goals for a professional football record of thirty-three for the year. Namath again played only the first half and went out with the Jets leading 17–7 as Babe Parilli took over for the second half.

The Jets went into the final regular game of the season with a season record of 10–3. However, a number of Jet players were hurt in the Cincinnati game, causing significant concern with the postseason coming. Don Maynard suffered a hamstring injury, George Sauer a right elbow problem, Dave Herman a sprained ankle, and Bob Talamini a neck injury.

The regular season finale in Miami turned out to be a blowout for the Green and White. With a final score of 31–7 the Jets completed the regular season winning four games in a row and with an 11–3 record. Another big bright spot was the return to action of Emerson Boozer, who ran the ball seventeen times for 83 yards. Boozer had missed the previous two games because of an ankle problem. One of the regulars who didn't play in this game was Don Maynard, who had a conversation with Weeb Ewbank before the game. "I told Weeb, 'If I suit up and play and then I take off on my instincts running my routes I might hurt myself worse. I don't need to play.' Weeb said to me, 'You got a lot of yardage this year going for you.' I told him that it didn't matter, and as a result Bake Turner caught a long touchdown pass. Over the years when someone says to me I could have gotten more yardage if I played that game, I just tell them I traded a few yards for $15,000, which turned out to be the winner's share in the Super Bowl."

Also in this game Jim Turner kicked a 49-yard field goal for his thirty-fourth of the year. Turner's 145 points for the season was third best in professional history behind Paul Hornung and Gino Cappelletti.

No matter how they did in the championship game, this was the best season in Jets history. It showed that the club had fully matured as a top football team. Looking back, only the tough loss in Oakland kept them from winning the last nine games of the regular season. But, as fate would have it, two weeks later the Jets would get an opportunity to avenge that game and play their archrivals, the Oakland Raiders, at Shea Stadium for the AFL Championship.

6. The AFL Championship

"I just took a deep breath and felt a sigh of relief."
—Matt Snell

The Jets had two weeks to get ready for the AFL Championship game. Practice was very focused. In many players' minds this championship game was more important than the potential one they might play against the NFL champion if they won. At that particular time the AFL-NFL Championship game had not yet been given the name "Super Bowl."

Before practices started for the championship game, Weeb Ewbank had a talk with Dave Herman, the outstanding right guard for the Jets. "I remember Coach Ewbank came up to me before our first practice when we were getting ready for the Raiders and said, 'Dave, Sam [Sam Walton, a rookie offensive tackle] has been making some mistakes, and we cannot afford to make mistakes in a championship game. I want you to think about moving over to tackle because I know you are not going to make mistakes.' Then he said, 'I also think you can do it physically, too.' And that became my huge challenge because back in those years when you played offensive guard the unwritten rule in professional football was that you weighed 250 pounds. That was Lombardi's rule in Green Bay, and

Weeb's rule with the Jets. So, here I am moving from guard at 255 pounds, to play offensive tackle against Ike Lassiter who was 6'5" and weighed 300 pounds. So it was a new position for me playing against a guy that was bigger than me. My line coach, Joe Spencer, and I worked really hard to come up with a game plan. I ended up making Lassiter have to go up over the top of me instead of around me, and it worked. It wasn't a lot of fun and it was an anxious time for me."

By this time, after a few years working together, an important bond had been formed between Coach Ewbank and his star player, Joe Namath. In speaking with Joe, he related, "My relationship with Coach Ewbank was one of the best relationships I had with a coach in my career. He certainly was one of the most influential people for me personally. Before I ever played a down for the Jets he had an impact on me. He actually influenced me in making the decision to be a Jet. Coach Bryant at Alabama didn't tell me what to do, where to go, how to do things. But, he did offer the advice to get to know the people you're going to work for. Weeb Ewbank coached Johnny Unitas, my football hero, who I watched growing up. To have an opportunity as a quarterback to play for Coach Ewbank is where it started."

When the Jets realized they would be playing the Oakland Raiders for the AFL Championship, the game took on added meaning. The Raiders, coached by John Rauch, were a terrific team and had a great season, winning thirteen and losing only two. They had just walloped Kansas City 41–6 in a playoff game to decide their division title. The Jets-Raiders rivalry was huge even though the teams were in different divisions. The rivalry was due in part to the fact that former Brooklyn native Al Davis ran the Raider organization. As witnessed by his tenure as president of the AFL earlier, he was as fierce a competitor you would ever see, and he wanted to win. "Just win baby" had been a slogan of his for a long time. And, the previous year, Namath had his cheekbone fractured when hit by defensive end, Ben Davidson, in a game in Oakland. Add to this mix the "Heidi" game earlier in the season and you had the makings of a terrific championship football game. Matt Snell said, "I was glad when I found out that we were playing the Raiders for the championship. We had classic battles against them, but they seemed to always come out on top."

"The rivalry between us and the Raiders was very good," said Jim Turner. "It was a big deal because we had Namath and they had a great team with Al Davis looking over them. The Raiders played what Ben

Davidson described to me as 'creative Raider football.' Because of Joe and the fact that they had a terrific team made it a perfect rivalry."

"We always had good, tough ball games against Oakland," commented Don Maynard. "At the same time things happened to stir up a rivalry. Like the hit by Ben Davidson on Joe Namath, and Weeb coming from the NFL, and Al Davis himself. Heck, Al Davis had a rivalry with everybody. The media liked to build things up, but we were just two good teams."

"I think the rivalry goes back to Al Davis more than anyone else," said Johnny Sample. "Al Davis was a great football man. He instilled competition, playing hard, and winning every game, particularly the big games. And whenever Oakland came to New York to play in Shea Stadium, it was always a big game for Al because he came from Brooklyn. I think he got the Raiders hyped up to play us."

Walt Michaels recalled the preparations for the playoff game with Oakland. "We actually prepared like any other team. We played every team pretty much straight up because we felt we could get to the quarterback. I thought we could rush Lamonica. We knew he was going to throw deep passes. We wanted to take that away from him. I always thought we had an advantage at Shea Stadium. I always felt teams were intimidated when they came to Shea with the winds and the airplanes going over with the noise. I always felt that if the Jets moved out of Shea Stadium, there goes a big home-field advantage."

A pretty good indication of how good the Jets' season had gone up to this point was when three members of the team, Joe Namath, George Sauer, and Gerry Philbin, were named to the AFL-NFL All-Pro Team. Thirteen Jets were named to the AFL All-Star Team.

The day before the championship game there were reports that Raider quarterback Daryl Lamonica, who had hurt his thumb on his passing hand against Kansas City, might be hampered because of soreness and the weather. The Jets had a question mark in Don Maynard. He had pulled a hamstring and didn't play in the last regular season game. There was some concern that he might not be able to run deep patterns. "There was never any doubt that I wouldn't play in the championship game," said Maynard. As it turned out, at least in the Jets case, that injury had little effect on the outcome of the game.

That same day as the Jets worked out at Shea Stadium, Randy Rasmussen remembered how real the Raiders-Jets feud was in everyone's mind. "We were going through a walk-through practice at Shea Stadium and Weeb saw someone cleaning seats in the stands. He sent someone up to check out that person. He thought it could be one of Al Davis's spies."

In the early morning hours of December 29, 1968, Shea Stadium was about as dreary and quiet a place as one could imagine. As usual for this time of year, the stadium was cold and windy. In a few hours more than 62,000 screaming fans would fill the stands to see a classic football game.

"We wanted a chance to redeem ourselves against Oakland because of how we played out there during the season," recalled Ralph Baker. "We thought there was some lousy officiating in that game that cost us. I felt we should have won that game. Still, the fact was that we gave up two touchdowns in the last minute or so, and it didn't sit too well with us."

Like the Jets, the Raiders had a strong-armed quarterback in Lamonica, one of the talented young quarterbacks in the AFL. With Namath, Lamonica, Len Dawson and a few others, the AFL was particularly strong at that position. It was to no one's surprise that both Namath and Lamonica were able to deal with the elements at Shea.

"Playing against Daryl Lamonica wasn't that difficult," recalled Johnny Sample, "because you know that three out of five passes were going to be bombs."

The Jets opened up a 10–0 lead after one quarter as Namath threw a 14-yard touchdown to Don Maynard and Jim Turner kicked a 33-yard field goal. On the touchdown pass from Namath, Maynard said, "We were in a slot formation left, and I wound up in the slot so I ran a down and out pattern. Joe made a great pass and I scored."

Oakland came roaring back in the second quarter to cut the lead to 10–7 with a 29-yard Lamonica touchdown pass to Fred Biletnikoff. Jim Turner kicked a 36-yard field goal for the Jets, and the ageless George Blanda kicked one from 26-yards out for Oakland. The first half ended with the Jets up 13–10.

In the third quarter, the Raiders opened the scoring with another field goal, this time a 9-yarder by Blanda to tie the game. Namath came right back with a drive capped by him throwing a 20-yard touchdown pass to tight end Pete Lammons. At the end of three quarters the score was 20–13. In the fourth quarter the Raiders added another field goal to bring the score to 20–16, before things got really interesting. With the ball and a four-point lead, Namath threw a pass toward Don Maynard that was intercepted by Raiders cornerback George Atkinson at the Jet 37-yard line. He ran it back to the Jet 5-yard line where Namath knocked him out of bounds. Oakland scored a touchdown on their first play on a Pete Banaszak 5-yard run. The Raiders had now taken the lead over the Jets 23–20. With the stiff wind, the cold, and what had just happened, the crowd acted like the temperature was below zero.

But the crowd did warm up a little when the Jets got a good return on the kickoff by Earl Christy to their own 32-yard line. Namath then took control. On the first play he connected with George Sauer who snagged his seventh catch of the day. It gained ten yards and gave the Jets a first down at their own 42-yard line. Then, one of the biggest plays of the game occurred. "I remember earlier in the game, I said something to Namath," recalled Don Maynard. "I said, 'Joseph, I got a long one in me when you need it.' So, when we got into the situation of being behind, I remember Namath saying in the huddle, 'No penalties, we're going to go for it.' And the wind was blowing really tough and we were going from the out into the closed end of the stadium. The play was called and I took off on my route. Joe's pass was coming to me around the ten o'clock area. All of a sudden the wind catches it and my hands and head begin to go around. I turned completely and caught the ball around the two o'clock area. After the catch my momentum carried me out of bounds on the six-yard line." Maynard, who had a sore hamstring, beat George Atkinson on the 58-yard play, the same guy who had made the interception earlier. "It was the greatest catch I ever made," said Maynard. "I mean the greatest in my career. There's no doubt about it." A few plays later Namath hit Maynard again, this time in the end zone for a 6-yard touchdown pass to put the Jets back in the lead 27–23. "When Joe called the play for the touchdown in the huddle, I was the number-one receiver on the play," recalled Maynard. "As the play started, because of the coverage, immediately I became the number-four receiver. So Joe first looked at Sauer, then Lammons, then Billy Mathis, and was pumping his arm. Each guy was covered and I was doing a delayed route that I'm supposed to do since I wasn't number one. I turned back in and Joe drilled it about three feet high off the ground and I caught it away from the defender."

The crowd went wild, but everyone knew that there was still over seven minutes left in the game. The Raiders would have plenty of time to score and possibly win the game.

The Jets kicked off, and the strong-armed Lamonica was able to move the Raiders down to the Jets' 26-yard line. With the Raiders trailing by four points, John Rauch decided not to try a field goal and on fourth down Verlon Biggs dropped Lamonica for a 6-yard loss.

The Jets took over on downs, but were unable to kill the clock. After a Curly Johnson punt, the Raiders once again had a chance to come back. From their own 15-yard line, the Raiders moved to the Jet 12-yard line where Lamonica tried a little flair pass to halfback Charlie Smith. He was open, but the ball went a little behind him and fell to the ground. Not sure if it was a lateral or incomplete pass, Jet linebacker Ralph Baker alertly picked it up and started to run. The referee blew the play dead. The officials ruled it was a lateral rather than an incomplete pass, but the ball could not be advanced. In any case, it meant the Jets got the ball and a chance to once again run out the clock. But it was not to be, as the Jet offense stalled and Oakland got the ball back in their territory with forty-five seconds to go in the game. The Raiders only chance now was for Lamonica to throw a few long passes, but fortunately for the Jets he couldn't connect for a touchdown. It was a wild game that came down to the wire, but the Jets' defense held on and the team was able to capture their first AFL Championship.

"Lamonica was notorious for pulling games out at the end," said Randy Rasmussen. "That pass he threw behind Charlie Smith is vivid in my mind." Randy said there was one thing that stood out in that game for him. "I remember playing against Dan Birdwell and I chop-blocked him on one play and he said, 'If you do that again, I'm going to kill you.' It wasn't so much the words, but the way he said it. He was an intense guy."

When the game ended a few of the Jet player's hoisted Coach Ewbank onto their shoulders. It was an emotional moment. "I thought I caught a couple of tears coming down under his glasses," said Pete Lammons. Weeb Ewbank became the only coach to win titles in both the NFL and the AFL.

In the locker room after the game Coach Ewbank was given the game ball and then promptly carried into the showers by some players, fully clothed and still holding the ball. I imagine he didn't care about getting soaked right at that time.

"Looking back at that game," Larry Grantham told me, "I remember the interception Joe threw, but I also remember that once we got the ball back Joe went to work and completed that first-down pass to Sauer. After that, the long pass and the touchdown toss to Maynard are very vivid in my mind. It was a sign we could handle adversity and showed how great Namath really was." Joe had a simple answer to any doubters that the Jets might not recover after the Raiders took the lead. "Of course I thought we could come back," he said.

Emerson Boozer remembered, "I knew we had a very good team going into the championship game against the Raiders. When we beat them I just realized we could go all the way."

Even though he only completed 19 passes in 49 attempts, Namath still threw for three touchdowns, two to Don Maynard and one to Pete Lammons. Matt Snell and Emerson Boozer ran for 122 yards between them. Although it was many years ago, some of the players recalled their thoughts immediately after the championship game. Snell said, "I was so caught up in the game. I was so happy we won the championship in front of our fans who had struggled and stayed with us even though we hadn't done much over the years."

"I remembered thinking about the play-calling that day," Dave Herman said. "We had a lot of confidence in what we could do offensively. It was such a mental and physical game for me because of the new position on the line. I had to really think quickly when Joe changed a play at the line of scrimmage. I had to remember I was playing tackle, not guard." I also asked Dave if Coach Ewbank talked to him after the game about how he played his new position. "Coach Ewbank came up to me and said, 'Dave, that was a great job.' I was really tired and I said, 'Thanks.' He then asked, 'Will you do it again?' I said, 'I'll be happy to do it if it will help the team.' And then I thought about the defensive player I might be playing against in the next game. If it was Bubba Smith, then he was heavier, taller, and a better athlete than Ike Lassiter!"

"After we beat Oakland in the AFL Championship game," said Johnny Sample, "I thought now that we were going to be in the NFL-AFL Championship game we were going to win it because the Raiders were probably the second-best team behind us in football that year. I told Matt Snell in the locker room after the Raiders game that the next one will be easier."

"I'm not sure the celebration after the victory over Oakland wasn't bigger than the NFL-AFL Championship game," recalled Walt Michaels. "It was a hard fought game against Oakland and winning the AFL Championship was important for all of us.

It wasn't long after the victory over the Raiders that the Jets found out they would be playing the Baltimore Colts for the NFL-AFL Championship, as it was then labeled. The game, soon to be dubbed "Super Bowl III," would take place two weeks later in Miami, Florida. The Colts had just shut out an excellent Cleveland Browns team 34–0 in the NFL Championship game in front of over 80,000 people in Cleveland. It was the first shutout the Browns had absorbed since 1958. It was the powerful Colts' fifteenth win of the season, their fourth shutout of the year, and the sixth game in which their opponent failed to score a touchdown. Needless to say, the Baltimore Colts were a terrific team. In most people's minds they were the best team in all of professional football, and certainly much better than any team the AFL would put up against them. Some football "experts" even considered this Colts team one of the best teams ever to play professional football. In two weeks, at the NFL-AFL Championship game, the Colts were confident they would prove that true.

Meanwhile, the Jets were still celebrating their victory. For some players the game against the Raiders was more important than the NFL-AFL matchup. For others, the next game would give the Jets and the AFL an opportunity to prove they were on a par with the long established NFL. In any case, both teams had two weeks to get ready for a game that would turn out to be one of the most significant ever played in professional football. A game that would change the face of professional football and help make the Super Bowl the most promoted and most expensive sporting event in the world.

JOE AND WEEB—WHAT THE PLAYERS THOUGHT

George Sauer, one of Joe's key receivers, when asked how he was able to work so well with Namath related, "We talked a lot during the week. We also practiced a lot, and he always wanted to try something new. Coach Ewbank let us try things if we thought it could work. Much of our success was due to the offensive line. Our line was great."

When Larry Grantham was recently asked about all the problems going on in the country during the season and throughout the postseason he replied, "I knew about the protesters and about Vietnam, but I'll tell you how perceptive Namath was. One time there was some stuff in the newspaper about him and he said, 'If you believe what's in the newspaper then you don't believe we're getting a lot of people killed in Vietnam.'"

Dave Herman gave this insight on Weeb, "I am constantly asked about the Jets' success. I tell older people and young kids alike that preparation makes the results. We were a team that worked as hard as any, and we worked smart because Coach Ewbank was a smart practice coach as well as a smart game coach. He was a guy from the NFL who had won a championship so he knew what he was doing. Weeb was also a great offensive line coach as well as a superb head coach. With the great defensive line players against us we had to be good, and Weeb made sure we were."

Don Maynard of course had a lot of things to say. A real student of the game, he had this to say about Joe Namath's importance to the team and his ability to be a great quarterback: "A lot of people don't know that I played and watched and learned and suggested a lot of things to over twenty-five professional quarterbacks. When Joe came along I told him, 'Joseph, I'm going to make you a better quarterback, and you're going to make me a great receiver, but we're going to talk on every play. I'm going to teach you how to communicate, and we're going to make our deal the greatest thing in the world.' Joe was a great listener and he was a great student of the game. And with Pete Lammons, George Sauer, Bake Turner, and me, we had the best passing attack in America. In eight years playing with Joe we had one busted play and it was the first pro game Joe played. He threw it one place and I was already going the other way. I came back to the huddle and he said I called this play and I told him I'd explain later. We turned that one play into maybe six touchdowns in the future because I told Joe, 'You read the defensive back, you don't have to read me, you've already told me what to do in the huddle, and I will do that, but we're still going to work off the defensive back. If he comes up we're going to go for it, if he stays off we'll run the quick out.' So from then on we never had any miscommunication. We also had hand signals that we could change. I'd put up two fingers and he knew it was play sixty-two, or four fingers would be play sixty-four. If I tapped my head it was another pattern, clenched fist another. I also told Joe to get rid of the ball quicker and taught Joe to read the safety. I knew football—a lot of it is common sense. And Joe was able to see everything. You couldn't get to Joe as a defensive player from the left side. Joe had the great release with great strength in his arm, but his greatest ability was anticipation of what to do in the passing game. It didn't hurt that he also had four receivers he could count on and never had to worry about them cheating on the route."

Maynard also had feelings about Weeb Ewbank. "I loved him. He was also a good listener. If I wanted to change something he would listen. If you could prove a play would work he would let you change it."

Dave Herman gave Namath lots of praise. "He was a team player all the way. Joe came a year after I got there, so we stayed together for nine years. Never once did he ever say to me or anyone else that if they would have done this, or they would have done that, we would have had a better opportunity. He was a team player then, and he is still a team player now. That's what I remember about playing football with the New York Jets—the team attitude. Joe just came across as an individual outside the game. In that and many ways he was ahead of his time. Sure, he was an individual and a lot of younger kids could identify with him, but I think that they identified with him in a positive way— being a leader and doing what it takes to get himself ready to play the game. We were lucky to have him as our quarterback. He was a great player. But, he was also a great teammate. I always tell people that far and away Joe was one of the best teammates I ever played with in my nineteen years of high school, college, and pro football."

Defensive tackle John Elliott had similar feelings. "He was great. Joe shouldered a lot of pressure for the whole team. I couldn't have dealt with what he had to deal with. The writers made him almost bigger than life. But, on a personal level, he was a great teammate."

"Joe was as good a quarterback as any that ever played the game," remarked offensive guard Randy Rasmussen. "I rate him high in his ability to read defenses and his poise in calling plays. Joe did a lot of checking off at the line of scrimmage. Half the battle was getting the right play called, and Joe had enough poise and confidence to stand up there and change plays. He was great at that. And, he was just one of the guys as far as a teammate. The great part about Joe is he could be anywhere and if you had a chance to speak with him he would just talk to you like you and he were friends. He took a lot of kidding from everyone and gave it out, too." When asked if Namath got down if things weren't going well, Randy said, "I think Joe was always the same. He understood the game and knew we had a good defense to help out."

"Joe was a tough quarterback," said Jim Turner. "He wouldn't get mad when we went for a field goal. Other quarterbacks come off the field cursing and upset. He would always check with me on the wind, particularly at Shea Stadium. He would always ask me where I wanted the ball and let's go for it. He knew that three points were important. As far as a teammate, he was the best. He was fun and he wasn't full of himself. Anytime there were jokes played in the locker room you could bet guys were playing them on Joe. He wasn't sacred." Billy Hampton, equipment manager for the Jets in 1968–69, confirmed this. "He was great in the locker room. He gave it and took it like everyone else."

"Joe was an outstanding teammate," said Johnny Sample. "I've never played on a team that had any better teammate than Joe Namath. He was great to all of the guys, not only me, but offensive players, defensive guys, and special teams people. Joe got along very well with all the guys on the team. Whenever we went out Joe always picked up the tab for everybody. He would listen to you if you had a problem and if you didn't want to go to Weeb about something, Joe would go to Coach Ewbank if you wanted him to do it."

"Joe and I had a very good relationship," commented Walt

Michaels. "He was a class act. He was ready to play no matter what anyone thinks. If anyone could give you one game, and I played with Otto Graham, and you needed an important win, Joe Namath would be at the top of the list. He just made everything look so darn easy. He could make a ten-yard pass look exciting."

7. Super Bowl III—The Difference Between Arrogance and Confidence Is Ability

"A chicken ain't nothin' but a bird."
—John "Curly" Johnson

C oming off the high of beating the Raiders, if the Jets had a choice, they would have played the NFL-AFL Championship game the week following that win. But, like today, it was decided there should be a two-week break between the respective league championship games and the "official" championship game. While it hadn't as yet been officially titled the Super Bowl, many fans and sportswriters were calling it just that. Dave Anderson, who covered the Jets for the *New York Times* during this time, remembered, "Pete Rozelle and the league didn't like the name 'Super Bowl,' but they eventually surrendered to it."

The first two championship games between the NFL and the AFL saw the Green Bay Packers, under Vince Lombardi, win pretty handily over the Kansas City Chiefs and the Oakland Raiders. "The Packers had won the first two Championship games. As a result of that nobody really believed in the AFL," said Anderson. "That's why the Colts were seventeen-point favorites over the Jets." Still, there was a lot of interest in the game, particularly in New York City. "There was a tremendous amount of hype in New York," continued Anderson. "The fact that they were such overwhelming underdogs made it a big story. Everybody thought the Colts were just going to walk through the game."

After three days off following their victory over the Raiders, Coach Ewbank decided to take the Jets down to Miami for ten days of practice and to get them acclimated to the warm weather. As it turned out, the warm weather wasn't close to the heat that was starting to come out from the opposing players. Namath, whose lavish lifestyle and outspoken personality was not always thought of in the best of terms, particularly by opposing players, just happened to mention to whoever would listen, that in his opinion, Earl Morrall, the Colts starting quarterback against the Jets, "was not equal to the top young quarterbacks in the AFL." He said that in addition to himself, "guys like Daryl Lamonica in Oakland, John Hadl at San Diego, and Bob Griese of Miami, were all superior." Namath also shared this observation, "I study quarterbacks, and I assure you the Colts have never had to play against quarterbacks like we have in the AFL."[1] Needless to say, it didn't take long for the Colts to react. Earl Morrall said, "He's got his newspaper space, and that's what he wants. A lot of players have opinions on other players that would have writers running for their typewriters if they expressed them."

"I have a lot of respect for Joe," Colts defensive end Bubba Smith said. "But a football player who is real good doesn't have to talk. The Green Bay Packers were real champions. They never talked. They never had to. That's the way I visualize all champions, dignified and humble. All this Namath talk isn't going to fire us up." To which Namath replied, "If they need newspaper clippings to fire them up they're in trouble."[2]

Colt defensive end Billy Ray Smith had this to say about Joe: "He hasn't seen a defense like ours in his league. We have twenty variations of our blitzes. I think reading our defenses will be a new experience for him. When he gets a little older he'll get some humility." Joe certainly got the Colts' attention.

While this back and forth banter was going on, the fact remained that the Baltimore Colts had established themselves as one of the best teams ever in the National Football League. Their record had proved that they not only possessed a terrific defensive team, but also a very good offensive unit as well. Superbly coached by Don Shula, the only tarnish on an out-

1. TheSportingNews.Com—*History of the Super Bowl.*
2. Ibid.

standing season had been the injury to their great quarterback, Johnny Unitas. In their last pre-season game earlier that year Unitas, while trying to complete a pass, was knocked down and suffered a tear on the inside of his right elbow. He ended up having trouble with his throwing motion and the Colts went to Earl Morrall, who they had fortunately acquired earlier as insurance to Unitas. Morrall ended up having a tremendous year and was named the Most Valuable Player in the NFL.

Joe's comments about Earl Morrall became headlines and created a stir. It wasn't long after that he decided it was time to really get the folks excited. While receiving an award as pro football's Player of the Year at the Miami Touchdown Club, Namath bristled at some Colts fans in the audience mocking the Jets. He decided to say what he thought, hence the infamous "guarantee" of a Jet victory in the championship game, even if the Jets were 17-point underdogs. His prediction had some effect on his teammates as well as on the Colts.

Dave Herman recalled, "I said to myself, 'Joe, what are you doing!' I then asked Joe if he remembered that I was playing a new position and would be up against 6'8", 320-pound Bubba Smith, and if he was trying to get him psyched up against me? Joe just told me, 'I'm not worried about you.'"

Jet defensive tackle John Elliott wasn't troubled. "I didn't think much of it. Where I'm from that's how we always talk. We say we are going to do something and do it."

"I wasn't shocked," Gerry Philbin said. "In watching films of the Colts we saw they could be beaten. They played an offense that was so detectible. Our defense was more advanced than a lot of NFL teams."

Coach Ewbank wasn't too happy. Equipment manager Billy Hampton remembered, "Weeb was pissed off. He came over to me and said, 'What the hell did he say that for? Goddammit, I told them to keep their mouths shut. I don't want to fire up the Colts.' He just walked away shaking his head."

Matt Snell was less concerned; "If you have been around Joe for a couple of years you can expect anything. I just felt, what's the worst thing that can happen? There's no pressure on us. It's on the Colts. In the papers in Florida they had comparisons at all the positions. The only position we were rated at least equal was quarterback."

"After Joe made his prediction it was all over the papers, radio, and television the next day," recalled Johnny Sample. "I asked Joe, 'What are you doing?' Joe said, 'We're going to beat them aren't we?' I said, 'Yeah, we're going to beat them.' And Joe said, 'If the Colts play the way they played in some of their games, we should win the game by thirty.' Looking back, he was right."

Pete Lammons related where the basis of Joe's optimism came from. "We were sitting down watching film of the Colts. It seemed like every team they played was very predictable. They would never change a play at the line of scrimmage. With Joe, we always did that. And most of the teams they played didn't have very good passing quarterbacks like Joe. So I said out loud, 'Damn coach, if we keep looking at these films we're going to get overconfident.' Everyone laughed. I sort of predicted a win, but Joe said it on the outside and he's gotten all the credit for it."

"The one thing that really stood out when we were watching film of the Colts," said Randy Rasmussen, "we realized the way they played they didn't look as difficult to us as maybe other people thought. We matched up better against them than the Raiders. We were getting two stories. One from the outside telling us that we were going to get killed and the other from ourselves saying we thought we could beat them easier than the Raiders. The only question mark I had going into the Super Bowl game was Unitas and would he play?"

The Colts felt differently about Namath's comments. Earl Morrall said recently, "I thought he was just putting the spotlight on himself. The writers probably made more out of it than they should have."

"I used it in the meetings and had the headlines posted up on our bulletin board. From that standpoint we tried to get the most out of it," Don Shula told me. "In reality, the Jets were a very good football team with a great quarterback and a very good coach."

"As far as preparing for the game, the practices were very focused," said Johnny Sample. "It was good we came down to Florida early. The hotel was nice. All the people I met down in Florida were into the game. I owned a ticket agency at the time. I sold entertainment tickets. The president of the hotel where we were staying asked me to try and get him some tickets for the Super Bowl game. I told him that I probably could get him a few so I said to him, 'Exactly how many do you need?' He said, 'Whatever you can get.' Every minute I wasn't practicing I was on the telephone, calling people who owed me favors. I got him 220 tickets for the game. It was great for my business and on top of everything I got two free suites at the hotel."

Placekicker Jim Turner related his view of the preparations for the

Super Bowl game, "The coaches had developed great game plans. The players were very relaxed. Of course, we had Pete Lammons and Curly Johnson who kept everybody loose. And the best thing we did was come to Florida early and enjoyed the nice weather."

"We looked at the Colts on film and I figured we played at least three teams in our league who were similar to what they were doing," said Walt Michaels. "We knew they were overconfident. The looked predictable on offense. I had tremendous confidence in our defense and their ability to understand what I was trying to get across to them."

On the day of the game, as Jet players got on the bus for the ride over to the Orange Bowl, there was a sense of nervousness and apprehension. While they were somewhat confident, they knew they were playing an outstanding Colts team that had proven over the season to be one of the most dominant NFL teams of all time. The ride over was unusually quiet so the Jets' team philosopher decided it was time to offer some words of insight. Without any cue he blurted out the now famous words that altered the mind-set of Jet players and coaches for this historic game. "A chicken ain't nothin' but a bird." That was it. Nothing more, nothing less. Curly Johnson had done it again. His wit and wisdom had come to the rescue. "Everybody was a little tight and tense and it broke the team up," said Larry Grantham. "It meant nothing and yet it meant everything. It changed the mood of the team in an instant."

Also on that bus was the Jets' "artist-in-residence," LeRoy Neiman. "Somehow when the players were boarding the bus to come to the game I just got on with them. A lot of people tell me that they've seen footage of me getting off the bus just like I was part of the team. I remember Curly Johnson's remark. He was a funny guy. He used to kick with an old-fashioned football shoe. I actually made a drawing of that shoe."

In the Jet locker room as the players put on their uniforms and got ready for the game that would change their lives, a little humor was still left. Equipment manager Billy Hampton had brought his family with him down to Florida and his five boys were running around the locker room. Billy said, "When Weeb Ewbank saw all my kids he yelled out in front of all the players, 'That goddamn Hampton. He has to get a vasectomy so he has no more kids.' "

Pete Lammons recalled another light moment before the game. "A big dilemma for Coach Ewbank was who he was going to introduce before the game, the offense or the defense. He just couldn't make up his mind.

We were in this meeting before the game and there was a long silence. All of a sudden Namath says, 'Weeb, why don't you just introduce the seniors?' Everybody laughed and he decided on the defense."

Before the players went out for the start of the game both coaches had some final thoughts. Coach Ewbank simply said, "Don't get fancy. Let's do the things we do best and do them well. Don't lose your poise. We've only lost our poise one time this season and that was at Oakland. We can't let it happen again."

Don Shula's advice to his Colts team was also pretty simple. "Don't wait for them to lose it. Be aggressive. We have to win it ourselves. Namath is a great passer and we have to put a lot of pressure on him because of his great receivers."

Winston Hill recalled, "Right before the game all the starters were so psyched up. Everyone wanted to be in on the kickoff at the start of the game. Weeb was running around trying to keep the starters off the field for the kickoff."

So, after all the hype, banter, and controversy, it was game time. With a national television audience and over 75,000 people in the Orange Bowl, it was time to finally play. The Jets won the coin toss and at 3:05 P.M. EST the NFL-AFL Championship game began.

On their very first possession the Jets showed they were not going to be a pushover. On his third carry of the opening series Matt Snell bulled over Colts' safety Rick Volk, who had to leave the game groggy and rubber-legged. He would return, but would require hospital care after the game. "I remember when Matt Snell knocked the Colts' safety out of the game," said *New York Times* writer Dave Anderson. "It showed the Colts the Jets were tough."

"That play was a tone-setter for us," said Randy Rasmussen. "After the play was over the whole stadium knew the Jets were there and weren't going to be intimidated by the Colts." When I asked Randy how Coach Ewbank was on the sidelines during the game he said, "I never knew Weeb to be nervous. The only thing I noticed was that he adjusted his glasses a lot during the game. He had two great coaches running the offense and defense in Clive Rush and Walt Michaels, and had confidence in them. Once the game started all Weeb had to do was walk up and down the sidelines. He always chewed ice and I did notice he was doing that a lot more during this game." Jim Turner added, "He didn't seem nervous to me. I thought he was more relaxed in that game than the AFL Championship game against Oakland. He and his coaching staff were so well prepared, and the players were, too."

"To me Coach Ewbank was always the same," recalled Don Maynard. "We went into every game on offense and defense with everything pretty well set. Weeb was like me, quietly confident. Maybe on the inside he was different, but on the outside I thought he was probably the same as any other time."

Johnny Sample didn't see it quite the same way. "Weeb was a little more hyper in the Super Bowl game," he said. "He was prancing a little more than usual. You have to understand that he was playing against his old team on national television in a championship game between two leagues. The game meant a lot to him. Looking back it keynoted Weeb's coaching career. That game is the reason he made it to the Hall of Fame."

Although Snell ran well, the Jets were unable to get into scoring position and were forced to punt to the Colts' 27-yard line. On the Colts' first possession they were able to get the ball all the way down to the Jets' 27, but a field goal attempt by Lou Michaels, Walt's brother, was no good as it went wide to the right. With the Jets in possession of the ball deep in their own territory, wide receiver George Sauer fumbled and the Colts recovered on the Jets' 12-yard line. After two plays only gained six yards, on third down Earl Morrall threw a pass that was deflected by Jets' linebacker Al Atkinson and bounced off the shoulder of the intended receiver, Tom Mitchell. It was intercepted in the end zone by Jets' cornerback Randy Beverly. The Jets had escaped without being scored upon.

Even though they hadn't moved the ball yet, Don Maynard knew the Jets' offense would be effective. "Namath checked off for a long pass to me," said Don. "I beat their zone defense by five yards and Joe's pass was just a couple of inches too long. But that pass made the Colts aware I could beat their coverage whether I was healthy or not. So the Colts doubled and occasionally triple covered me the rest of the game. It opened up other opportunities for our receivers."

With the Jets starting from their own 20-yard line they began to move the ball with a combination of passes with Matt Snell and Emerson Boozer runs, making their way down to the Colts' 4-yard line. Namath then handed off the ball to Snell, who behind blocks from Winston Hill and Boozer ran it in for a Jet touchdown. Jim Turner's point after gave the Jets a 7–0 lead. After fumbling the ball and stopping the Colts from scoring and then scoring themselves, the Jets had proven to everyone this was going to be a much closer game than most people thought.

Artist LeRoy Neiman remembered Matt Snell's touchdown, "I was on the field around the 40-yard line with a terrific *New York Times* photographer by the name of Barton Silverman," said LeRoy. "He was a guy with great instincts on where the action might happen. I remember Barton telling me he was going to go down to the end zone. I figured I would go down there with him and all of a sudden the Jets came down the field and Matt Snell made that run into the end zone and we were right there. And I made a drawing of it."

Johnny Sample recalled, "After the first quarter, Namath came up to me and said, 'What do you think?' I said, 'Man, they can't move the ball at all. If they don't come up with some new plays, they might not score.'"

The Colts took the ensuing kickoff and, with the help of a 58-yard run by Tom Matte, reached the Jets' 16-yard line. Earl Morrall then tried a pass to Willie Richardson that was intercepted by Johnny Sample. Once again, the Jets were able to escape a Colts' score.

The Colts did get the ball back again with time running out in the first half. They were able to get into Jets' territory and with twenty-five seconds left Morrall took the snap and handed off to Tom Matte. Matte started to take off but suddenly stopped and flipped the ball back to Morrall. It was the old flea-flicker that had worked well for the Colts earlier in the season. The ball was supposed to go to wide receiver Jimmy Orr, who was waving his hands, wide open at the 10-yard line. For some reason Morrall didn't see Orr and instead threw the ball toward Jerry Hill. The Jets' Jim Hudson intercepted the pass, and again the Jets were able to avoid a Colts' touchdown. Asked about this play after the game, Morrall said, "I had to turn to my right to get the ball back from Matte and when I looked up I didn't see Orr. I saw Hill and I went for him." At the end of the first half the Jets had the lead 7–0.

Some writers in the press box thought Orr might have visually mixed in with a band that was nearing the field to perform at halftime. Don Shula told me he thinks that's what happened. "The first half we had so many opportunities to score. We moved the ball well. Of course, Earl not seeing Jimmy Orr wide open downfield right before the half hurt us. The band was starting to come out on to the field. I think Jimmy blended in with the band members."

At halftime Coach Shula told his players, "We're making stupid mistakes, and we're stopping ourselves. You've got them believing they're better than us." The Jets on the other hand were now filled with confidence and were told by Coach Ewbank to "keep doing the things that we're doing."[3]

Many people thought Shula would switch from Morrall to Johnny Unitas at halftime. Most Colts fans thought he should have gone to Unitas earlier in the game. In my interview with Coach Shula he explained, "The decision I made was to stay with Earl. He had a great year and a great game against Cleveland to get us to the Super Bowl. Unitas was still not 100 percent in practice. The third quarter ended up with us really never having the ball, the Jets controlled it. So, when I finally made the decision to bring in Unitas there wasn't a whole lot of time left in the third quarter. In the fourth quarter John did take us in for a touchdown and that's where all the backlash comes from."

"I was worried Unitas might play," recalled Johnny Sample. "I had been teammates with him in Baltimore and I knew what he could do."

When the second half started it didn't take long for adversity to strike the Colts. On the very first play of the half Tom Matte fumbled and Jets' linebacker Ralph Baker recovered on the Colts' 33-yard line. The Jets couldn't move the ball, but Jim Turner kicked a field goal from the 32 to give the Jets a 10–0 lead.

On the next Colt possession they weren't able to do anything as Unitas started to warm up. On the other side of the field, the Jets were also worried about their quarterback situation. Namath had some previous problems with his right thumb, and it started to bother him during the game. Namath's backup, Babe Parilli, was sent in. He managed to get the Jets down in Colt territory where Jim Turner kicked his second field goal of the game to make the score 13–0. Just as important though, Namath would return to the game.

Johnny Unitas finally replaced Morrall at this point. Morrall told me in a recent interview, "We weren't getting any points on the board. John had been injured, but was working out. He was a great player and Coach Shula tried to stir things up. Was I surprised? Yes and no. I had proven that I could bring the team back before, but Johnny Unitas was Johnny Unitas."

I asked Walt Michaels if he was surprised that Johnny Unitas didn't come into the game earlier? "No, not at all," said Walt. "Morrall had a great year and Unitas was hurt. I think Shula did exactly what he should

---

3. Ibid.

have done. Of course, we dominated the third quarter on offense and the Colts didn't get a lot of chances with the ball."

When asked what his thoughts were when Unitas did finally come into the game, Randy Rasmussen said, "You got the feeling on the sideline that hold on, something might happen. I think there was a quiet lull on our bench at that time."

Johnny Sample remembered when Unitas came into the game. "I told the guys in the defensive huddle that he's just a quarterback like anybody else, not believing what I was saying. I said, 'All we have to do is keep playing the way we've been playing.' But, there was a stigma about John Unitas."

Shula, however, had been deadly accurate. The Jets effectively controlled the ball in the third quarter. The Colts managed only seven offensive plays with a net gain of ten yards.

Two minutes into the fourth quarter the Jets were able to score on another Jim Turner field goal, this time from nine yards out, to give them a 16–0 lead.

On another Baltimore drive in the fourth quarter the Jets made their fourth interception of the game, the second by cornerback Randy Beverly. With less than four minutes remaining, Unitas led the Colts downfield, finally scoring on a one-yard run by Jerry Hill. With the point after, the score was now 16–7. The world was watching one of the most incredible upsets in sports history.

As the clock ticked down the final seconds of this astonishing event, a few players picked up Coach Ewbank and put him on their shoulders. It would be a fantastic ride for the only man to ever coach world champions in both the AFL and NFL. "The only problem with the ride on the players' shoulders for Coach Ewbank," Ralph Baker told me, "was that somebody pulled on his leg and he ended up with hip problems the rest of his life."

Bedlam broke loose as the game ended. The famous footage of Joe Namath running into the locker room with his finger signaling "number one" has been shown thousands of times since that day.

"I remembered as the clock was winding down, thinking about warming up before the game and during introductions. There didn't seem to be a lot of people pulling for us," said Randy Rasmussen. "When the game turned in our favor and then toward the end, I thought there was nothing but Jet fans at the stadium. As soon as the game was over I ran over to Johnny Unitas to shake his hand. Believe it or not he was my absolute hero when I was a kid in Nebraska. I grew up a Baltimore Colt fan. When I caught up to him he shook my hand but he looked upset. He didn't say anything. I guess the Colts were embarrassed. It didn't make me feel less happy about winning the game, but it was something I had to do."

In the Jet locker room there was plenty of excitement but not as much hollering as one might think. Maybe it was because the players believed they could win so it didn't come as such a big surprise to them. After the game Gerry Philbin was quoted the next day, "We didn't make us three touchdown underdogs."

"I think the NFL will be ready for us in about two years," Johnny Sample was heard yelling sarcastically across the locker room. "The reason why I said that," recalled Sample, "was because of what Vince Lombardi said after Super Bowl II. He said the AFL is not good enough to play against the NFL. I had that quote from a newspaper in my pocket in the locker room and pulled it out and held it up."

By defeating the Colts, the Jets brought themselves and the AFL to parity with the NFL. After years of demeaning coverage by the press and steadfast NFL fans, the AFL had won bragging rights. It truly was a time for the AFL to gloat. In winning the Super Bowl the Jets earned $15,000 while the Colts' losers share would be $7,500. Philbin said, "I hope the Colts didn't spend $15,000 thinking they were going to win." Joe Namath yelled, "I'm only talking to the New York press. They're the only ones who believed in me." He forgot about that a few minutes later.

Praise was coming from everywhere, offense and defense alike, in the Jet locker room. *The Daily News* got some choice epithets: Walt Michaels, the architect of the stingy Jets' defense said, "It was execution and the great play of our safetymen. And, I can't say enough about our linebackers."

"It was the offensive line," said Matt Snell, who ran the ball 30 times for 121 yards. Asked about his thumb Namath replied, "Nothing hurts now." And, when asked about his guarantee, he said, "I always had confidence we would win, but didn't know what to expect. But, I had a good time. When you go out and play football you're supposed to have a good time." Joe added, "We got some kind of defense. Usually sixteen points isn't enough to win, but with our defense it is." Defensive tackle John Elliott was quoted, "How about our defense? I want to know who's got the number one defense now?"

Speaking more about his team's defense in the game, Walt Michaels told me, "It was a tremendous team effort. Whenever you get a lot of in-

terceptions like we had in that game it means that people are working together. It was a dedicated team-oriented defense. They played to their
strengths and played off each other. They talked a lot and they knew offense. As an example, Jim Hudson, one of our safeties was a quarterback
in college and he could stand out there and know pretty much what play
the opponents were going to run. He was definitely underrated on our defense."

Over in the dejected Colts' locker room there was disappointment
and yet some praise for the Jets. "The story of the game was simple," Don
Shula said in an interview. "We didn't do it, they did. We had all the opportunities in the first half. We didn't make the plays we made all season.
They deserved it." In my recent interview with Coach Shula reiterated his
praise for Namath and the Jets. "I don't think it's been talked enough
about how good a quarterback he was. We made a living that year on the
blitz and no team was able to figure it out or do anything about it. Namath
and Weeb figured it out. When we did blitz, Joe got rid of the ball on
quick passes. The Jets did everything they had to do to beat us. It wasn't a
fluke win for them. They played very well and Weeb coached a great
game. Namath was exceptional and he was as good or better than adver-
tised."

Defensive tackle Billy Ray Smith, who had said earlier in the week
that Namath needed to learn a little humility, told a reporter, "We
couldn't get to Namath all afternoon. He was everything we expected."

Immediately after the game, Namath was given the game ball by his
teammates and then named the Most Valuable Player of the game. In a
very humble moment, Joe said he was giving the game ball to the AFL as
a symbol of its coming-of-age in professional football. Matt Snell recently related how he felt: "When the game was over I was totally ex-
hausted. I ran the ball a lot. It was a great feeling because we were
vindicating the whole AFL."

Walt Michaels remembered the Jet locker room after the game. "It
was kind of quiet. We all felt the AFL Championship was bigger to us at
the time. Over the years I think we have all come to realize the significance of that Super Bowl victory."

All of this was not lost on Weeb Ewbank, who had nurtured the Jets
to the pinnacle of their sport. Weeb recounted to a group of sportswriters
on the field that earlier in the day, before the game, he ran into Carroll
Rosenbloom, his former boss with the Colts who invited him and his wife
to a postgame victory party he was hosting. His answer to Rosenbloom

was he couldn't make it because he and his wife had a party of their own to go to.

On the bus ride back to the hotel Billy Hampton remembered driving by the Colts' hotel. "The best part was when we went by the headquarters of the Baltimore Colts. They had set up a tent for a party after they won and when we went by after the game there was nothing going on in the tent. When we got to our hotel the place was jumping. It was a great time."

Back in New York the city was going wild. Through all the civil turbulence that had been going on, and still occurring, the city had put off its gloom for the time being. Everyone was now celebrating his or her new-found champions. Mayor Lindsay sent his congratulations. It read:

> To Weeb Ewbank:
>
> On behalf of all New York citizens, our congratulations to the players and management of the New York Jets. Your smashing triumph is the greatest upset in professional football. We are looking forward to welcoming you World Champions back to New York City.
>
> Sincerely,
> John V. Lindsay, Mayor of New York

"The Jets win helped the city a lot," David Garth recollected. "The feeling at City Hall was if the Jets can win the Super Bowl, we could do anything."

Joe Namath recently reminisced, "Championship! We did it. We achieved our goal. We had been growing together. The heart of the team had been jelling for some time. The season didn't happen in six months. We worked hard at building an attitude and belief and we got there. It was an achievement that was very difficult to attain, and everyone (on the team) was special."

Looking back at the success of the Jets during the Super Bowl season Winston Hill said, "Our quarterback, Joe Namath, was not only great, he was smart. Namath called his own plays. He didn't come out of the game because he got dinged. The unselfishness of the players is another thing that stands out on that team. I moved around to different positions. That was what all of us did on the Jets. We were unselfish. I might have made the Hall of Fame if I had not agreed to move to other positions at some time or another. Also, Namath, Matt Snell, and Johnny Sample weren't just teammates, they were people to be reckoned with. They are three people who possessed ways of making mature decisions. They played on principles and succeeded on principles."

"I don't think a lot of us realized the magnitude of Super Bowl III at the time," recalled Larry Grantham. "We really felt like Oakland was the key game to win. I thought we still had to beat the Giants to gain credibility with New York fans. A few of us had suffered all those years. We all felt like second-class citizens to the Giants. We had to beat the establishment to be thought of on the same level." When told that Namath had said, "Winning the Super Bowl was great for guys like Grantham and Maynard because they had laid the groundwork for the rest," Grantham said, "That was nice for him to say. The guys who were with the Jets for a couple of years couldn't have felt the same way that those of us who had been there with the Titans felt."

It was a great time. The sports world was shocked and professional football would never be the same. There would be no more looking down at the AFL. But some people just could still not believe it. Emerson Boozer, the Jets stalwart running back, had this noteworthy experience, "Right after the Super Bowl a lot of people asked me if the game was 'fixed.' I guess people just couldn't believe we could win. I just tell them it was fixed because we were the better team."

When the Jets returned to New York City they were welcomed as heroes by their fans. Even though they had accomplished a remarkable feat and uplifted the spirits of all New Yorkers when they sorely needed it, the city did not give them a parade. "Maybe, they weren't thinking we could win," recalled former Jets public relations director, Frank Ramos. Or maybe the Mayor was worried about a riot breaking out if all those crowds could not be contained? There was however, a celebration at City Hall with Weeb Ewbank, the coaches, and most of the players in attendance. On the steps of City Hall Mayor John Lindsay presented Joe Namath with a key to the City and read a proclamation extolling the virtues of the team.

On the other side of the world fans like Stanley Kuchlewski also shared the joys of victory. "I was a sergeant in the infantry with the 82nd Airborne Division. I was at a firebase when the Jets were playing in Super Bowl III, in this bunker made out of sandbags. I was a big Jets fan and tried to follow them as much as I could. I actually heard a little of the 'Heidi' game that season on someone's radio. It was 4 o'clock in the morning over there in Vietnam when the Super Bowl was on. Somehow I got a small radio and found one of the few English speaking AM stations that had the game on. So, I'm in my sleeping bag in Vietnam listening to the game. It kind of brought me back home a little bit. During the game I found myself thinking about things back home. It was great to listen to the game. It made me forget where I was for a little while. When the Jets won there were a few guys around wanting to know what was happening. I was so proud of being from New York City that I bragged about it all day. There weren't a lot of things that could bring you away from the war. There were very few times you were taken away from it. This was one of them."

Around the same time as the celebration at City Hall, after almost eight months of negotiations at the Paris peace talks, U.S. and North Vietnamese delegates agreed on the shape of the table to be used when the South Vietnamese and National Liberation Front joined the negotiations. It had taken Henry Kissinger, the leader of the U.S. delegation, that long to accomplish this simple step. It would be a harbinger for the future course of the talks.

Less momentous, but long-lasting results came out of the Jets' championship win. It is generally accepted that the Jets' victory changed the face of professional football like no other game ever had. Dave Anderson summarized it well. "After the Jets won the game took on added meaning. It really became the 'Super Bowl' and that's when the importance of the game really started to grow and has led to what it is now. Also, after the Jets won the game, it strengthened the desire of the AFL owners to stay together. Soon after the Jets' victory they had a league meeting to discuss re-alignment (for the upcoming merger of the two leagues) in 1970. The AFL owners demanded they stay together and they did. Three teams from the NFL had to come over and join them: Baltimore, Pittsburgh, and Cleveland."

That victory was not positive for everyone, at least initially. Don Shula remembered: "It's the toughest loss I ever had to deal with. The magnitude of the game, the circumstances surrounding it, the Namath guarantee, and then the Jets' victory caused repercussions not only after the game, but also into the year that followed. It affected my relationship with Carroll Rosenbloom, which had a lot to do with my ending up in Miami. Our relationship was never the same after that game. After we beat Cleveland in the NFL Championship game he put his arm around me and told everyone, 'This is the last head coach I'm ever going to hire.' And after the Super Bowl, the embarrassment to him because he was doing so much business in New York and also having an apartment there was hard for him to handle, and he found a way to pass that down to me. The magnitude of that victory gave more power to the AFL to negotiate with the established NFL in the merger. It played a big part in that because it gave the AFL credibility. No doubt it was also difficult for the fans of Baltimore."

Thomas D'Alessandro, mayor of Baltimore back then, recently commented, "Baltimore was a city going through many of the problems that New York was going through at the time. It was a time of tremendous confrontation. And there was enormous loyalty to the Colts. The loss in Super Bowl III stayed with us in Baltimore a long time. While in many respects it changed the whole complexion of football, in reality it was a downer for us, no question about it."

Soon after the City Hall celebration most of the players scattered to their homes around the country, but it wasn't over for the Jets. They still had to prove themselves to some. Larry Grantham reminded me of what he had said earlier, "We hadn't beaten the Giants, so in New York we were still second-class citizens." Noted sportswriter Robert Lipsyte added, "The Jets were the second team behind the Giants, who were seen as the white establishment team. The Jets were feisty and working class. They supposedly represented working class people."

Matt Snell recalled, "People always tell me how important that win was. I guess soon after we won I started to realize it wasn't just important for the players. A lot of people saw us as the blue-collar worker who got the job done. That's a great feeling for me. Also, I remember how a New York sportswriter came up to me and said that we wouldn't be considered real champions until we beat the Giants."

Not too long after the Jets got their chance to show all New Yorkers and NFL diehards that the Super Bowl was no fluke. The following summer during the exhibition season the Jets beat the Giants at the Yale Bowl in Hartford, Connecticut. Gerry Philbin has some vivid memories of that experience. "I felt we had one more big game to play after the Super Bowl. We were always mentioned behind the Giants in New York. Even after we won the Super Bowl people kept saying, 'You haven't beaten the Giants yet.' So playing them in the Yale Bowl that summer became a big thing for me. When we beat them it finally gave us credibility in New York City. After we won that game I came back to the city with a friend. We went to P.J. Clark's where there were always a lot of Giants fans and Giant management, even Howard Cosell was there. So I go into Clark's with this sign that was six feet long and three feet high that said, 'Jets

Number 1' with the final score painted on it in green. I sit down in Clark's with the sign draped over me and everyone is hissing me. There's this Giant fan sitting at a table really giving it to me so I go over to him and hit him right over the head with it. Right then we officially became a rivalry."

"Philbin was right," said Dave Anderson. "Some people in New York said the Super Bowl was a fluke. Even though the Giants weren't a good team then, the old New York establishment still doubted the Jets." Even Don Shula knew about the Giants specter haunting the Jets. "Even after they beat us some people in New York didn't give the Jets the credit they deserved until they beat the Giants." Finally, the Jets had nothing more to prove.

And so there you have it, the first leg of the Trifecta. The Jets had truly performed a sports miracle and the city had a championship, something they hadn't seen in a while, certainly not in football. Around the same time, while the people in New York were savoring the Jets' win, the war in Vietnam again took another tortuous twist. Early in February, despite government restrictions, President Nixon authorized Operation Menu, the bombing of North Vietnamese and Vietcong bases within Cambodia. The war was expanding and the public was concerned.

But, for sports fans, there was something to look forward to; the baseball season was just around the corner. Spring training was only a few weeks away. Both the Yankees and Mets were coming off bad years in 1968. There really was no reason to think that anything much different would happen in 1969. No one was prepared for what was about to take place.

SUPER BOWL III—INSIGHTS AND REMEMBRANCES

The following excerpts are from interviews conducted with some of the Jets and Colts who participated in Super Bowl III. Also, sportswriters, politicians, and fans add their thoughts about that historic game.

Dave Herman: "The instincts we had as a football team and the intuitiveness to play the game the way it is supposed to be played made that Super Bowl very memorable. To find a group of guys on offense and defense and special teams that could play, and then share the same goals with the same type of team attitude was great."

Winston Hill: "I believed we were good. I didn't think there was anybody I couldn't play against and block. I thought if we gave Namath time he would pick the Colts apart. I didn't know we were going to run as much as we did. My most vivid memories are about personalities and my teammates. What we accomplished could only happen through perseverance and determination. I was glad we won it for New York because it's the place in the universe that's unlike all others."

Walt Michaels: "Winning was the greatest because of all the garbage we had to take. We didn't belong in New York because of the Giants. We didn't belong in the NFL because we weren't good enough. We capped the season off by disproving a lot of things and most important, people are still talking about it."

Pete Lammons: "Winning the Super Bowl was something outstanding. Anytime an underdog comes up and wins it changes the whole picture. In our case, we were huge underdogs and lo and behold we came through. It made people, especially in New York, feel good."

Larry Grantham: "A lot of us weren't very happy about Joe's pregame prediction of a win, but Joe was Joe. We were pretty confident ourselves. After seeing a lot of film you could really diagnose the Colt team. Tom Matte wasn't going to beat you deep. Jerry Hill was a fine fullback, not a great runner, but a pretty good blocker. Jimmy Orr and Willie Richardson were the wideouts, however we thought the only guy who might beat us was John Mackey. So Walt Michaels, our defensive coordinator, came up with a great defensive game plan. We double-covered Mackey wherever he went.

Jim Turner: "I remembered going to a function that off-season in Richmond, Virginia. Billy Ray Smith from the Colts was there. I almost got into a fight with him. He told the people there,

'If we played the Jets again we would kick the shit out of them.' I said, 'Billy, you lost. Take it like a man.'"

Johnny Sample: "Personally, for me, I wouldn't have a radio show here in Philadelphia if it weren't for that game on January 12, 1969. I wouldn't be in a position to have a corporation that is doing well financially if it wasn't for that game. That game, for three and half hours, made my life comfortable today."

Earl Morrall: "It certainly was the lowlight of the year. It was devastating for all of us because up to that point we had a phenomenal year, the team and myself. The Baltimore fans were very disappointed like we were. We were expected to do better. We were on top of the world when the game started and the bottom of the world when it was over."

Ron Swoboda (grew up in Baltimore): "I was rooting for the Colts. I always felt Unitas should have played more."

Mario Cuomo (former governor of New York): "I followed the Jets. As a matter of fact, I told Namath at a dinner that he was my hero and I bet on him in the Super Bowl. He asked me, 'How many points did you get?' I told him 16. And, he said. 'You should have gotten more.'"

David Halberstam: "The Jets were a joy to anybody who cared about underdogs."

Barry Levinson: (movie director originally from Baltimore): "Coming from Baltimore I despised New York teams. When the Colts lost to the Jets it was devastating. I didn't get over that loss for a long time. I watched the game with friends and we were all stunned because it was a loss that seemed inconceivable."

Mike Francesa (popular sports talk show host on New York radio station WFAN): "The Jets had become a good team and with Joe Namath, they had a guy who really was the first sports hero in our culture. Ali and Namath were the first crossover athletes. Namath actually transcended sports. He was bigger than sport. He was the first athlete who really was a culture icon. Ali was in exile at this time. Namath was this figure bigger than life.

He wasn't just an athlete. The Jets' win elevated Namath more than the Jets."

Drew and Tracy Nieporent (owners of famed New York restaurants such as Nobu and Tribeca Grill): "The Jets' win was unbelievable. It was Namath putting his money where his mouth was. The team had balance and had other great players besides Namath. They deserved that win. They were second-class citizens in New York behind the Giants. They were tremendous underdogs. Nobody thought they were going to win.

Ray Romano (comedian, star of *Everyone Loves Raymond*): "I was only twelve then and a big Met fan. But when the Jets won they made me think, maybe the Mets can win, too."

Robert Wuhl (actor/writer): "I was a senior in high school and a big Jets fan. I was also a big Joe Namath fan. I remember watching Super Bowl III and everything was going the Jets' way, but I didn't want to see Johnny Unitas play. I wasn't worried about Morrall; it was Unitas I feared. To this day I feel that if they had brought Unitas in earlier, the game would have ended up differently."

(From left to right): Don Maynard, the New York Jets leading pass receiver; Jets coach Weeb Ewbank; George Sauer; and quarterback Joe Namath get together during practice. *(Photo courtesy of New York* Daily News.*)*

Joe Namath goes on the defense at Shea Stadium as he meets members of the *Playboy* Bunny touch football team, of which he was the honorary coach. The former Alabama star said, "Bear Bryant never told me I'd run into anything like this." *(Photo courtesy of New York* Daily News.*)*

New York Jets Joe Namath and Don Maynard are surrounded by reporters after winning the AFL Championship 27–23 over the Oakland Raiders. *(Photo courtesy of New York Daily News.)*

New York Jets quarterback Joe Namath (12) hands off the football to Matt Snell (41) during Super Bowl III in Miami, Florida, on January 12, 1969. The Jets beat the Baltimore Colts 16–7. *(Photo courtesy of AP/Wide World Photos.)*

DAILY ⚅ NEWS
NEW YORK'S PICTURE NEWSPAPER ⓡ

Vol. 50. No. 173 Copr. 1969 News Syndicate Co. Inc.   New York, N.Y. 10017, Monday, January 13, 1969★   WEATHER: Sunny and cold.

SUPERDUPER!

B'way Joe Jolts Colts By 16-7

Joe Namath, who belittled the highly-touted Baltimore defense in pre-game interviews, gains his vindication in Miami dressing room after the game. Burned cork beneath his eyes is to cut down glare of the sun. He completed 17 of 28 passes—without an interception—for 195 yards. Fullback Matt Snell carried 30 times for 121 yards and a touchdown. The Jet total rushing yardage was 142. Meanwhile, the Jet defense, tops in the AFL, rushed super-sub Earl Morrall into three key interceptions. They stole another on the subbing Johnny Unitas. The 18½-point favorites had to scramble to score before the finish. The Jets' 16-7 Super Bowl triumph was witnessed by 75,377 Orange Bowl fans and a nationwide TV audience of millions.

Other stories and editorial on page 60; other photos centerfold, back page.

Front page of the *Daily News*, January 13, 1969. *(Photo courtesy of New York Daily News.)*

Mayor John Lindsay pins a flower on the lapel of New York Jets coach Weeb Eubank at Kennedy Airport as City Council President Francis X. Smith (to the right of Lindsay) and other dignitaries look on. *(Photo courtesy of New York Daily News.)*

Fans cheer the Jets after their stunning Super Bowl upset of the Baltimore Colts. New York's first winners in six years were saluted at City Hall. *(Photo courtesy of New York Daily News.)*

Nobody we knew would ever have dreamt of claiming that luck had anything
to do with the fact that our Mets were only a half game behind the Chicago
Cubs. OK—so maybe a black cat walked onto the field to get acquainted with
the Cubs and Leo Durocher, their manager. The Mets won 7–1. *(Photo courtesy
of New York Daily News.)*

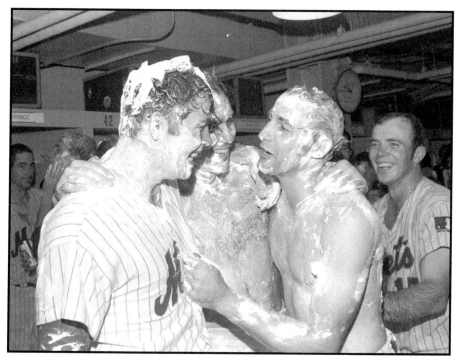

New York Mets Ron Swoboda, Art Shamsky, and Ken Boswell celebrate as the Mets clinch the N.L. Eastern Division title. Catcher Jerry Grote looks on. *(Photo courtesy of New York* Daily News.)

New York Mets get in line to cut an album in West 54th Street Studio. *(From left to right):* Art Shamsky, Ken Boswell, Tug McGraw, Ed Charles, and Ron Swoboda harmonize. *(Photo courtesy of New York* Daily News.)

Tommie Agee's great catch in the seventh inning of Game Three of the 1969 World Series verses the Baltimore Orioles. *(Photo courtesy of New York* Daily News.*)*

Fans flood the field as the New York Mets defeat the Baltimore Orioles 5–3 in Game Five of the 1969 World Series. The best banner of them all flies over the heads of the fans who believe in miracles. They also believe in the Mets. Let them have a field day. *(Photo courtesy of New York* Daily News.*)*

Mrs. Joan Whitney Payson, owner of the Mets, receives a special *Daily News* Page One during a ceremony at the News building. *(Photo courtesy of New York* Daily News.*)*

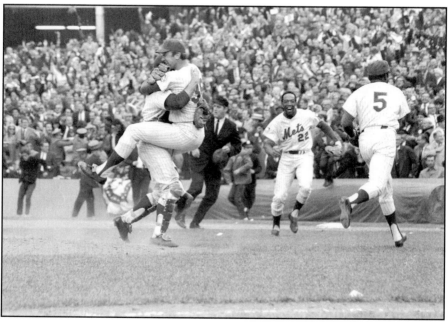

The New York Mets defeat the Baltimore Orioles 5–3 in Game Five of the 1969 World Series. Mets winning pitcher Jerry Koosman jumps on his batterymate, Jerry Grote, after Cleon Jones caught Davey Johnson's fly ball for the final out of the year. Donn Clendenon (background), who put the Mets back in the game with a homer in the sixth, rushes in to join the celebration. *(Photo courtesy of New York Daily News.)*

The 1969 New York Mets in Vegas, where they were one of the first teams to warble in public. *(Photo courtesy of AP/Wide World Photos.)*

(From left to right): The 1969–70 New York Knicks starting five—Dick Barnett, Walt Frazier, Bill Bradley, Dave DeBusschere, and Willis Reed—rejoice in the dressing room after winning their fifth playoff game against the Milwaukee Bucks by a lopsided score of 132–96, and with it their first National Basketball Association Eastern Conference title since 1953. *(Photo courtesy of New York* Daily News.*)*

New York Knicks verses Baltimore Bullets. Knicks Dave DeBusschere *(left)* and Walt Frazier get position on Bullet Gus Johnson (25) for a rebound in the first period. *(Photo courtesy of New York* Daily News.*)*

New York Knicks captain Willis Reed (19) could lend little more than moral support to the Knicks in their decisive 107–100 victory over the Los Angeles Lakers in Game 5 of the 1969–70 NBA Finals at Madison Square Garden. Hampered by a hip injury, he was helped off the court by trainer Danny Whelan *(left)* during the first period. *(Photo courtesy of New York* Daily News.*)*

Kids have a ball as Walt Frazier entertains them with autographs and banjo playing outside Gracie Mansion on 86th Street and East End Avenue, New York City. *(Photo courtesy of New York* Daily News.*)*

New York Knicks verses Milwaukee Bucks. Fans celebrate New York's win over the Bucks 4–1, in the Eastern Division NBA Playoffs at the Garden. *(Photo courtesy of New York* Daily News.*)*

DAILY NEWS

NEW YORK'S PICTURE NEWSPAPER ®

New York, N.Y. 10017, Saturday, May 9, 1970

MORE THAN TWICE
THE CIRCULATION
OF ANY OTHER
PAPER IN AMERICA

WILLIS, CLYDE DO IT

Knicks Whip Lakers, 113-99, for Title

NEWS photos by Dan Farrell
Wilt and Willis (foreground) head-
to-head.

NEWS photo by John Duprey
Frazier goes up in first-half to score
two of his game-high 36 points.

NEWS photo by Dan Farrell
Walt Frazier lets ball roll
off his palm for score in
second period. Ref Richie
Powers indicates foul
committed on play by
Jerry West (l.). In addi-
tion to high scoring and
record-tying 19 assists,
Frazier, the Thief of
Bagdad-on-the-Hudson,
played superb defense.

Kings
Of Sport

← Injured hip and
all, Willis Reed (l.)
guards Wilt Chamber-
lain as The Stilt pre-
pares to pass out to
teammate in first half.
Reed, a question to start
game, hit first shot and,
though hobbling, helped
Knicks to first cham-
pionship in their history,
113-99. —Story p. 28
NEWS photo by John Duprey

Daily News back page, May 9, 1970. *(Photo courtesy of New York* Daily News.*)*

PART III

THE METS

8. The Mets Are Born

"I'll never make the mistake of being seventy again."
—Casey Stengel

In 1958 the Dodgers and the Giants and the National League abandoned New York City for greener pastures. A short time later a few people began laying the groundwork for the birth of a new team and the league's eventual return. This group included two lawyers, George McLaughlin and William Shea, who tried contacting other National League teams in hopes of luring them to New York. Their idea was eventually frustrated which left them with only one option, to form another baseball league.

In July 1959 the Continental League was established and franchises were awarded to New York, Toronto, Denver, Houston, and Minneapolis-St. Paul. There would be other franchises in the near future. The owners of the New York team were Joan Whitney Payson and a gentleman by the name of Dwight Davis. The theory behind filling the rosters for these new teams was simple. "The supply of young players can be unlimited," said Bill Shea. "They haven't been given the opportunities. The risk of a big league career with only sixteen teams has been too great. The young players have to wait too long for their chance. With twenty-four or more big league teams they'll get their chance."[4]

With Mayor Richard Wagner's help, the plan was that the new team in New York City would play their home games at the old Polo Grounds for one year and then a new stadium would be built on the site of the World's Fair in the Borough of Queens.

Needless to say, the owners of the sixteen Major League teams weren't happy about the new Continental League. This was an especially sensitive time for them as Congress was beginning to take a look at baseball's "reserve clause" within the context of antitrust laws. This clause was standard in every player's contract and bound them to a team forever. Over the years that clause was the main issue creating friction between the players and owners, eventually leading to player strikes and ultimately to free agency. Faced with the establishment of a new competitor and the fervent desire of their founding cities for big league baseball, the Major League owners decided to look into the possibility of expansion. With their eyes firmly on money, the owners thought about new, untapped geographic areas and large admission fees into their leagues. No less important in the owners' minds was the specter of creating new advocates for a Congressional inquiry into the "reserve clause" from the states represented by the upstart league's teams. The threat of the new league and the resulting ramifications rattled the big league owners.

In August of 1960, the Continental League disbanded with the knowledge that four of its franchises would be accepted into the major leagues. The National League announced new expansion teams in Houston and New York City. The American League awarded franchises to Los Angeles and Washington, D.C.

With the deal now consummated to bring the National League back to New York City, Joan Whitney Payson would be the new team's majority owner. Her qualifications were simple: a passion for the game and money. Her family, the Whitneys, and her husband's family, the Paysons, were scions of New York society and truly wealthy. Mrs. Payson had been a Giants fan and loved baseball, and would be the first woman owner in the major leagues. She did have one other "love" in her life, thoroughbred horses. She was one of the founders of Greentree Stables, which over the years had had their share of big winners.

Mrs. Payson paid $3 million for eighty-five percent of the new base-

---

4. George Vecsey, *Joy in Mudville* (New York: McCall, 1970).

ball team. The other minority owners were G. Herbert Walker and M. Donald Grant, both business associates and her friends. Mrs. Payson, and particularly Donald Grant, would rule the team from the top, but they needed someone to run the day-to-day operations. They found their man in George Weiss, the person responsible for putting together the great Yankee teams of the '40s and '50s. The Yankees fired Weiss in November of 1960, only a few weeks after they let go of their manager, a wise old baseball seer by the name of Casey Stengel.

On March 14, 1961, George Weiss was named president of the New York National League team that was to begin play in 1962. Rumor had it that Weiss was given the title of president because when the Yankees fired him he agreed not to take another job as general manager. It sounds strange that someone would agree to that when being fired, but who knows? In any case, Weiss was going to be the general manager of the new team in New York City.

It was time now for the New York Metropolitan Baseball Club to find a "name." Fans were put to the task of finding one. The name had to fit five basic criteria: 1) meet public and press acceptance; 2) be closely re-lated to the team's corporate name; 3) be descriptive of the metropolitan area; 4) have a brevity that readers would like; 5) have historical back-ground referring to the Metropolitans, the name of the New York team that played in the American Association in the 1880s. After a screening process, Mrs. Payson would be the final judge.

Two months later Mrs. Payson decided on the name "Mets." After sorting through countless names that the fans submitted, it turned out that it was right there in front of everyone. History repeated itself and maybe some common sense, too.

Now came the process of trying to find a manager for the new team. The difficulty in this was determining what direction the team would be taking in the first few years. Should it be someone who would have the patience to work with young players in the developing stage of their baseball careers? Or should it be someone who would be able to lead veteran players who had been around the big leagues for years? A third factor might be the most important. With the loss of both the Dodgers and Giants the city was hungry for a National League team. The fact that this was New York and, of course, the Yankees were still the Yan-kees, the Mets would need a person who was able to deal with the noto-rious New York press and be a public relations master at the same time. While I'm sure George Weiss looked over a list of possible candidates, one name came right at him, a person he had worked with for a number of years. A person who knew only success in the big leagues and someone who knew how to handle the press. In September of 1961, they named their new manager, seventy-one-year-old Casey Stengel, a natural for the Mets.

"I think Casey was hired strictly because of his name value in New York," sportswriter and radio host Maury Allen said. "George Weiss hired him because of his name and it was kind of a zinger to the Yankees. Weiss thought that Casey would give the Mets an identification and credibility that no other manager could do." Allen also recalled a comment that Casey made when the Yankees fired him, "I'll never make the mistake of being seventy again."

So with a new name, a new manager, and lots of excitement, what was left? Just the small matter of finding a few players to populate the new team. As Bill Shea suggested when he was promoting the Continental League, it should not be a problem. But in reality there were two problems. The first wasn't the ability to get players; the problem was getting good players, even though the National League agreed to put a pool of players together from the existing eight teams. The second problem was the National League general managers were able to manipulate their major and minor league rosters so as to ensure available players in the pool would be aging veterans and fringe players who most likely wouldn't make the big leagues if it were not for expansion.

On October 10, 1961, the first expansion draft in National League history took place at the Netherland-Hilton Hotel in Cincinnati. George Weiss and the Mets had decided that since it was New York and many of the new team's fans were old Giant and Dodger fans, perhaps they should have a few locally recognizable names on the team. With their first pick they selected a catcher by the name of Hobie Landrith from the Giants. When it was over, the Mets had selected twenty-two players, including Gil Hodges, a star from the old Dodgers. Here is a list of the other players. Some of these names might sound familiar:

Don Zimmer	Lee Walls	Roger Craig	Al Jackson
Jim Hickman	Choo Choo Coleman	Joe Christopher	Bobby Gene Smith
Ed Bouchee	Elio Chacon	Jay Hook	Sherman Jones
Bob Miller	John Demerit	Ray Daviault	Sammy Drake
Felix Mantilla	Chris Cannizzaro	Craig Anderson	Gus Bell

The cost of these players, while some were more than others, was close to the $1,800,000 that the Mets were required to spend in the dispersal draft. One of the original drafted players, Lee Walls, would end up not playing for the new expansion Mets. He was traded in December 1961 to the Los Angeles Dodgers for Charlie Neal and $100,000. I don't know if he realized at the time that it might be a blessing for him that the trade happened.

Soon after the draft, the Mets were able to pick up some other veteran players like Frank Thomas and Richie Ashburn. Okay, so it wasn't the '27 Yankees, but it was a National League team back in New York City. On October 28, 1961, ground was broken in Queens, not far from LaGuardia Airport near the World's Fair site, for a new stadium to be the home of the New York Mets. For all the fans who had longed for a National League team back in New York City, their hopes and dreams had become a reality. They now had one. The team would start play in 1962. With a new stadium coming soon, things couldn't be brighter. It wouldn't be long before they realized what they really had.

As the Mets were putting together their roster for their initial season they announced the hiring of their three-man broadcast team. The trio included Lindsey Nelson, Bob Murphy, and Ralph Kiner. They all had their own style about them plus they had the experience the Mets wanted. "They actually hired Bob Murphy first," said Kiner. "They also wanted a guy that was known nationally and they picked up Lindsey Nelson. I had just obtained a broadcasting job with the White Sox and the Mets called me. They were looking for an ex-player. It made my decision easier to come to the Mets because I wasn't replacing another announcer." Kiner, of course, was one of the best power hitters of all time in the major leagues, albeit many of his years playing were with the Pittsburgh Pirates, one of the worst teams of his era.

In November, the Mets unveiled their circular logo. Sports cartoonist Ray Gatto designed it. The shape of the insignia, with its orange stitching, represented a baseball. There was a bridge in the foreground that symbolized that the Mets, in bringing back baseball to the National League, represented all five boroughs. The skyline in the background had special meaning. It was made up of different buildings in different boroughs. The colors the Mets chose were orange and blue. Ironically, it was the old New York Giant orange and the old Brooklyn Dodger blue. Over the years since the logo was developed in 1961, little has changed.

9. The Early Years

"It was sort of like finishing in tenth place in a beauty contest."
—Ralph Kiner

"Lose 100, have some fun, and interview Casey after the game."
—Ron Swoboda

On February 19, 1962, New York Mets pitchers and catchers opened spring training in St. Petersburg, Florida. The Mets were using Huggins Field, the former spring training site of the Yankees, as their workout base. They would play their spring training games at Al Lang Field downtown, sharing that facility with the St. Louis Cardinals. Huggins Field was about an 8–10 minute ride to downtown St. Petersburg. I always wondered about this setup. Even in 1968 when I joined the Mets, you would practice at Huggins Field and then the players would pile into taxicabs, in uniform, and go the games at Al Lang Field. It was a strange setup. After the games they would have cabs standing by to take the players back to Huggins Field to shower and change. I always wanted to get into one of those cabs and just say, "OK, take me here or take me there." Just go out straight from the game in uniform. I never did it. Now I often wish I had.

Spring training is always a time of optimism for every big league team. The Mets were no exception. They lost their first exhibition game to the Cardinals, but then actually won the second. So things weren't so bad. At this stage in their young life they couldn't possibly have thought about what the season would bring in terms of wins and losses.

"The first spring training in 1962 with the Mets was fantastic," said Maury Allen. "Everything that happened everyday was considered a big story. If a player got a hit in a game or pitched a couple of good innings you could write about the guy. Most of the stories then were about who the players were and the fact that some of them were back in New York, like Gil Hodges. There was so much Brooklyn and New York connection. Readers really got caught up in it. People were so happy when the Mets came into existence."

In an interview Lindsey Nelson did with Casey Stengel in spring training in 1962 Ralph Kiner related that Stengel said, "You gotta start with the catcher cause if you don't have a catcher you're gonna have a lot of passed balls." He went on about the team and got to the right fielder and couldn't think of his name. He knew who the right fielder was going to be, but just couldn't think of his name. So he said, "Well now, out there in right field we're gonna have a fella that played for the Pittsburgh Pirates and the Cincinnati Reds." And he went on and on and on until he thought of his name and said, "And if he plays for us like he did for the Pirates and the Reds, he'll ring your bell and that's his name, Gus Bell."

When asked about those spring training days in 1962, former Met broadcaster Bob Murphy said, "We just followed Casey around. We figured we would try and stay as close to him as we could. He always had something to say and most of the time it was positive. Actually, when I think about it, Casey was the best public relations guy I ever saw."

The Mets finished spring training in 1962 with a record of 12–15 for a winning percentage of .444. Do you think Casey Stengel, or any of the players or coaches would have chosen that percentage over the one they had at the end of the upcoming season?

The Mets opened the 1962 season in St. Louis against the Cardinals. Actually, they were rained out the first scheduled game but managed to lose the next to the Cardinals 11–4 on April 11th. That game was an indication of things to come as the Mets gave up sixteen hits and allowed three stolen bases, while making three errors and grounding into two double plays. Not a pretty start.

The team opened their home schedule on April 13th, a Friday. Somehow, there seemed to be messages all around. The Mets had spent around $400,000 to "fix" up the Polo Grounds. They weren't going to spend a whole lot of money since ground had been broken in Queens for their new stadium. Even though a little more than 12,000 people showed up for the home opener, once again the Mets lost. This time to the Pirates 4–3. The Mets proceeded to lose seven more games in a row to start the 1962 season with nine losses in a row. That tied a National League record for consecutive losses at the start of a season. And, they did it in their first year!

However, on April 23rd, the Mets finally won beating the Pittsburgh Pirates by the score of 9–1. Shouts of "Break up the Mets" from the players were heard in the Met locker room. The Mets would not lose 160 games that season. They did lose the next three, though.

The early part of the 1962 season was not kind to the Mets. Poor pitching, errors, busted plays, careless fielding, and lack of hitting all added to their woes. While they did win a game here and there they also had another bad losing streak. This time it was seventeen games. After forty-eight games, a little less than one-third of the 1962 season, the Mets record was twelve wins and thirty-six losses.

There was one thing that was happening that was positive. A hardcore group of fans was developing from the old Dodger and Giant fan base. But the Mets were also starting to get a few new fans; either they were interested in the novelty of the new team or maybe they just hated the Yankees. In any case, a new phenomenon was starting to develop. More and more fans were bringing signs and banners. Some of the early banners said things like:

"Good grief, Mets."
"East is East and Mets is Mets."
"What me worry? I'm a Met fan."
"Ashburn for President."

At first, most of the banners were made of bedsheets that were large and blocked the view of people trying to watch the games. Then as the banners began to be carried around the stands it created more problems for fans watching, so consequently the Mets front office was not happy with this new fad. Reluctantly, the Mets realized that the people making the banners did buy tickets and spend money, and therefore, it would be a wise decision to allow the banners to be displayed. Also, *Daily News* columnist Dick Young called this new banner phenomenon part of the "new breed" that was growing interest in the Mets. It turned out to be one of the best decisions the Mets' front office ever made because banners and

the New York Mets became synonymous. The banner phenomenon became so popular that the Mets would soon start Banner Day at the park.

Banner Day got so big I remember that in 1968, and subsequent years
I was with the Mets, time was set aside between games of a doubleheader
scheduled on one Sunday during the season. Everyone who brought a
banner to Shea Stadium could come through the center field gate and parade their banner in front of all the fans who were there. It was great for
the fans. However, it wasn't too great for the players. The march of the
banners between games took at least an hour and a half. If you had extra
innings or long games in the doubleheader, you spent a very long day at
the ballpark.

As the Mets continued to play inept baseball, the amount of fans
started to grow. Not only did it grow, it became a little strange. Fans
would stand and applaud a simple catch by one of the infielders. Ordinary
plays became festive. Optimism was extreme. There was never a time in
the game when fans gave up. And the Mets rewarded them by losing.
There was no rhyme or reason for this love affair. It just happened.

The other thing the Mets did have, besides the fans, was the press.
The writers who covered the Mets knew that they had interesting stories
everyday. From Casey Stengel, they got Stengelese, a strange form of the
English language that was transcribed from sportswriters to sports fans.
And, there were the players, whose ineptness led to good copy. The writ-
ers loved the Mets because the Mets were interesting.

While Stengel and the rest of his misfits were losing the games but
winning the fans one new Met hero emerged from the depths. His name
was Marv Throneberry, or as he was commonly known, Marvelous Marv
Throneberry. Stengel had known Throneberry when he came through
the Yankee farm system and actually played for the Yankees in the '50s.
The Mets purchased him from Baltimore in May because they were looking for a left-handed batting first baseman. It didn't take long for Mets
fans to start their love-hate relationship with the Marvelous one. In a
game against the Cubs in June at the Polo Grounds the Mets had two runners on and were trailing 4–0 in the game. Throneberry was up at bat and
he hit a ball into the gap between center and right. By the time the ball got
back into the infield two runs had scored and Marv stood at third with a
triple. Or so he thought. Cub first baseman Ernie Banks got the ball from
the pitcher and stepped on first base, claiming that Throneberry never
touched the bag. The umpire agreed. Marvelous had not stepped on first
base and was called out. Stengel stormed out of the Met dugout to argue.

But before he could get in the face of the umpire, Mets' first base coach Cookie Lavagetto stopped him. "Casey, it won't do any good," he said. "He missed second base, too."

Marvelous had arrived. The Mets had their new hero. Throneberry didn't realize it at the time but he actually took the pressure off everyone else on the Mets. The fans loved him because they expected the worst and most of the time they got it.

There are countless other Marvelous Marv Throneberry stories. Too many to write about. They all fit in to what the 1962 Mets were. Losers. The word "loser" was automatically spoken right after the word "Mets." The team was constantly being made fun of on television and in the newspapers, except for the New York sportswriters, who still had fun dissecting Stengelese and continued to write fun-type stories.

As the season went on there was absolutely no indication the team would get any better. However, they were starting to scout and sign young players who one day might lead them to greener pastures. One of those young players was a seventeen-year-old local high school phenom from the Bronx by the name of Ed Kranepool. Ed, or the Krane as we later called him, would become a key member of the 1969 Mets and my teammate. He grew up a Bronx Bombers fan but ended up signing with the Mets. "In 1962 there was no baseball draft," Kranepool said. "I was a Yankee fan growing up and the Mets were just starting. I thought I had a better chance of making it to the big leagues with the Mets." The Mets had him work out at the Polo Grounds even before he graduated high school. After he signed with the Mets, the team took him on a road trip to California. However, he didn't play in a game on that trip. They ended up sending him to the minor leagues where he split time at Syracuse, Knoxville, and Auburn, New York. As it turned out, his earlier thinking paid off. He did make it pretty fast to the big leagues. He returned to the Mets in September 1962, played in three games and got his first big league hit, a double, in the last game of the season. Kranepool commented, "The Mets were a bad team then. Everyone knew who I was and I guess people thought I was the answer. People forgot that I was seventeen years old playing in the major leagues. Looking back at the time, the National League might have had the greatest array of pitchers in their history. I'm not sure I was physically and mentally mature enough. I had to learn the game." Ed must have learned a few things about the game because he ended up with an eighteen-year major league career all with the Mets. He still holds a few team records. Over all the years I've known Eddie he did teach me one important thing. His words of wisdom were, "Make sure you find a seat near the exit when you go to certain events. You might want to leave early." Eddie is the best at "exit strategy" I have ever seen.

Another 1969 Met, coach Joe Pignatano, was also there as a player during the 1962 season. He was catching the last game of the season and in his last at-bat of the year, has the dubious distinction of hitting into a triple play. Joe always says, "That's a great way for people to remember me."

So, the New York Mets first season started badly and ended badly. However, National League baseball was back in New York. It was a year that also saw the evolution of new cult-like baseball fans. And, it was a year that showed the world how bad the Mets really were. The final record for the team in their first year of existence was 40 wins and 120 losses, 60 and one-half games out of first place.

"I think one thing is forgotten in all of this," said Maury Allen. "Nobody knew anything about the Houston Colts and nobody recognized the two expansion teams in the American League. But the Mets brought immediate attention because of Stengel, and also the players quickly recognized the whole New York scene and the fact that they were entertainers as well as being ballplayers."

Bob Murphy said, "It was actually pretty easy to work in 1962. Casey was so pleasant to be around. I knew the team was going to lose. I thought they would lose 100 games. I only missed it by 20."

In 1963 the Mets did show some improvement. They won more games than they lost in spring training. However, Grapefruit League games don't count in the standings. When the "real show" was over their final tally was 51–111. While their record improved somewhat from 1962, it didn't affect their place in the standings. They again finished dead last in the ten team National League, only forty and a half games out of first place.

There was some progress in one area at the beginning of the 1963 season. The Mets "only" lost their first eight games of the year as opposed to the year before when they lost their first nine. Well, improvement is improvement.

In the spring of 1963, the team purchased the contract of Duke Snider from the L.A. Dodgers. Duke, who had been a favorite with the fans when the Dodgers were in Brooklyn, was at the end of his career. He would get one last hurrah in front of New York fans. The Mets had also acquired other players like Ron Hunt and Larry Bearnarth. Marvelous

Marv was still there, too. The team also decided to take the now eighteen-year-old Ed Kranepool to New York with them at the end of spring training. In May, the Mets released Gil Hodges so he could become the manager of the Washington Senators. For that favor the Senators sent the Mets Jimmy Piersall. Known for his bizarre behavior, Piersall lasted only a couple of months.

Somewhere around this time, sportswriter Dick Young started calling the Mets "lovable losers." That name stuck to the team for a long time.

One day Casey Stengel had a conversation with Ed Kranepool, who was struggling at the plate and having trouble adjusting to big league pitching. "Casey told me to come out early to the Polo Grounds, take extra batting practice, and he was going to watch me from his office way out in center field where the clubhouse was," said Krane. "When I went out to take extra batting practice Duke Snider was standing behind the batting cage. Casey had told me, 'When you take batting practice I want you to hit every ball to left field. I want you to get your eye on the ball so hit everything to the opposite field. And if you hit one ball to the right side of second base I'm going to send you to the minor leagues tomorrow.' So when I started taking batting practice my one intention was not how hard I was hitting the ball, but where I was hitting it. No matter where the ball was pitched I was doing everything to hit toward left field. It was difficult because some pitches were inside, but I knew what I was trying to do. When Snider saw this he said, 'What the hell are you trying to do? Why are you hitting like that? You have to pull some of those balls toward right field.' Being frustrated and struggling, I turned around and said, 'Duke, mind your own business. You're not doing too good yourself.' Well, Duke took this as a personal attack on him. After batting practice I sought out Snider and apologized to him and told him what Casey had wanted me to do. And he said, 'Well, now I understand what you are trying to do.' Meanwhile, some of the press were there and heard me blast Duke and tell him to mind his own business. They wrote a big story the next day about how a young player ripped into Duke Snider. It made me look bad. I wasn't able to live that down for months." Apparently, Casey must have liked a little of what he saw when Eddie was taking batting practice because he wasn't sent to the minor leagues the next day. However, Kranepool did add, "The Mets aggressively tried to change my style of hitting, but what it did was retard my progress because I just couldn't do the things they asked me to do." In July the Mets finally did send Krane to Buffalo, their AAA team in the International League, to play everyday and work on his hitting. He was recalled later and finished the season in the big leagues.

While Kranepool ended up staying with the team, the Mets finally had enough of Marvelous Marv Throneberry. In May of 1963, they sent him to Buffalo. Thus ended the career of one of the most memorable characters to ever grace the Mets uniform. His fielding, hitting, demeanor, and his love-hate relationship with the fans, became folklore. One cannot have a conversation about the early years of the New York Mets without mentioning the word losers and of course, Marvelous Marv Throneberry.

"The writers, broadcasters, all the media took it as it was," Ralph Kiner remarked about the Mets' first couple of years. "The fans were happy. It was sort of like finishing in tenth place in a beauty contest. It wasn't bad."

"What was fascinating about the Mets then was Casey Stengel's sense of what they were going to be," said Maury Allen. They came in as an expansion team and had a lot of players that were recognized in New York. But, it didn't take long for Stengel to realize that there wasn't a great deal of talent and that most of his players were going downhill in their careers. What Casey did was emphasize the fact that there was a team back in New York in the National League, and if people had patience they were going to see a good baseball team in a few years."

Final attendance at the Polo Grounds for the 1963 season was a little over one million, a very respectable total. The Mets had increased their newfound "loyal" fans. The team had improved, albeit only a little. There was some hope that in 1964 the hapless Mets would be better.

In 1964 came the opening of Shea Stadium. The original name that was chosen was Flushing Meadow Park, but it was decided to name it after attorney Bill Shea, who was very instrumental in bringing National League baseball back to New York City. It took twenty-nine months to build and cost $28.5 million. It was the first stadium capable of converting from baseball to football by moving the lower stands on motorized tracks. The luster of the new stadium was diminished by its location right beneath the flight paths of LaGuardia Airport. The noise of huge passenger jets constantly taking off and landing led to a large number of complaints over the years from fans and players alike. Batters didn't like to hit and pitchers didn't like to pitch when the roar of a plane's engine was blasting noise over Shea. I must admit that in my particular case, whenever I was batting at Shea Stadium, I can't recall ever stepping out of the batter's box because a plane was flying over. Maybe there was a time when the pitcher stepped off the rubber because he was uncomfortable, but I can honestly say it didn't bother me when hitting. It was, however, a really good excuse for striking out or giving up a home run.

The location of Shea, other than the noise, turned out to be perfect for residents of all five boroughs of the city, especially Queens. Add to that the close proximity to Nassau and Suffolk Counties in Long Island, most areas in Westchester County, and even Northern New Jersey, and Shea was an easy destination to reach—as long as traffic wasn't bad.

Spring training in 1964 was the normal Met stuff. The boys went back to their losing ways with a final Grapefruit League record of 10–17. There were a few roster changes, but not many people thought they would improve. Duke Snider ended his time in New York being sent to the Giants just before the season started.

The regular season started off surprisingly well for the "lovable losers." They only lost four in a row to start the season, a notable improvement from the first two years. All was not bad at the start. The Mets had their new ballpark.

Opening day at Shea Stadium was festive with banners, excitement, and, of course, excited fans. 48,736 showed up to see the Mets in their new home. What they saw was the Mets lose. It didn't take long to see that this was going to be another long season. After nineteen games they were 3–16.

The Mets did make one significant move at this time. They acquired veteran shortstop Roy McMillan from the Milwaukee Braves. It was important, not so much for the impact on wins, but because of his influence on Bud Harrelson. Bud would eventually develop into a terrific fielder and become the Mets' starting shortstop for a number of years. He would be part of the highly underrated "up-the-middle" defense that became one of the most important reasons the 1969 Mets became world champions.

The year 1964 was filled with interesting moments. On May 31st, the Mets played a doubleheader against the Giants. After losing the first game, the second game went twenty-three innings with the Mets, of course, losing. The two games lasted almost ten hours. Ed Kranepool had the best line about that day, "I wish it had gone longer. I always wanted to play in a game that started in May and ended in June."[5]

On June 21, 1964, Jim Bunning of the Philadelphia Phillies pitched a

---

5. George Vecsey, *Joy in Mudville* (New York: McCall, 1970).

perfect game against the Mets. At the time it was only the eighth perfect game thrown in major league history.

In recognition of the new stadium, Major League Baseball held the All-Star game at Shea in 1964. The National League won the game on a home run by Philadelphia's John Callison. The big excitement for Met fans was Ron Hunt, who had been voted onto the National League team as their starting second basemen.

At the very end of the season the Mets had a chance to be a factor in the National League pennant race. If they could sweep the Cardinals in St. Louis it would create a three-way tie for the pennant between the Cards, Reds, and Phillies. The Mets won the first two contests but lost the final to the Cards' ace, Bob Gibson. That last-day victory over the Mets put the Cardinals into the World Series against the Yankees.

The Mets again finished last in the National League, something they were used to. However one big bright spot was that attendance grew significantly. Their home attendance for the year at Shea was 1,732,597. More and more fanatics were joining the Met army of fans.

In talking about the Mets first three years Ed Kranepool had this commentary. "It was very frustrating because as a young player growing up I was accustomed to winning teams. I was always getting accolades with a good club. The Mets were a bad ball club. No matter what you did, it was never enough. For me the situation was very uncomfortable."

On how it was broadcasting the Mets' games in the early years, Ralph Kiner remarked, "Nobody expected a lot so that made it easier. It was almost like a movie out of Hollywood. The first year at the start of the season we lost nine straight. The second year it was eight. The next it was four. Each year you could say the Mets improved a little."

Their final record for the 1964 season was 53–109. It was a slight improvement from the year before. Still, the fans loved them and most of the writers provided strong support. "Most of us in the press understood that if we wrote funny things about the team and kidded them about it, they would be more accepted as opposed to being put down," said Maury Allen. "That was led by Dick Young. We followed his attitude that it was great to have a National League team back in New York. It was fun writing about the Mets back then."

Before spring training in 1965, the Mets signed Yogi Berra as a player-coach. The Yankees had recently fired him as manager. Yogi's apparent crime came from taking the Yankees to the seventh game of the 1964 World Series and not winning it. Although he hadn't played in a while, George Weiss and Casey Stengel didn't care. They also signed ex-Brave star, Warren Spahn, as a coach and pitcher. Spahn, however, would be released in July after compiling a 4–12 record.

Spring training wasn't much different than previous years. The Mets won eleven and lost fifteen, but were starting to find some more good prospects. One was Ron Swoboda, who made the big league club after spending a year in the minors. Ron would turn out to be a player the fans adored. Not totally in the Marvelous Marv way, but very close. When asked about his early years with the Mets, Ron, whose nickname soon became Rocky for obvious reasons said, "Lose 100, have some fun, and interview Casey after the game." On his remembrances of Casey, Swoboda remarked, "He was this little guy with a bum leg he got from being run over by a taxicab. His face looked like it was taken from Mt. Rushmore. He had a wonderful sense of humor. He called me 'Saboda.' He never called me by my first name." Ron would never run out of things to say. Sometimes he would not think about something before giving an opinion and it would come out a little harsh. Now, as well as back then, I'm never surprised at anything Swoboda says on any topic.

The Mets opened the 1965 season in Cincinnati. Every game of the series was rained out. Ralph Kiner remembered a comment made after the final game of that series had been cancelled, "Someone said it was the best start the Mets ever had."

A little later in the season a play occurred that exemplifies a typical Mets–Ron Swoboda situation. I was a member of the Cincinnati Reds and we were playing the Mets at Crosley Field in Cincinnati. The Mets were trailing by three runs and had the bases loaded with Swoboda at the plate. Two things were unusual at Crosley Field. One was an uphill terrace that ran all along the outfield. It was a moderate embankment that went 10–12 feet down on an approximate 30-degree angle from the base of the outfield fence. Over the years I saw that terrace eat up many outfielders going after fly balls. The second unusual feature was a short center field fence no more than 380 feet from home plate that was made of concrete, but which changed to wood about halfway up. Any ball hitting above the concrete was a ground rule home run. It was well known, and fairly evident to everyone, that if a batted ball hit the wood it would just drop straight down. So, Swoboda is batting with the bases loaded and hits a ball off the top of the wood in center field and it drops down. Home run, right? Not so! Here is the story as Swoboda tells it: "I hit the ball off John Tsitouris. It hit the wood wall in center field above the concrete fence. That signified a home run. The ball just dropped straight down. In fact, the center-fielder just nonchalantly tossed the ball back to the infield. I thought it was a home run, but the umpires ruled it in play. The runners didn't know what to do. There was mass confusion. When it was finally sorted through, I ended up with a single and one RBI. We lost the game by two runs. Yogi Berra was our first base coach then. He argued the play and was thrown out of the game." After the game the writers asked Yogi what he said to the umpires. Yogi related, "I told that umpire that if anybody couldn't hear that ball hit the wood, they're blind." That was typical of Swoboda and the Mets (and Yogi, too) in 1965.

The biggest thing that happened to the Mets that year was on July 25th. Stengel, while getting out of a friend's car, hurt his hip. It was diagnosed as a fracture and Stengel would require surgery. The Mets named coach Wes Westrum as interim manager. As it turned out, Casey would never return as manager of the Mets. On August 30, 1965, the Mets sadly announced the retirement of the legendary Casey Stengel. The most important piece of the Mets' early history was gone.

The rest of the year didn't fare much better for Wes Westrum than previous years had for Casey. The Mets finished the season with a record of 50–112. They actually regressed by three games from the previous year. Of course they finished in last place—again.

Not all was lost, though. The Mets again drew close to 1.8 million fans to Shea that year. The fanatics were strong and growing. More important, on the field some familiar names were starting to crop up. Names that would eventually help turn the sorry franchise into a winner. Cleon Jones and Frank "Tug" McGraw joined Ron Swoboda, Ed Kranepool, and Bud Harrelson in the Mets picture. Even with another miserable year the future did not look so bleak.

Wes Westrum was retained as the Mets' manager in 1966. The team made one move over the winter that would turn out to be one of their best ever. They acquired catcher Jerry Grote from Houston. Grote would turn out to be one of the best defensive catchers in baseball, and another key component of their future success.

Another positive event occurred for the Mets in early April 1966. The club won a special lottery for the rights to a right-handed pitcher out of the University of Southern California by the name of Tom Seaver. Originally signed by the Atlanta Braves in February 1966, Seaver's contract was voided by Commissioner William Eckert on the basis that the USC season had already started when he signed. The right to sign Seaver was up for grabs and the name of every team willing to match the Braves' offer was also thrown into the hat. The Mets' fortunes changed that April day in 1966. By winning that lottery, their future could only go in a positive way. And, it did, except it didn't happen overnight.

The Mets season record for 1966 was 66–95. They drew more than 1.9 million at home. For the first time in their history the team didn't lose 100 games and, for the first time in their history they didn't finish in last place. The Chicago Cubs had that distinction in 1966. How bad were the Cubs!

On November 14, 1966, the Mets announced that George Weiss would retire and be succeeded by Bing Devine. Devine worked for the Mets since being let go as general manager of the St. Louis Cardinals the previous August. I knew Bing Devine as a youngster growing up in St. Louis. The Cardinals scouted me, but I ended up signing with the Cincinnati Reds. A little later down the road Bing Devine would have an effect on my life.

After Devine became general manager he started to bring in players who would eventually help make the Mets winners. In November of 1966, he traded for Don Cardwell. After the season started he acquired Ed Charles and Ron Taylor.

However the 1967 season would be another bad year for the Mets. On September 21st, Wes Westrum resigned. He just couldn't take it anymore. Coach Salty Parker took over for the remaining eleven games. The Mets would finish the season with a record of 61–101. Another year of 100 losses and last place again. On top of that attendance slipped for the first time. The Mets lost almost 350,000 paying customers from the previous year.

The only real positive in 1967 was Tom Seaver. He finished the season with a record of 16 wins and 13 losses, had an earned run average of 2.76, and was named National League Rookie of the Year. He was "Tom Terrific," and it was the beginning of a brilliant Hall of Fame career.

Shortly after the season was over the Mets announced Gil Hodges as the new manager of the team. Gil had been successful as manager of the Washington Senators in the American League. They were not a good team, but Gil helped them improve every year he was there. He was another natural for the Mets. Hodges still lived in Brooklyn, had many ties to New York City, and he knew how to manage.

Soon after the Hodges announcement Bing Devine made another player move. He traded for me. That's right, me. I was living in St. Louis and had just come off a season of injuries playing for the Cincinnati Reds. The worst were back problems that would plague me my entire career. I had just arrived home from the hospital after exploratory surgery on my back and was feeling terrible. Early in the morning I got a call from Bob Howsam, general manager of the Reds. When Howsam identified himself my first thought was that he was calling to see how I was feeling. So before he could say anything further I said, "Mr. Howsam, thanks for calling. I feel great and I'm looking forward to next season." The bubble burst when he replied, "That's good, because we just traded you to the Mets."

Well, you can imagine. First of all, when you get traded for the first time it's a shock. All my baseball friends were with the Reds. I came up from the minor leagues with all of them. That was bad enough. But, traded to the Mets! I just thought it was the worst thing that could happen. I hated New York. People there called me "Auttie." They didn't talk right. And the Mets were the worst team in baseball. "Please Mr. Howsam, this can't be true," I said to myself. Mr. Howsam must have picked up on my despair because he said, "Listen, this could be good for you. Bing Devine, the general manager of the Mets is going to call you in a little while. Good luck. Bye." I didn't get another word in. But I remembered Bing Devine from my days in St. Louis as a kid so maybe it wouldn't be bad after all.

About an hour later I got the call from Mr. Devine. We did our pleasantries and he said, "The Mets have been trying to get you for a while and I followed through. It's a great organization, and even though we've been struggling for a few years we have a bright future. Plus, New York is a great place to play. The fans are great, the press, everything." Well, after we hung up the telephone I can honestly say I felt a lot better. Bing Devine's call helped a lot, and from my initial reaction of despair upon hearing of the trade came a feeling of acceptance. Everything was going to be fine. Except two days later I picked up the St. Louis newspaper and read that Bing Devine was just named general manager of the Cardinals. That's right, he was returning to the Cardinals. Two days earlier he had told me how good the Met organization was and how great New York City was, and now he left to come back home. It was the longest winter in my life.

Shortly after Devine left Johnny Murphy was named general manager of the Mets. He had been an assistant general manager with the Mets and was a great relief pitcher with the Yankees during some of their many glory years. Soon after he took over, Murphy completed a trade that brought Al Weis and Tommie Agee to the team, two more players who would figure into the glorious future. That deal also affected Cleon Jones. Agee and Jones had been best friends growing up in Mobile, Alabama. Cleon openly lobbied the Mets to try and get Tommie. "What do you think of your buddy Tommie Agee?" Johnny Murphy asked Cleon one day. "We might be making a trade for him." Cleon told Murphy, "If you get Tommie you won't have to worry about center field anymore."

Spring training in 1968 started with an air of professionalism. Team veterans and writers who covered the team in previous years talked about this new approach. Something was different. It was Gil Hodges. "The minute the Mets got Gil Hodges with his physical presence, things changed," said Maury Allen. "As early as spring training in 1968, you could sense that the Mets were going to be a serious team. It was going to be a serious competitive training camp." For sure. It also gave me a chance to meet one of my boyhood heroes. When Gil Hodges was named manager he brought the coaches who had been with him at the Senators. Rube Walker was his pitching coach, Eddie Yost his third base coach, and Joe Pignatano the bullpen coach. The same Joe Pignatano who hit into a triple play in his last at-bat as a Met. The final coach was Yogi Berra, who Gil carried over from the 1968 Mets staff, as his first base coach. I was in heaven. It was a chance to meet and work with one of my idols. Both growing up in St. Louis, Yogi and I had something in common. Well, something is better than nothing. When one actually meets one of their heroes it is something special, and it wasn't any different for me, except Yogi had no idea who I was. During drills in spring training, or if he was hitting fly balls to the outfielders, he just didn't know who I was. He would call out a name that didn't come close to my mine. In the clubhouse he would walk by me and just sort of grunt and keep walking. That can be very demoralizing to a young player. This went on for about ten days until we had our first spring training game against the Cardinals.

That first spring training game started in an auspicious way when future Hall of Famer Bob Gibson hit Tommie Agee in the head with the first pitch. This was Tommie's first game as a Met. No one can prove it, but maybe that was Gibson's welcoming Tommie to the National League. It worked because Tommie had a tough spring, a miserable start to the season, and a very difficult year in 1968.

In that same game I got a base hit. While running toward first base a revelation came to me. This was it. My chance for Yogi to call me by my name. He's got to call me something because the first base coach does have a job to do. He usually tells the runner the situation in the game, how many outs there are, if the pitcher has a good move over to first, and so forth. After rounding first base and going back to the bag I saw Yogi move toward me. I felt like it was going to happen. Yogi was actually going to acknowledge me. When he got right next to me he said, "Hey!" I looked at him and said, "Yeah Yogi, what is it?" I waited with heightened anticipation. He said simply, "Pay attention, you're on first base." That was it. No "Art." No "Shamsky." Nothing! Later that spring I finally asked him to say my full name three times out loud so he would remember it. He and I often laugh about it now.

Joe Pignatano remembered a Yogi story that spring. "Early in spring training in 1969, Yogi got a call from his wife and asked her if everything was alright. She said, 'Yes, I went to see *Dr. Zhivago.*' And Yogi said, "What the hell is wrong with you now?"

When spring training broke in Florida we traveled to Phoenix to play a few games against the Giants. From there the team went to Palm Springs to play against the California Angels. Then it was off to San Francisco for the opening game against the Giants and their ace, Juan Marichal. Not a bad trip to get ready for the season. I started in left field that first game, but we lost to 5-4. It was the Mets' seventh straight opening day loss.

Plenty of new faces showed up on the team in 1968. Besides Agee, Weis, and myself, second baseman Ken Boswell and left-handed pitcher Jerry Koosman joined the club. Jerry was now the number two pitcher behind Tom Seaver and would turn out to be one of the toughest left-handed pitchers in the game. Additional new hurlers included right-handed pitchers Cal Koonce and Nolan Ryan. Nolan, who couldn't throw strikes at this point in his career, would miss a lot of time because of his military commitment. When he returned at various times during the year, Hodges would start him occasionally, primarily in the second game of a doubleheader. Many times he would return to the club and throw batting practice to get some work in. Talk about hitters pissing and moaning. Everyone hated to get in the cage against him. No strikes and invariably trying to impress Gil and Rube Walker the pitching coach.

A few weeks into the season, on April 15th, we played a game in Houston's new Astrodome. The Astrodome was a scary looking building from the outside. It was round and looked like some sort of alien spacecraft. It was even scarier on the inside. Most of us had never played indoor baseball before. It was a new experience and the stadium was tough to hit in. The roof had sections of glass that were barely tinted. Day games became things of beauty because both teams had trouble seeing pop-ups and fly balls. It was even tough to see the ball during night games because the lighting was bad. One particular night everyone was having trouble seeing and as a result the game went twenty-four innings. We finally lost 1–0 on an error by shortstop Al Weis. The game took over six hours and was the longest 1–0 game in major league history. It was not a good evening for the team and even worse for Tommie Agee. He went 0–10 in the game. That's what you call a tough game at the plate. It was indicative of the year he would have.

"Tommie had a miserable first year with the Mets in 1968," said Cleon Jones. "We used to talk about it a lot. Tommie wasn't a student of hitting. I remember I had a chance to hit .300 that year if I got three hits the last game of the year. The night before, Tommie wanted to go out and I told him I wanted to get some rest because I needed to get the hits the next day. Tommie said, 'Well, I'm having a bad year so it doesn't make any difference to me.' I missed hitting .300 and after that Tommie would frequently say to me, 'Don't you wish you had gone out?' "

While we weren't breaking any records in 1968, we were competitive. Seaver and Koosman were a very good one-two punch and the pitching and defense kept us in most games. We were a little less than a .500 ball club through the middle of the season. The one thing that we did have, though, was harmony. It was a clubhouse filled with people who genuinely liked each other. We had a few "characters" and some loners, but, all in all, the 1968 Mets were a team that pulled for each other.

One of the main reasons the clubhouse was so good was Ed Charles. He had bounced around the minor leagues for many years. When he started out, black players just didn't get the opportunities like the rest of us. He finally got a chance with Kansas City and, lucky for all of us, found his way to the Mets. Ed had the fortitude and temperament to deal with the good and the bad. Plus, he was a heck of a player. He was the poet laureate of the Mets. When things would go bad Ed found some good in it. He was the "glass is half filled" father figure that made all of us who spent time with him better for it. It was Ed, with his poetry, wisdom, and good play, who held the locker room together. In his late thirties in 1968, he was undeniably our team's spiritual leader. He would probably deny that, but, to all of us, the "old man" was special. Let me rephrase that. Is special.

When asked about being the elder statesman on the club, Ed said, "I had been around a long time. I knew the role that Gil Hodges wanted me to play." Eventually, Ed would be nicknamed "The Glider." "That came about one afternoon when Jerry Koosman was pitching," Charles remembered. "Every time he pitched I would get a lot of ground balls at third base. One day a batter hit a smash at me, and I nonchalantly scooped it up and threw the guy out at first. Koosman got all excited and ran over from the pitcher's mound and said, 'That was one hell of a play.' I looked at him and said, 'I was just doing my job.' Koosman replied, 'You sort of glide at the ball. That's it. You're "The Glider" from now on.' If I hit a home run in a game I would go on Ralph Kiner's postgame show," Ed continued. "He would ask me what the pitch was that I hit. I would always say it was a slider no matter what. Then Bob Murphy started saying, 'Don't ever throw a slider to The Glider.' Since then everybody knows me as The Glider."

Although the team at this point was far from becoming a National League power, there were signs the future would be brighter. The one common denominator was Gil Hodges. The more the season progressed the more the players knew who was in charge. Gil was not the friendliest person to talk to, but the one thing we did know was that if he had something to say to you, he said it. We didn't have a lot of meetings. He took care of a lot of things in spring training. Things like being on time and acting as professionals were conveyed in what I would call, "the Gil Hodges way of doing things." Back then the only thing most players had that today would look a little out of the ordinary was sideburns. Many of us had the Beatles look; long muttonchop sideburns that were part of the sixties look. After all, if it was good enough for Joe Namath, it was good enough for us.

Once during the 1968 season, Gil decided to have a meeting before a game. We had played poorly for a while and were reverting to some old Met habits. I mean we were missing cutoffs, throwing to the wrong bases, things like that. When Gil got mad he looked twice as big as he really was. His veins would pop out in his neck and he looked like he was ready to kill. Thankfully, that didn't happen very often. But at this meeting it did to the max. Gil was getting madder and madder as he's telling us how bad we're playing, and we're doing this thing awful and that thing terrible. All of a sudden he looks at me, Boswell, Grote, Swoboda, and a few others and says, "Not only that, those sideburns look like shit." Well, needless to say we were shaken up. Was that the reason we're playing so bad? After the meeting we put our heads together and came up with a solution. We would trim our muttonchops just a little and see if that passed the test. It must have because there was never another word spoken about it. Nobody ever wanted to see Gil that mad again.

We had a number of players missing games during the 1968 season due to military commitments. Besides Ryan, Kenny Boswell, Tug McGraw, and Bud Harrelson all missed games during the season because of the military. It was an unavoidable circumstance, but it gave opportunity to reserve players. If we were in the middle of a pennant race it would have been interesting to see how well we handled it.

By the time September rolled around everyone knew that Gil Hodges had firmly established himself as a manager with a purpose. Put simply, that purpose was to be professional and win. Even Tom Seaver got a lesson from Gil. "I was pitching against the Giants in San Francisco in 1968 and was ahead 7–0," said Tom. "All of a sudden I turned around and the score was 7–6. This is when the Giants had Mays and McCovey. They had a heck of a team. I ended up winning the game 7–6, and the next day Gil called me into his office. He shut the door and I thought I was dead. He said, 'You were very unprofessional yesterday. I don't care what the score is, how many people are in the ballpark, you let the game get away from you. From now on you go about your business this way,' and he outlined how I should do it, A, B, C. Then he said, 'That's all.' I never said a word. I was glad to get out of there alive."

As the 1968 season was winding down we were in Atlanta for a night game. Gil threw batting practice before the game and in the second inning he started to feel ill. Gil was a heavy smoker and a person that kept many things inside. He was taken to a hospital where it was determined he had suffered a slight heart attack. Recovery was assured although he would need to stop smoking, exercise, and watch his diet. He spent the following winter relaxing and getting ready for 1969.

The 1968 season ended with a record of 73 wins and 89 losses. While we didn't have a great year, we had a higher win total than we ever had and twelve more than the year before. We finished in ninth place, not last, and drew over 1.7 million people to Shea. A major bright spot for the year was our pitching. Jerry Koosman won 19 games and Tom Seaver 16. Both had earned run averages below 3.00. The pitching staff as a whole had 25 shutouts and an ERA of less than 3.00. It wasn't a great year, and it wasn't a bad year. It was a year that showed real promise for the future. With the pitching we now possessed and a fine defense all we needed was some timely hitting.

For the rest of the country the Vietnam War was still in the forefront of the news everyday. At the end of October President Johnson announced a complete halt to U.S. bombing of North Vietnam. But soldiers were still dying everyday.

I stayed in New York City in the winter of 1968. The city had put its claws in me. I learned that New York City is really one of a kind. The more time you spend there the more you realize there's never enough time to do everything you want to. The city energizes you. Many professional athletes who come to New York never understand what it means to be playing there. If you play for any one of the city's major sports teams, be prepared for anyone, anytime, recognizing you and coming up to "chat." And, be prepared for what they might say. There is never a dull moment in New York City. After a few months I fell in love with the city. And, I got used to "Auttie." It's Artie in New York City lingo. I was okay with it now.

On Election Day, November 5th, one of the closest elections in our nation's history took place. Richard Nixon with 43.4 percent of the popular vote defeated Hubert Humphrey who garnered 42.7 percent. George Wallace received 0.4 percent. The next week, National Turn in Your Draft Card Day was observed with rallies and protests throughout the country. As author David Halberstam related recently, "It was a very tough time because we were in a war that didn't work." Everyone was glad to see 1968 come to an end.

THE BIRTH OF "BASEMENT BERTHA"

Bill Gallo, the venerable cartoonist/columnist for the New York *Daily News* for sixty years has created some of the most memorable images in sports history. One of those is Basement Bertha, created in the early days of the Mets. I asked Bill where he got the idea. "In 1962 the Mets were awful. I used to draw Casey Stengel a lot," recalled Gallo. "My managing editor wanted me to do other things about the Mets. The team was very popular even though they were losing. One day there was a rainout and I drew Casey in the cellar hanging up his wet clothes. Casey needed a sidekick. I needed something downtrodden. Why don't I have a washer-woman there? So I put this frizzy hair woman in the drawing with Casey. The next day I got lots of calls on the character. Now she needed a name. She was a basement girl so I called her 'the last place Bertha.' I kept doing it and eventually shortened her name to Basement Bertha. She started getting mail at the *Daily News* and became very popular. Pearl Bailey wanted to make a doll out of her. When the Mets won the World Series in 1969 she wasn't a loser anymore so I tried to kill her off. I asked the readers how to get rid of her. The *News* got tons of mail saying not to get rid of her, so she stayed."

10. That Remarkable Season

"I've always said the Mets won it, we didn't lose it."
—Ron Santo

Around the time pitchers and catchers were scheduled to report to the warm and sunny climate of Florida for the opening of spring camp, New York City residents were not so lucky. On February 9 and 10, 1969, fifteen inches of snow fell in the metropolitan area. While Manhattan was quickly and repeatedly plowed, the streets of Queens remained blocked for days, and Mayor Lindsay was blamed. Many thought the Lindsay administration was catering to certain constituencies.

When spring training got into full swing the Mets brought two young players into camp, Wayne Garrett and Rod Gaspar. Pitcher Jim McAndrew had been recalled the previous season and had a good shot to be a starter. The pitching staff was shaping up nicely. The Mets also had Amos Otis in camp. They wanted him to play third base. There was only one problem; he didn't want to play third base. But, he reluctantly tried to learn a new position. The Mets had Ed Charles and Wayne Garrett in the wings if the experiment didn't pay off. It didn't, and the two spring backups would form a very good righty-lefty platoon at third base during the season. A natural outfielder, Amos would eventually be traded and end up having a wonderful career in the American League.

The coaching staff remained intact from the year before. In describing them Joe Pignatano told me, "Rube [Walker] was one of the best pitching coaches ever. He was a player's friend, too. Eddie Yost was the intellectual. He came out of NYU and would talk about applying the elements, basically thinking about the game and certain situations. Yogi was dumb like a fox. We all got along together. Yost taught us cribbage and the coaches played all the time. Only Rube would cheat a little when we were playing partners."

Spring training was a great time of the year. If a player pretty much knew he made the team, there was really no pressure. It was five or six weeks of just getting into better shape to start the season. That's how I felt in 1969. I had become friendly with everyone on the team. I now felt acclimated and, given the opportunity to play, could put up some numbers. And Yogi now knew my name.

Three days into the exhibition season, I was taking some throws from Ken Boswell during practice at Huggins Field, just trying to work out at first base in case I needed to play there during the season. While taking throws in the dirt something "popped" on my lower left side. It hurt, but I continued practicing. Finally I decided to go see our trainer, Gus Mauch, former New York Yankees trainer for many years. I just said, "Give me something so I can play." I always thought it was important to play and stay out of the trainer's room.

After taking a pain pill we went over to Al Lang Field. While taking infield practice I felt an excruciating pain down my left leg to my kneecap. I went down on my knees and that was it. I did not play another inning in spring training that year. The doctors told me to rest and I spent the whole month of March in bed in a hotel room. The only time I got out of bed was to go to the bathroom. I started the 1969 season on the disabled list with an injured back. It was early April and my world was as bleak as could be. I was depressed and scared. Was my career over? My life was in flux; it was a terrible time for me.

That wasn't all the distressing news. Early in March, in a L.A. courtroom, Sirhan Sirhan admitted killing Robert Kennedy, and on March 10th James Earl Ray pleaded guilty to assassinating Dr. Martin Luther King Jr. He would later retract his guilty plea. The country would be on edge for months.

The rest of the spring for all the other Mets, however, was proceeding favorably. In Gil Hodges' second year as manager everyone and everything was pretty well set in the way he wanted things done. The team had a good spring winning fourteen games and losing ten. Over the winter Major League Baseball expanded again, and the National League added two new teams, Montreal and San Diego. There now would be two six-team divisions, East and West, in each league, and for the first time in history there would be a playoff system. The division winners would play a series to determine who would compete in the World Series. The Mets, of course, were in the Eastern Division of the National League.

Another major change in baseball was the lowering of the pitcher's mound. Pitchers like Bob Gibson had been so dominant in baseball, particularly in the National League, that the decision was made to lower the mound and give the batters a little bit more of a chance. I guess somebody felt sorry for the poor hitters.

The Mets opened the 1969 season against the newly formed Montreal Expos amid unsettling news swirling around the country. U.S. combat deaths in Vietnam had reached 33,641, topping the number killed during the Korean War. At Shea Stadium, on a cold, windy day, the Mets did their usual thing and lost. It was a wild game, with Montreal pulling it out 11–10. The next day, April 9th, before our game started, we heard more bad news. Mayor John Lindsay met with top union officials and asked for their help. The Mayor told them the city was in big financial trouble. We later learned of a student takeover of the main administration building at Harvard. The following day 400 state and local police cleared the building.

The Mets won that game against the Expos, but lost seven out of the first ten games in 1969. It was starting out to be another typical year for the Mets and an all too familiar continuation of difficult times for the citizens of our city and country.

After my twenty-one days on the disabled list were up I was feeling okay. Okay meaning well enough to think about playing. If you have ever had a bad back you know that at any minute something can happen, and you're back to square one. I was ready to take that chance and get back to action. Arriving at the ballpark the day after my stint on the disabled list Gil Hodges called me into his office. Johnny Murphy was also on hand. Gil asked me how I was feeling, and I said fine. He said, "Well, you missed all of spring training." I said, "No I didn't. I played in three games." Gil said, "That's not spring training. You need to play some games." I said, "Okay, I'm ready to play." I saw where this was going. Gil then said,

"We're going to send you to Tidewater. John and I agree." I then said the ultimate stupid thing, "I don't need spring training to play on this team." They both just looked at me. I wanted to take it back as soon as I said it. I regrouped and said, "I mean I just want to play." Gil, having recovered from my shocking statement, said, "You'll be back as soon as you're ready." I walked out of Gil's office quite dejected. But I, too, needed to know. I could fool others but not myself. So, unhappily, I went to Tidewater. It turned out all right and I was back in ten days.

The night I came back to the Mets I had pinch-hit a single and drove in a run against the Atlanta Braves. Life was a lot brighter now. Soon I began sharing right field with Ron Swoboda. The year was better already for me and the Mets, but the city was experiencing more unrest. On April 22nd, black and Puerto Rican students padlocked the gate at City College, demanding the student body reflect the racial makeup of the city's high schools. At the time, admissions standards were high and few applicants from the most disadvantaged high schools were admitted. In response, the Board of Education announced a policy of open admissions to begin in 1970.

We played respectably and after the first thirty-six games were 18–18. Incredible as this may sound, it was the farthest into the season the Mets had ever been at .500. When we reached that milestone some of the writers covering us thought it was a big step. They began asking the players what we thought and suggested we should celebrate. Tom Seaver had the best response. He said quite simply, ".500 is nothing to celebrate."

Maybe those words by Tom affected the team. From that point on we started to play better. Subtle yet important things were changing with our team. We started to win games that we lost in the past. Close games where small things were done right on the field turning a potential loss into a win. We found ways to win games as opposed to finding ways to lose. Don't get me wrong, at this point nobody thought about winning the Eastern Division title or even visualized hopes of a pennant. But we were a better ball club than the Mets had ever been in our history. More important, we were starting to have faith in our own abilities. Positive things started to happen.

"Going into 1969 there was a lot of optimism," said Ken Boswell. "By spring training I knew we had some talented guys and had made some good trades. I thought we could beat some teams. And Gil Hodges was such a stickler for fundamentals. We were learning how not to beat ourselves. At some point during the 1969 season we started to really believe in ourselves." Jerry Grote also remembered an early sense of optimism. "I remember spring training in 1969 and having a good feeling about the team. I thought if we could just start winning some close games you never know what could happen."

The real transformation started around the end of May. At that same time New Yorkers received some news that confirmed what they had all felt for quite a while. A new report documented that the city was the center of the most severe inflation the nation had seen for more than a hundred years. As if that wasn't enough, the report also revealed the city was on the verge of economic disaster. It seemed like the Mets got better as the city's woes got worse. From that point until the second week in June we won eleven games in a row. It was the longest winning streak in Met history. At that moment we knew we had a good team. "At the beginning of the season I thought it might be the same old stuff again. I mean the losing," recalled Ed Kranepool. "But, when we won eleven in a row against some good teams I knew things were changing."

While we were playing better there was still a piece of the puzzle missing. The club needed more right-handed power. Johnny Murphy knew this and made a great move. On June 15, 1969, he traded for Donn Clendenon. Donn had spent a number of years on very good Pittsburgh Pirate teams with Roberto Clemente and Willie Stargell. Together they made Pittsburgh a terrific hitting team. Donn was eventually drafted by Montreal from the expansion pool. "Joe Brown thought he would put some of the veteran players from the Pirates, who were older and making a little money, on the expansion list," Clendenon said. "But it backfired when some of us got picked." Donn went to Montreal and was then traded to Houston. He decided he did not want to go to Houston. Commissioner Bowie Kuhn ruled that Donn was the property of Montreal and the Mets made a deal for him. "Johnny Murphy called me before the trade to the Mets. I couldn't wait to come," Clendenon told me recently.

Most people didn't realize at the time how important Donn would become for the 1969 Mets. That importance was not only on the field, but in the locker room as well.

"When Clendenon joined us," Ron Swoboda said, "we started to win more and began to jell. Clendenon had a way about him. He had been on a good team. He could annoy the crap out of you, but he had this way where you could get back at him. Suddenly, we were a real good team."

Another important factor helping the team tremendously was Tommie Agee bouncing back from his miserable first year with the team. He was a different batter at the plate in 1969. "We put in a lot of work over the winter working on our hitting," said Cleon Jones. "I started watching Tommie. There were no films then, but I watched him and figured out what he needed to do. All I had to do was holler at him when he was hitting and tell him to kick his foot toward the plate so he could stay back. That was the only time he ever listened to me."

By now Gil had pretty well set the lineup. Everyone knew his role on the team. There were three everyday players: Bud Harrelson at shortstop, Cleon Jones in left, and Tommie Agee in center. Jerry Grote caught most of the games, but was spelled by J. C. Martin and on occasion by Duffy Dyer. The other positions were platooned. At first base Donn Clendenon and Ed Kranepool shared duties, second base Ken Boswell and Al Weis, third base Ed Charles and Wayne Garrett, and right field Ron Swoboda and myself. This constituted the basic set for both right-handed and left-handed opposing pitchers. Once in a while Gil altered it, but most of the time that was it. Most of us who were platooning didn't like it. It's not easy to play the game that way. It's very difficult to get into a rhythm and extremely difficult to put up great stats at the end of the year. I don't mean this in a selfish way; it's just the facts. A baseball player wants to play—all the time. While you might have some personal feeling about the situation, most of us back then never complained. I didn't, although I was frustrated at times. In my particular case, due to my experience in spring training and the first part of the season, I was thankful for having a career again. But the main reason the guys didn't complain was because it worked. Hodges got the most out of his players and in each platoon position there was productivity.

"I didn't like it," said Donn Clendenon on being platooned. "Once you platoon you get labeled. It's a difficult way to play. Hodges knew how I felt, and I respected his honesty when he and I talked about it. But no player I knew liked it." Ed Kranepool added, "It wasn't the greatest situation, but it worked in 1969. At least there was some stability knowing when you were going to play. Before Hodges got there no one knew when they were going to play."

In June, New York City and the nation were still going through some trying times. Along with the war protests and racial strife, civil unrest was continuing countrywide and locally. Earlier that month, nearby Hartford, Connecticut, experienced four days of looting and violence with over 200 arrests being made. At the end of the month an uprising came from a previously unheard-from quarter. Gay rights activists took part in what was called the "Stonewall" riots in New York City that marked the beginning of the modern day gay rights movement in the United States. It started in the early hours of June 27, 1969, in Greenwich Village. Police raids on gay bars in New York were common then and on this night seven plainclothes and one uniformed policeman entered the Stonewall Inn near Sheridan Square. They cleared the bar out as patrons fumed on the street outside. As the crowd became hostile, tensions, built on years of harassment, led to a confrontation between police and people in the street. Cops used their nightsticks to try and quiet the crowd. As more and more people gathered to support the angry crowd, a chant of "Gay Power" began. The protests continued for five days as the gay rights movement rose to the surface and began to grow as a result of this famous confrontation.

Back at the ballpark things were also different. In the first seven and one half years of their existence the New York Mets never played an important game or series, at least one that was crucial to the team. Sure, the Mets played the Cardinals at the end of the 1964 season in a series that helped determine the National League champion, but they never competed in one that really meant anything to them. Now the time had come.

On July 8, 1969, the Mets began a three-game series with the division leading Chicago Cubs. In the preceding few weeks, with our steady, improved play, we had moved into second place in the Eastern Division. Manager Leo Durocher, a man that Met fans would grow to hate, led the Cubs. They possessed a very good team, including future Hall of Famers Ernie Banks and Billy Williams, along with a bevy of first-class players like Ron Santo, Randy Hundley, and Glenn Beckert among others. Their starting pitching was outstanding. Future Hall of Famer Ferguson Jenkins was one of the best pitchers in baseball. Billy Hands and Ken Holtzman were two other star hurlers. (Holtzman and I had gone to the same high school outside of St. Louis. Although I was a little older, we had known each other since we were kids.)

By now Met fans had tasted success. We were playing well and showing promise. Isn't that what Met fans wanted from the very start? Big crowds were nothing unusual for Shea Stadium. This series against the Cubs was what Met fans had waited so long for. It would also mark the beginning of one of the best rivalries in baseball. Ferguson Jenkins recently told me, "The rivalry between the Mets and the Cubs was pretty fierce. It started because we were in the same division, and the Mets were coming on strong. It seemed like every game was important."

With over 55,000 people in the stands, the first game of the series lived up to everyone's expectations. The pitching matchup was Jerry Koosman against Ferguson Jenkins. I remember Fergie would pitch with a heavy, hundred percent wool shirt underneath his baseball uniform. And he never perspired. No matter how hot it was, he never perspired. "I was always in shape," Jenkins said. "I ran in long sleeve wool shirts and got used to it. I was comfortable with it and maybe it psyched out some batters." It turned out to be a pretty good pitchers' duel and the Cubs were leading 3–1 going into the bottom of the ninth. But this was a different year for the New York Mets. With runners on second and third, Cleon Jones came up to the plate. He promptly ripped a single to tie the score. The stadium went crazy. I walked and then Cleon and I moved to second and third on a groundout. With first base open the Cubs decided to pitch to Ed Kranepool. Krane had certainly seen his share of losing with the Mets and didn't want it to continue. Intent on making contact with the ball he hit a soft blooper over the shortstop. With both the shortstop and left fielder desperately going for the ball it fell between them for a base hit, driving in the winning run. It was fate that Ed should get this key hit. "It was great when I got the hit that won that game. It made me feel like we were turning it around after all the years of losing," Ed recalled.

The crowd went wild. It was like Met fans had just witnessed a revelation. The team went wild, too. Everyone ran out on the field, congratulating Krane and each other. We were now a team on the move. That moment is what I call, "The true beginning of the 1969 Mets."

The following night it was Tom Seaver against Ken Holtzman. Seaver was on his way to a fantastic year, capable of throwing a gem every time he went to the mound. This night would be one of those never-to-be-forgotten games. From the first inning Tom was masterful. With a 4–0 lead going into the top of the ninth he was pitching a "perfect game." It was a packed house at Shea Stadium, and this was every Met fan's dream. Witnessing a game that meant something and a potential perfect game as well. But, it was not to be. With one out in the top of the ninth, Jimmy Qualls, a little known outfielder, forever etched his name into Mets history. He hit a semi-line drive to left center for a base hit. It ruined Seaver's perfect game. Tom ended with a one-hit shutout, but more important, we were only one game behind the Cubs in the Eastern Division standings.

The next game's pitching matchup scheduled Bill Hands for the Cubs versus Gary Gentry. We got a dose of reality losing the game 6–2 in front of another big crowd. Even though we lost the last game of the series, the tone had been set for the rest of the season. The Cubs knew we were for real, and we knew we could play. There was going to be a pennant race, but this time the New York Mets were going to be in it. "That was a big series," said Ferguson Jenkins. "The Mets gained a lot of confidence. Not only against us, but also against everyone."

We split the next two games with the Montreal Expos and immediately left for Chicago to open a three-game series against the Cubs. It was time for their fans to do their thing, which is simply love their Cubbies and hate the opposition. Unlike Shea Stadium, Wrigley Field has bleachers in right and left field. The people who sit out there are known as "bleacher bums." When you are on the opposing team playing in the outfield at Wrigley Field you enjoy hearing every expletive imaginable. And it's usually directed at you. I heard words that I didn't even know existed.

One time I recall the Mets visiting Wrigley on a hot but beautiful day. Playing in the outfield in front of those bleachers I kept hearing a screechy woman's voice directing invective my way. Whoever it was got on my case early. Halfway through the game I made the last out of an inning. Running out to right field I heard that voice again. It just didn't stop. She didn't let up. Not able to stand that screeching any more I decided, against my better judgment, to say something to her. I turned around and tried to find her. It wasn't difficult. There she was at the ledge of the bleachers' fence screaming at me. "The Mets suck, you suck," and a lot of worse things. To my surprise, the woman with the screechy voice wasn't some ugly, beastly looking lady. It was this beautiful girl wearing a bikini top, screaming at me and at the same time putting on suntan lotion. I did a double take and couldn't say a word. She was gorgeous. It was difficult matching that voice to the person. I just shrugged and figured it was a bleacher bum that loved her Cubbies. You have to give Cubs fans credit for sticking with their team. They hadn't won a World Series in a very long time.

We lost the first game of the series to the Cubs 1–0. Ron Santo, the Cubs' third baseman, had started a trend where he would jump and click his heels after a Cub victory. He would do it on his way to the Cubs clubhouse located in the left-field corner of Wrigley Field. After they beat us that day Santo did his thing. As we watched Santo after the game, most of us made the usual comments accompanied by expletives. Needless to say we didn't think too highly of it, and Ron's heel clicking didn't continue because we won the next two games at Wrigley. At this point we definitely were contenders.

When I talked to Ron recently I asked him why he did that particular exhibition. "I started clicking my heels with every home victory starting in June of 1969," Santo said. "We had lost the first game of a doubleheader and won the second game in the bottom of the ninth to keep us in first place. I was always an emotional player. I carried my emotions on my sleeve. I ran down the left-field line to our clubhouse and didn't realize I had clicked my heels. That night it was all over the television. The next day, when I got to the ballpark, Leo Durocher called a meeting. He says, 'Can you click your heels again? We ought to make that our victory kick, but only at home when we win.' So, from that moment on, when we won at home, I would run down toward our clubhouse doing it. The fans really got into it. I actually got telephone calls from friends on other teams saying, 'Our pitchers don't like that.' My response to them was 'too bad.' I ended up getting knocked down a lot, but it didn't matter. As soon as we dropped into second place I never clicked my heels again." It should be noted that Ron has since had serious health problems, through which he has persevered, displaying guts and true determination. He related his ordeal to me. "I just had my third operation in three years. I lost my right leg in 2000 and left leg in 2001. I also lost my bladder, which was cancerous. It was contained and I am recovering and doing very well."

Our next series was in Montreal and we didn't fare too well. Cleon Jones got into a fight with the Montreal catcher in one game. He tried to score from second base on a single and got tagged hard by the catcher, Ron Brand. Cleon came up swinging, and they got into it. When it was over the umpires threw Cleon out of the game. After losing the first three games of the series we finally won the second game of a doubleheader on a run-scoring bunt for a base hit by Bobby Pfeil. Left-handed reliever Jack DiLauro saved the game for us. Both Bobby and Jack joined the Mets earlier in the season from Tidewater, our Triple-A club. DiLauro had come up when the Mets traded Al Jackson. Pfeil was called up when Bud Harrelson had two weeks of military obligation. He ended up staying even when Buddy returned. "I originally came up for two weeks to replace Bud Harrelson," recalled Pfeil. "At the end of the two weeks I went up to Gil Hodges and said, 'My wife is in Virginia, what do I do?' He replied, 'She's *your* wife.' I didn't know what the hell that meant. He then told me, 'They [the front office] don't want you here, but I want you here, so you will be here the rest of the year.'"

We weren't able to leave Montreal on time Sunday evening to return to New York because of airplane problems. This aggravated a lot of the players. It was the All-Star break, which meant we would have three days off except for maybe a workout on one day. We wanted to be home in New York, not in an airport, to utilize the days off. But here we were in the early evening in the Montreal airport. Lou Niss, our traveling secretary, bore the brunt of the players' wrath even though he had nothing to do with the situation. One thing has been a fact since baseball and travel began: The traveling secretary is always going to be the person taking the blame for just about everything. If a bus is one minute late or your room is not available upon checking in, or God forbid your meal money is a dollar short, the traveling secretary is the person responsible. The perfect traveling secretary is a person who can handle the pressure, doesn't care, and is a little hard of hearing. Lou Niss fit all those criteria. In any case, we were stranded in the Montreal airport, but did get a meal and a chance to watch an historic event—the lunar landing and walk on the moon's surface by Neil Armstrong and Buzz Aldrin. I remember thinking about two things simultaneously. How great this event was for the United States and how screwed-up the country was at the same time. It was one incredible technological achievement during a very bad time in our country's foreign and domestic history.

We worked out on Tuesday minus Cleon Jones, Tom Seaver, and Jerry Koosman. Their stellar play got them selected to play in the All-Star game. Gil Hodges also went as a coach. Perhaps it would have been better if the team didn't have the days off. We split the next four games against the Reds and then on July 30th played the Houston Astros in a double-header at Shea Stadium. Using the word "played" is somewhat of a misnomer—we were massacred in both contests. In the first game the Astros set a record by hitting two grand slam home runs in the same inning. It wasn't pretty, and the fans were restless. They were starting to expect better things from us. The second game was even uglier, but contained a significant incident for the 1969 Mets.

While we were were getting clobbered, again, Houston batter John Edwards, who was a former teammate of mine with the Cincinnati Reds, hit a slicing ball down into the left-field corner. Cleon Jones went after it, but very gingerly. When the play was over and Edwards stood at second base, Gil Hodges started for the mound. Even the usually faithful Shea Stadium crowd was booing. I was in right field at the time. Whenever Gil would go to the mound, either to talk or change pitchers, he never stepped on the first-base line. He was superstitious like most of us and never came close to the line. This time he barely missed it. I had great vision then and

I remember thinking that he came as close as I have ever seen. It looked like he missed it by an inch or less. I figured he was a little upset. After all, we're in the second game of a doubleheader after getting our asses kicked in the first game, and the second game is going the same way. As Gil got to the pitcher's mound he kept walking. I said to myself, what did Harrelson do? The next thing I see is Gil walking right past Buddy toward Cleon. Holy shit! What is going to happen now? I'm thinking Cleon and Gil are going to go at it. I saw Gil stop in front of Cleon and after a few moments both of them began walking back toward the Met dugout. Gil took Cleon out of the game, and to this day there are many who think that event was the defining moment for the team that year. "Nobody knows what really happened except Gil and myself," Cleon told me recently. "All anybody knows is that he came out on the field and pulled me out of the ball game. But, this is what happened. The ball was hit down the left-field line and there was no way you were going to stop him from getting a double. So I ran after the ball the best way I could. It was soaking wet in the outfield that day and I had a bad ankle. When Gil walked out to me I was surprised as everyone else. First, I thought he was going to take out the pitcher. Then, I thought he was going to say something to Harrelson. But, then, when he walked past Buddy I looked back. I thought something had happened behind me. When I turned around he was walking right toward me. He got to me and said, 'What's wrong?' I said, 'What do you mean what's wrong?' He replied, 'I don't like the way you went after that last ball.' I said, 'Gil, we talked about this in Montreal. You know I have a bad ankle and as long as I wasn't going to hurt the team I would continue to play.' And then I said, 'Look down.' And he did. His feet were in water. He said, 'It is bad out here. I didn't know it was that bad. You probably need to come out of the game.' So I said, 'Fine' and we walked in together. A few days later we had a conversation and he said, 'You know I wouldn't embarrass you like that, but I look at you as a leader on this club. Everybody seemed like they were comfortable getting their tails kicked, and I didn't like that.'"

Gil had made his point. He wouldn't tolerate that kind of play and it was a wake-up call. "Everyone misinterpreted what happened," said Cleon. "But in a way it proved a point and woke us up. That was his way of trying to shake up the ball club."

Joan Hodges, Gil's wife, recalled, "Gil usually didn't bring the game home with him. But I remember when he got home that night after walking out to left field and taking Cleon out of the game. I had the television on and Gil sat down at the table and said, 'Why don't you turn off the TV?' I knew something was bothering him so I turned it off. He said to me, 'Why don't you talk about it?' I said I really would rather not. He said, 'Go ahead.' So I just said, 'Gil, I wouldn't have cared if you killed him in the clubhouse, but whatever possessed you to walk out to left field and take him out of the game?' And, he said, 'You want to know something? I didn't even realize I was doing it until I was past the pitcher.'"

None of us in the club understood then what the cause was, but the effect worked. We all knew Gil was a tough person, but if any player up to that time didn't think Gil was all business, he did from that point on. That moment had to be our lowest point of the year. Now six games behind the Cubs, we had to regroup.

One of the things adversity does is bring people together. While none of us would want the manager taking a leisurely stroll out to our position and then removing us from the ball game, we were a team and Cleon was our teammate. It was a wake-up call to all of us; in turn that made all of us care more about each other. The clubhouse was special before this all happened. After, it became even more so.

"Everyone got along," said Ed Charles. "It was one big happy family where guys just bonded together. Everybody had big hearts. Each one was up for the challenge. We didn't have big names, but we had some guys with experience. We cared for each other, and I think that's what really made our team."

"It was a close-knit group both on and off the field," said Cleon. "We all started to be hands-on with one another. We genuinely cared about each other."

"We had a good bunch of guys," recalled Jerry Koosman. "You had to keep up or you would get picked on all the time. We went out together. We liked to aggravate Nick Torman, our clubhouse attendant. He had a short fuse. Then, of course, there was Clendenon. I knew he was going to be a lawyer. He liked to talk. He was always creating havoc."

Rod Gaspar gave his take. "It was a great clubhouse. We got along well. My problem was my nickname, 'P.P.' While only a few people knew how I got the nickname, I had to take a lot just from that. I learned to give a lot, too."

"We had a great clubhouse," Tom Seaver explained. "Cleon had a great sense of humor. Sometimes he would talk so fast you couldn't understand him. Agee was the only one who understood him. It was the Alabama language; it would bring tears to your eyes you would laugh so hard. With Koosman, Clendenon, and Tug, it was enough to keep us loose."

Of course we had Yogi around, too. There weren't many days that went by when something he did or said didn't have us laughing. Yogi threw batting practice once in a while. Except his batting practice was awful. It was slower than slow. I recall one time I complained to him about it. He told me to "Go complain to a coach."

Rube Walker was also terrific. Even though he was the pitching coach, he would mix in with the other players. He would walk by Kenny Boswell and myself, stop and say things like, "You guys are exciting ballplayers." We would just laugh. I always wondered if Hodges told him to do things like that since Gil didn't frequently communicate with many of us. It was fun. We were really a close team.

Our other coaches were great, too. Eddie Yost, our third base coach, was an outstanding baseball person. He was a stickler for fundamentals like Gil. He knew the game and was fun to be around. Joe Pignatano was the bullpen coach. He was in charge of keeping order in the bullpen. Sometimes that could be a little difficult because of people like Ron Taylor and Tug McGraw. Joe tells this story: "One day I came out to the bullpen before the start of a game, and there's a chef out there with three buffet dishes with sternos underneath them. I said, 'Who might you be?' He said, 'I'm waiting for coach Pignatano.' I said, 'You found him.' He then handed me a bill for three hundred and seventy-five dollars. He told me that McGraw said he shouldn't worry, Coach Pignatano would pay for it. I told the guy the game is about to start and you can take the bill and all the food and you know what you can do with it. I caught McGraw lying on the floor in the tunnel laughing. We ate the stuff in the clubhouse that night. By the way, Tug paid the bill."

Joe Pignatano was famous for his vegetable garden in the Met bullpen. "In 1969, around the beginning of April, I saw a little tomato plant coming out of the ground in the bullpen against the far fence near the parking lot," Joe recalled. "I told the groundskeeper to leave it alone. I was going to take care of it and wanted to see how big it would grow. It got to be a foot high and I dug it up and moved it to the bullpen side of the outfield fence. It grew well and I got about eight to ten tomatoes. I never took them home; we ate them in the clubhouse. I think it all started when the stands got moved around for football at Shea Stadium. Someone must have dropped part of a tomato down between the stands and nature took its course. Before long, I planted radishes, pumpkins, zucchini, peppers, and a few other vegetables. None of the grounds crew ever complained. When I went on the road they looked after them for me."

After the Astros fiasco and our awakening, we beat the Braves three in a row at Shea. That modest three-game winning streak stopped there, because we lost three out of four to the Reds in Cincinnati. We won the next three out of four against the Braves in Atlanta, but then went to Houston, and guess what? We lost three in a row in the Astrodome.

It's crazy the way it works sometimes. We couldn't beat the lowly Astros in 1969, but had no problems with the mighty Braves. That's what makes the game so interesting. On a down note, on August 12th, the country was traumatized by news of five murders in California by members of a cult led by Charles Manson. One of the victims was actress Sharon Tate, wife of movie director Roman Polanski. The murders were vividly gruesome and the next day the cult members murdered two more people. It seemed like the world was going insane.

We came home for a long home stand on August 16th, opening with a doubleheader sweep against San Diego. Tom Seaver pitched a 2–0 shutout in the first game for his seventeenth win and Jim McAndrew was the winner in the second. McAndrew was turning out to be the perfect fourth starter on a team that had three of the league's top pitchers: Tom Seaver, Jerry Koosman, and Gary Gentry. Toss in Nolan Ryan, Cal Koonce, and Don Cardwell as spot starters and you have something pretty good going.

As if war, protest, and riots were not enough, weather became a huge factor for tragedy and despair. On August 17, 1969, Hurricane Camille, a category five storm, hit the Mississippi coast, killing 248 people and causing billions of dollars in damage. It was almost as if Mother Nature was trying to beat down our spirits, too. Amid this tragedy the Mets kept their composure. We won four more in a row, including the last two against the Giants, for a six-game winning streak. In that streak our pitchers threw three shutouts and didn't allow the Padres or the Giants to score more than three runs in a game.

On August 21st, the Giants beat us, stopping the streak, but then we swept three games from the Dodgers before leaving on a West Coast swing. Every single game at Shea during the home stand brought huge crowds. Banners were everywhere, and the fans were as loud and energetic as ever.

The road trip started in San Diego with us winning three straight games to make it another six-game winning streak. Seaver, McAndrew, and Koosman all pitched well in that series.

We were supposed to have a day off in San Francisco but Gil had us practice. It also cost the coaches a golf game. "We were supposed to play golf in San Francisco, but Gil decided to have a workout so that killed the golf game," recalled Joe Pignatano. "Yogi said, 'After the workout we can go deep-sea fishing. A friend of mine has a boat.' So, I said, 'Great, but I get a little seasick once in a while.' Yogi replied, 'You mean you get seasick on water?' I just told him we'd do it another time."

In the first game in San Francisco Juan Marichal shut us out. But then we won the next two out of three on the weekend. In the bottom of the ninth with the game tied, Rod Gaspar made a terrific play that kept us in the game. "We had the 'McCovey shift' on," Gaspar recalled. "I was way over in left-center field. There was a runner on first base. Tug McGraw was pitching and threw McCovey a screwball. He hit the ball down the left-field line. I ran over, picked it up, and fired a strike to Grote who tagged out the runner trying to score the winning run. Jerry thought there were three outs so he rolled the ball back to the pitcher's mound. However, there were only two outs. McCovey kept running around the bases, but Donn Clendenon ran over from first base, scooped up the ball and threw to third to get McCovey. It was an important game for us and I was so glad I made a good throw home." Usually a very heads-up catcher, Grote's actions reverted back to the "old" days of the Mets when things like not knowing how many outs there were in the inning was the norm for some players. Maybe they would have just run off the field thinking the inning was over. But this was not the same old Mets. Clendenon's heads-up play was indicative of how far we had come as a team. Picking up each other was now the norm.

August had been a good month. We won twenty-one games while losing only ten. We were now twenty-two games over .500, and the Cubs were looking over their shoulders.

On September 1st, we lost the first game of a three-game series to the Dodgers in Los Angeles. I always loved playing at Dodger Stadium. You never knew who you might see sitting next to your dugout. Just before the start of a game one night, I saw the movie actor Randolph Scott sitting with a friend. Doris Day was always there. Movie stars could be seen at almost every game. I also remember leaving tickets for my uncle Tony who had been an actor and then a television network executive. At that time he owned his own drama school. After the game he waited with a friend of his to say hello to me. It turned out his friend was the famous Jerry Goldsmith, composer of many musical scores for Academy Award–winning movies. In Los Angeles you just never knew who you were going to see or meet.

We split the next two games with the Dodgers and flew back to New York feeling pretty good about getting through the West Coast trip in good shape. We were coming home for an important home stand. We anticipated huge crowds, and the Cubs were coming in. We were going to have to take care of business.

The Vietnam War again captured the forefront of public thought. Lieutenant William Calley was charged with six counts of murder in the deaths of 109 Vietnamese civilians in My Lai. No senior officers would ever be charged. The incident presented an embarrassing and tragic portrayal of good people doing unthinkable things in the grip of fear and uncertainty amid an unpopular war.

Although we were in the heat of a pennant race the players could not help being affected by all the issues facing the city and country. Ron Swoboda remembered, "Looking back then, we had the war, protests, and lousy economic times. It seemed like anything and everything could happen, and it did." Wayne Garrett recalled, "I was a young kid. I saw what was happening in the streets of New York. My baseball world was different than the real world. Once you left the ballpark the real world was pretty obvious."

Tom Seaver gave considerable thought to the situation. He recently gave me this perspective. "As a young professional athlete you are so engrossed in what you are doing that it is difficult to be totally emotionally involved in what is going on around you. That does not mean that we were not aware of events around us. The city was in a dire financial mess. The country was dealing with Vietnam and the demonstrations. All that was on the periphery of our lives every day. As far as me personally getting through all that, one of the good things was that I was working seven days a week and being in the middle of a dream on the baseball field. We did not live in a cocoon, we were aware of everything. But we had an outlet, a sense of relief going to work. However, every night on television you were seeing people being shot up and it was surreal. I was in the Marine reserves, and I knew I could have been there. I thought about that a lot. It could indeed be tough concentrating, but we were pros and whatever we thought about daily events outside the park, the public expected our full attention when playing." Tom exemplified this in our next game.

On Friday September 5th, we opened the home stand with a double-header against the Philadelphia Phillies. In the first game Seaver won his twentieth game, beating the Phillies 5–1. Tom became the first Met pitcher to ever win twenty games. The second game was a disappointing loss. We won the next two against the Phillies then awaited the Chicago Cubs, who were in first place, two and a half games in front of us.

It was the perfect setting for a pennant race. Even though it was a Monday night, a big crowd showed up to watch Jerry Koosman pitch against Bill Hands. Both pitchers were tough competitors. It was a fan's dream game. We were on the Cubs heels and they could feel it.

In the bottom of the first inning Hands wasted no time in trying to get his Cubs motivated. He threw the first pitch right at Tommie Agee's head. Tommie, of course, had the horrible experience of being beaned in spring training by Bob Gibson in 1968. This time he was able to dodge the bullet. In the top of the second inning, Jerry Koosman knew what was expected of him. Ron Santo was the first batter. Jerry wasted a pitch and then threw right at him, hitting him in the forearm. "Knowing Bill Hands," recalled Ron Santo, "he pitched inside so I thought nothing of it. When I went up to the plate I wasn't expecting anything. When Koosman hit me on the forearm I just went to first base. It was part of baseball." Koosman had a different take. "What started it was Bill Hands. On the first pitch to Agee he threw at his head. In the top of the second Santo was the lead-off hitter and I drilled him. A lot of people have talked about that being some sort of turning point for us, but I don't know. I recall wasting a pitch down and away first, and then I drilled him to not make it look so obvious. Santo always thought it was an accident. It wasn't." Both teams had sent a message. Ours was simple: "We are not going to sit around and let you try and intimidate our players." It worked. We were determined. Later, Agee hit a two-run home run off Hands, but another play from that game involving Tommie is well remembered. In the seventh inning Agee was on second base after a hitting a double. With the score tied 2–2, Wayne Garrett singled to right setting up a play at the plate. With the throw coming in from the rightfielder, Tommie and the ball arrived at home plate at almost the same time. Cubs' catcher Randy Hundley caught the ball and tagged Agee sliding into home plate. The umpire called him safe and the crowd went wild. The Cubs went crazy. It didn't matter. They lost the argument and the game 3–2 as Koosman struck out thirteen. We were only a game and a half behind them.

The next night, Tuesday September 9th, in front of another big crowd, we did it again. This time Tom Seaver pitched a great game and we beat their ace, Ferguson Jenkins, 7–1. I even got into the act by hitting a home run, as did Donn Clendenon. This game was not only an important win for us, but featured the most bizarre event in this incredible year of remarkable and unusual episodes. It was also one of the strangest incidents I've ever encountered.

In the top of the first inning with the Cubs at bat, a black cat appeared from underneath the stands near home plate and started walking toward the Cubs' dugout. As if on cue, the cat moved past the Cubs' on-deck circle and stopped. The cat just peered into the Cubs' dugout staring at manager Leo Durocher. Then, again as if on cue, the cat ran back under the stands.

"I was on the on-deck circle," remembered Ron Santo, "and I was very superstitious. It came out of the stands and walked right by me. Then it walked over closer to our dugout and just stared at Leo. It freaked me out a little."

"I saw the cat come out and it was strange to say the least," said Jerry Grote. "The look on the Cubs' faces was priceless."

Fergie Jenkins remembered it well. "I was pitching in the game, but I wasn't superstitious. The cat just casually walked in front of our dugout. Somebody tried to scare him off, but he didn't move. He just stared at our bench. I thought that was a little eerie."

Recently I asked Pete Flynn, who was on the groundskeeping crew that day, if anyone from the grounds crew had anything to do with the cat? He said, "I was just as amazed as anyone. No one from the crew had anything to do with that cat coming onto the field. As a matter of fact, I never saw the cat before that game or anytime after."

The following day most New Yorkers were talking about a big drug sweep in Brooklyn that netted seventy-four suspected drug dealers, and the impending race for mayor of New York City. John Lindsay lost the Republican primary in his bid to win re-election as mayor. He did get the tiny Liberal Party candidacy to at least keep him in the race. He was now ranked as a heavy underdog, just like the Mets at the beginning of the season.

We were moving fast. After our two-game sweep the Cubs had lost six in a row and we had won four in a row. We were only a half a game out of first place.

The next evening we played a doubleheader against the Expos. The first game was a close one. We were tied going into the bottom of eleventh inning, but won 3–2 on my roommate Ken Boswell's single. We were now tied with the Cubs for first place in the Eastern Division of the National League. At some point in the second game everyone at Shea Stadium learned the Cubs had lost in Philadelphia. That meant we were in first place all by ourselves. First place, can you believe it? The "lovable losers" were on top. We won the second game of the doubleheader behind Nolan Ryan and kept our hold on first place. Never before had the Mets ever been in first place. The Cubs had lost seven games in a row, and they lost first place, too. They had held on to the top position for one hundred and fifty-five straight days.

The following night Gary Gentry pitched a gem, a six-hit shutout against the Expos. Again, the Cubs lost, their eighth in a row. We were now in first place by two games and had a seven-game win streak going.

The next day we flew to Pittsburgh for a twi-night doubleheader, and it was memorable. We won both games by a score of 1–0. On top of that both pitchers, Jerry Koosman and Don Cardwell, drove in the winning runs, a feat that had never been done before. Cardwell was a good-hitting pitcher while Jerry liked to *think* of himself as a good-hitting pitcher. "Koosman started the first game and I was in the clubhouse listening to the game on the radio," recalled Don Cardwell. "After the game Koosman comes into the clubhouse. He's bragging about this line drive base hit that drove in the winning run. I told him he never hit a line drive in his life. It seemed to me that he was pumped up more about his base hit than pitching a shutout. In the second game, around the fourth inning, I hit a hanging slider into left field for a base hit that drove in the runner from second base for the only run in my game. I went eight innings and McGraw finished up. When I came into the locker room, Koosman said, 'I understand you hit a blooper.' Then we got into an argument over who hit the ball harder." Meanwhile, the Cubs finally broke their losing streak, but we were still two and a half games in front.

I had taken off those two games in Pittsburgh because of the Jewish High Holiday. This was a particular difficult decision for me. We were in the middle of a pennant race and this couldn't have been at a worse time. Finally I decided to discuss the situation with Gil Hodges. It was uncomfortable for me because I knew the significance of the games and quite honestly, Gil and I never really spoke much during the season. I thought about my conversation with him when I came off the disabled list earlier in the season. That made me more nervous. But, as I reflect on it now, Gil was the most straightforward manager I ever played for. He was honest and honorable, two outstanding characteristics. He simply said, "Do what you think is best for you. You'll make the right decision." I walked out of his office with more respect for him than ever before. On reflection, all I can say is thankfully, we won both games of the doubleheader and as far as I'm concerned both Koosman and Cardwell were terrific hitters who hit solid line drives for base hits to win the games. When I came into the clubhouse the next day, there was a big sign in my locker. It was right to the point: "Why don't you take off every day."

We won three out of four against the Pirates and moved on to St. Louis. On September 15th, the Cardinal starter was left-hander Steve Carlton. Carlton proceeded to strike out a major league record nineteen Met batters. It sounds like a Cardinal victory, right? Not quite, because this was fast becoming the New York Mets' year. Ron Swoboda, who struck out twice, hit a pair of two-run home runs to beat Carlton and give the Mets a 4–3 win. Swoboda remembered the game vividly: "I wasn't swinging the bat very well. I took some extra batting practice underneath the stands in St. Louis the day before. Ralph Kiner was helping me. He would help when you asked him. He didn't give me a lot of tips. Basically, he just observed and commented that I looked better doing this with my hands and things like that. Just the fact that he spent some time with me made me feel better. After some swings I did get more comfortable. I then started to swing the bat better. In the game against Carlton, he had great stuff. I struck out my first time up and then hit a home run. We took a 2–1 lead. I struck out my third time at bat and then hit another two-run home run. Both times I had two strikes on me. It was an amazing game in an amazing year."

After a rainout the next day we flew to Montreal to face the Expos in a two-game series. Once again our pitching came through as both Koosman and Seaver threw shutouts. For Jerry it was win number fifteen and number twenty-three for Tom. The last month or so encompassed a great run for the club. In the middle of August we were nine and one half games behind the Cubs. Now we were looking at them behind us.

The team came home for a series against the Pirates, starting with a doubleheader on Friday, September 19th. A small dose of reality hit us when we lost both games, but we were still four games in front of the Cubs.

Saturday the 20th saw Bob Moose pitch a no-hitter against us. I made the last out of that game. I had this thing about making last outs in big games that reached into October. Having lost three games in a row we needed to start winning again or our first place position would be in danger.

Mayor Lindsay had his hands full, too. That day, violence erupted again. Twelve people were arrested as cops were showered with bricks at a protest over an office building the State of New York was planning to build in Harlem. Local residents wanted low-cost housing or a school instead. Tensions in the city were very high.

Our situation was also challenging, but had an easier solution. We just had to win baseball games. And that we did, winning the next nine games in a row. It started with us beating the Pirates in a doubleheader on Sunday. Both Jerry Koosman and Don Cardwell pitched complete games. On Monday the 22nd, the Cardinals came to Shea. Every home game now had big crowds watching the lovable losers becoming lovable winners. Tom Seaver, who had not lost a game since early August, won his twenty-fourth, and the Cubs lost. We were very close to clinching the National League East.

On Tuesday, we beat the Cardinals again with Tug McGraw getting the win against Cardinal ace Bob Gibson. Buddy Harrelson drove in the winning run with a single in the 11th inning for the 3–2 victory. The Cubs lost again. The next day was Wednesday the 24th. Usually, around this date in September New York Met players were making plans to go home after the regular season. The longest-suffering Met, Ed Kranepool, remembered it well: "Before 1969 I never saw any improvement in the team. You knew you were going to be eliminated from a pennant race by the All-Star game." But it was going to be different today.

There was tremendous anticipation in the stands. The fans were hoping to be part of Met history. The players were also keenly aware of the ramifications. Donn Clendenon and Ed Charles homered and we jumped out to an early lead. Gary Gentry, lost in the notoriety of Seaver and Koosman, was having a strong outing against future Hall of Famer Steve Carlton. Gentry had a four-hit shutout going as Joe Torre, batting in the top of the ninth a little after 9 P.M., grounded into a game-ending double play. The victory made the New York Mets champions of the Eastern Division of the National League.

When the second the game was over, pandemonium broke loose. As if on cue, thousands of people ran onto the field. I had never seen anything like it. Ecstatic fans were taking the base bags, the pitcher's mound, and the turf. That's right. They tore up the turf for souvenirs. There was no crowd control. Even though it was only for the division, Met fans had witnessed their first championship and they weren't going to be short-changed on the celebration. When the field was cleared, seven fans had suffered fractures of some sort. All of the players were, of course, caught up in the exhilaration of this victory. Pete Flynn was one of the grounds crewmembers. He remembered the chaos: "When the crew saw what was happening to the field when the people all ran out, we didn't know what to think. When we saw all the torn up turf afterward, we knew we had our work cut out for us."

Needless to say, the locker room was bedlam. Most of the players on the team had never experienced a win and celebration like this in their big-league careers. I hadn't. It was wonderful. There was dousing of champagne everywhere. Everyone entering the locker room got it. We were the champions of the East. Nothing could take that away from us. Ed Kranepool commented, "I've gone full circle."

The next day newspapers and television were filled with Met stories. Every interviewer asked the same question. How could this team have done it? Everyone wanted to know. It didn't make a difference that it was only the beginning. There was a lot more to accomplish this season, but it didn't matter. We had come farther than anyone ever expected. To most, we already were a success; everything from now on would be gravy, except to the players. Once the hysteria subsided, the players knew there was still the regular season to finish and then the playoffs, whoever that might be against.

After the celebration we went to Philadelphia for a three-game series. With Koosman, Seaver, and Gentry pitching superbly, we won all three. As fate would have it, we went from Philadelphia to Chicago to finish the regular season against the Cubs. Whoever made the schedule in 1969 could never had known that the world would be so upside down for one team and so right side up for the other. The Cubs, with a terrific team, had somehow blown a large lead. That wasn't the worst part. The fact that their archrivals, the hated Mets, had overtaken them was a hard pill to swallow. For us, going to Chicago for that last series was like sticking a dagger into their wound. I'm sure the Cubs would have preferred to call off their season a few days early.

There wasn't much talk between the two teams. Before the games there was an unusual calm. Even the bleacher bums were not their usual hate-the-other-team selves. Don't get me wrong. There is never total quiet from the bleacher bums, but the Cubs' bubble had burst earlier, and we did not gloat in front of their fans or the Cub players. Maybe in the confines of our clubhouse, but not in front of them. Even the usually boisterous Ernie Banks was quiet. In a way it was sad. Ernie didn't have a lot of time left in his career to win a World Series. He deserved that chance. Always friendly and outgoing, he was what baseball was all about. When playing first base he would always sing a little and make people laugh. He would even get on the opposing players in a fun way. One time earlier in the season when Cleon was sporting a small mustache that either Gil didn't notice or ignored, Ernie started to yell at him while he was hitting. Ernie recalled, "I used to kid Cleon a lot about that mustache. He would always smile and then hit a line drive somewhere." But, now, in these last couple of games at Wrigley Field, Ernie was quiet.

We won the first game of the series to run up our winning streak to nine games. I drove in the winning run with a single in the twelfth inning. It was our 100th win of the season. One hundred wins in the regular season for the New York Mets rather than one hundred losses! Who would have ever imagined that? The next day we lost on the final day of the regular season. Our final regular season record was 100–62. Remarkable. I don't think anyone on the Mets really cared about the last game loss; we were ready to move on to the playoffs. On the Cubs' side it was totally different. "For me personally, I thought it might be my last chance to get into the playoffs or World Series," Ernie Banks said. "It was really disappointing for me, and as far as the city was concerned everyone was looking forward to a World Series in Chicago. It was a pretty sad three or four months after the season ended."

Ron Santo had a more positive view of that season: "Looking back, 1969 was wonderful. We were in first place from the get-go. I've always said the Mets won it, we didn't lose it."

Ferguson Jenkins observed, "The Mets made a great move in August and September. That's when they got strong, and the Cubs couldn't win consistently. It turned out the Mets were a much better ball club."

Fergie was right. We were a better ball club. When the regular season was over we finished eight games ahead of the second place Chicago Cubs. We had won thirty-eight of our last forty-nine games. It was an incredible run. We came from nowhere to somewhere. Everybody had contributed to the effort. The bottom line was we really were a team.

A few days before going to Chicago we found out we would be playing the Atlanta Braves in the first division playoffs in Major League Baseball history. The Braves had come out on top in the Western Division outlasting the San Francisco Giants to win the crown. The Braves had a very good ball club led by the great Henry Aaron. We beat them eight out of twelve times during the regular season. We weren't fearful of any team in the Western Division, except we were all happy we didn't have to play the Astros. They beat us ten out of twelve times during the season.

Back home in New York, the city was going wild about the Mets. Lines for playoff tickets grew at Shea Stadium as soon as the announcement came of their availability. All the newspapers and television stations would be covering the "Amazin' Mets" during the playoffs. The first two games would be played in Atlanta and the next three, if necessary, in New York. No one was looking past the series against the Braves. After all, hadn't the Mets pushed the envelope to the limit by just making the playoffs? Even if we didn't get past Atlanta, this Met team had accomplished more than anyone ever expected. Earlier in the year, if anyone had bet on us to get to this point, they would have made a bundle. We had certainly bucked the odds.

After the last game of the regular season in Chicago, we flew directly to Atlanta. Gil Hodges and Rube Walker aligned the pitching rotation exactly how they wanted: Seaver, Koosman, and Gentry in the first three games. "Gil and Rube were good at setting up the pitching rotations all year," said Joe Pignatano. "They came up with a five-man rotation. As a result we never had sore arms."

We knew our pitching staff was outstanding. And, with the defense, especially up the middle, we should be in almost every game. But in a short series you never know what is going to happen. Everyone knew the Atlanta Braves were going to be tough to beat. As far as I was concerned, Atlanta was going to start three right-handed pitchers in a row, so I was going to have an opportunity to play.

With visions of grandeur and confidence abounding, the 1969 New York Mets moved on to Atlanta to play the Braves in a best-of-five series for the National League Pennant. Could the impossible dream continue? Would there be more than just a division championship? The New York Jets won their playoff and went on to the Super Bowl. Maybe we would do the same. Maybe we too would pull off a miracle.

11. The Playoffs: Mets vs. Braves

"Bring on Baltropolis."
—Unknown Fan

E ven though there was a huge task ahead of us in the playoffs, the fact
we had won a championship, was still in our minds. To most of us it
seemed like clinching the Division Championship was tantamount to winning the World Series, but then again we had no idea what it was like to
win a World Series. The fact was most of us on the 1969 Mets had never
celebrated any sort of professional championship except maybe in the minor leagues.

The sight of masses of people running onto the field at Shea Stadium
after clinching the division title and subsequent fan and media adulation
rocked all of us. It was as if we had climbed a mountain and reached the
top, thinking that we, "the lowly Mets," had done the miraculous and accomplished so much. The team had been losers for so long that even the
division championship was a major victory. It being New York City, media
attention was focused on the players and most of us really got caught up
in the hoopla. Even before the season was officially over, more newspaper

columnists, magazine writers, and television reporters than ever before began following the team. It was still a wild ride for all of us, but it was also a special time for every member of the team, coaching staff, and Gil Hodges, too.

The National League Championship Series looming ahead created a constant bombardment of interviews, and the exposure was intense. The fact that Gil Hodges was our manager helped us to handle the distraction. He had a knack for putting things in their proper perspective, and gave us the quiet but strong guidance that we needed. Using dry wit and wry sarcasm, he worked hard to make us aware of the task ahead. We soon came to our senses and realized there was a long way to go. It was the beginning of a journey that none of us could imagine, or would ever forget.

This was the first year for the new playoff format, and even though we would be starting the series on the road, most of us didn't mind. We were a good road team and by opening the series in Atlanta we also got away from the New York City media circus. That did not hide the fact that we were all a little nervous and apprehensive about the upcoming challenge. No matter how well we had played from the middle of August through the National League Eastern Division championship, we were still inexperienced; most of us had never played in the postseason. We were also well aware that the New York Mets had recently been the laughingstock of baseball. All this entered our minds. Confidence was one thing, reality another. One of the people who helped in this regard was Rube Walker, our pitching coach. Sure, Rube's primary responsibility was the pitchers, but he was also a coach and person who related to every player. On the plane ride to Atlanta before the series, Rube went up and down the aisle telling jokes and trying to ease the tension. He made us laugh. Looking back, it was probably a deliberate action on his part. Rube was quite a person.

When we arrived in Atlanta, one major decision hung over us. We finished the regular season with twenty-six players and the roster had to be dropped to 25 for postseason play. Ken Boswell, my roommate on the road, and I discussed the situation as the season was coming to a close. Whoever it was going to be was someone who contributed to the success of the team during the regular season. Some thought pitcher Cal Koonce, who had been nursing a sore elbow the last month of the season, the likely candidate. However, it was decided that Bobby Pfeil, a reserve infielder, would be left off the roster. Conventional baseball wisdom then, as now, is that you can never have too much pitching. As pitching was our strength, most of us felt Gil and the coaches opted for that in making a tough decision. Still, all the players felt bad about the situation. All we could do was express regrets to Bobby and tell him that no matter what we considered him part of the team.

"I was disappointed," recalled Pfeil. "I didn't even know the roster had to be cut down at the time. I was a little hurt, but I also was in awe of what was going on all that year anyway. Maybe, it wasn't such a traumatic experience because it was such a great time in my life. I worked out with the team every day and I got permission to sit in the dugout. If somebody got hurt I couldn't play that day, but they could put me on the roster the next day. Considering I played eight years in the minor leagues I just looked at everything being so positive." There were a couple of consolations for Bobby even in his disappointment. His teammates voted him a full share of whatever postseason bonus money the players earned, and there was the possibility if things worked out, he could end up with a World Series Championship ring.

Since this was the inaugural year for the playoff system, nobody really knew what to expect in terms of fan interest or how the new format would play out. However, one thing we were sure of, the Braves were going to be a tough team to beat. Atlanta won the Western Division of the National League by three games over the San Francisco Giants and four games over the Cincinnati Reds. It was a close battle between all three teams in the closing weeks, but the Braves finished strong. In fact, as early as August 19th, the Braves were in fifth place in their division, but only three games behind the leader. They went on to win twenty-seven of their last thirty-eight games, including ten out of their last eleven, to win their division. They were hot.

But, then again, so were we. Like the Braves, we also finished strong. At the beginning of August we were nine and a half games behind the Eastern Division leading Chicago Cubs. We won thirty-eight of our last forty-nine games to surge to the top. We also won nine in a row going into the last regular season game before losing that one to the Cubs in Chicago.

Atlanta fielded a team of many veteran players, including one of the greatest of all time, Hank Aaron. One of the biggest thrills of my life came one day early in my career when I was playing first base for the Cincinnati Reds. Hank got on base and we started talking about hitting. I asked him how it felt knowing that he was going to get two or three hits everyday? (I actually thought he was doing that because every time I saw him play he was on base or hitting a home run.) He just said, "I don't get two or three hits every day, but if I don't get any one day I might get four the next." I thought to myself, "Is there anything better than talking to Hank Aaron about hitting?"

Along with Hank, the Braves had a powerful lineup. They had Rico Carty, Orlando Cepeda, Tony Gonzalez, Felipe Alou, and former Yankee Clete Boyer. A core of good and experienced regulars like Felix Millan, Bob Didier, and Gil Garrido supported them. Their bench strength wasn't great, but with solid pitching they had won ninety-three games in the regular season, so they had something going besides momentum.

The evening we arrived in Atlanta, I was reviewing their lineup in the sports pages of the local paper and thought, "It's the men against the boys, the veterans against the kids." This made me very anxious until I remembered that we beat them eight out of twelve times during the regular season. However, we hadn't played them since August 10th and both teams were on fire going into the playoffs.

As far as pitching, the Braves had three good starters, future Hall of Famer Phil Niekro, Ron Reed, and Pat Jarvis, all right-handers. Niekro's record for the year was 23–13, Reed's 18–10, and Jarvis's 13–11. The rest of the Braves' pitching staff really couldn't match up to ours, so for them it boiled down to powerful hitting and good starting pitching.

We certainly couldn't match up to the Braves in power. Aaron had 44 home runs that season, Cepeda: 22, Rico Carty: 16, and Clete Boyer: 14. As a team they had a total of 144 home runs versus our total of 108. Tommie Agee led the way with 26 for us. After that there was a big drop off to my 14, then Donn Clendenon with 12. It was pretty obvious to us we weren't going to overpower them offensively. Looking back, it was easy to analyze the Braves. When they hit home runs they usually won. They did not run much and therefore didn't steal many bases. Their defense was so-so. They would simply overpower you.

As far as we were concerned, our outstanding pitching was the primary reason we did so well. With Tom Seaver, Jerry Koosman, and Gary Gentry, our starting core was as good as any team in the major leagues, except maybe Baltimore. And, the rest of our staff proved its mettle over the course of the season. Jim McAndrew was our fourth starter, and in the bullpen we had pitchers like Tug McGraw, Ron Taylor, Don Cardwell, and Cal Koonce. And we also had young Nolan Ryan as a reliever on our staff. He would be a factor in the postseason, and as everyone knows, would go on to have a "pretty good" major league career.

We had a terrific hitter in Cleon Jones, whose .340 batting average far outdistanced the rest of us. He also had 75 runs batted in. Tommie Agee hit .271 and led the team in RBIs with 76. Ken Boswell hit .279, and I hit .300 and was fifth on the team with 47 RBIs behind Cleon, Tommie, Ron Swoboda at 52, and Ed Kranepool with 49. Donn Clendenon helped us greatly hitting .252 during the season with 12 homers and 37 RBIs. We did not overwhelm with power, but no one could beat us in clutch hitting. After the middle of August when we began our roll to the division title, everyone on the team had contributed key hits to help win important games. But a key ingredient to our success was defense. We had a solid defensive team led by exceptional strength up the middle. At shortstop was Bud Harrelson, at second base Ken Boswell platooning with Al Weis, and in center field Tommie Agee. Each were superb fielders providing up-the-middle defense that was as good as any in the majors. Equally important, with Jerry Grote behind the plate, we were blessed with the best defensive catcher in all of baseball.

Outstanding pitching, solid defense, and timely hitting, that was the formula for our success to this point, and what the team was really all about. With the Braves starting three right-handed pitchers the first three games, our left-handed hitting line-up would have an opportunity to play a lot. The hitters needed to be up for it because although we had the pitching, the Braves could score runs. The National League Pennant series was going to be a pretty good test.

Everyone on the club understood that this pennant series would be totally different than the regular season. We would have to prove ourselves worthy against the Atlanta Braves in our team's very first post-season. But, didn't the Jets have to do the same thing in the football playoffs?

If someone had said back in spring training that the Mets would be playing the Atlanta Braves for the National League pennant they would have shipped that person off to some quiet mental health facility. Here were two improbable teams. Before the beginning of the season the Mets were a 100 to 1 shot to win the National League Pennant. The Braves were more highly regarded—but not by a lot—they're odds were 50 to 1. Some act of fate brought these two teams together.

The National League Championship Series was scheduled to start at 4:00 P.M. on Saturday, October 4, 1969. To say all of us were nervous would be an understatement. Anticipation was killing us. The bus ride to the stadium seemed more quiet than normal, and the locker room the same. When we went on the field to warm up, I noticed Joan Payson, the owner of the Mets, being led to her seat. She was a grand lady, always very sweet, and really liked talking to the players when she had a chance to chitchat. I remember one time in 1968, I jokingly asked her if she had any spare horses she would like to give away. She didn't take more than a second to answer. She said, "Sure, talk to me about it at any time." Of course I never mentioned it again, but thought it remarkable of her to even consider it. When we won the division, I read a quote from her in the newspaper. It struck me then and I never forgot it to this day. She said, "I am so happy now. For so long people said things that weren't funny about the Mets. It broke my heart." She was one lady whose heart I would never want to break. All the players liked and respected her. As far-fetched as it may sound, wanting to repay her kindness and caring probably gave many of us an extra incentive to win.

In a season of so many weird, crazy, and unusual happenings, one funny item occurred at this time that really stuck in my memory. At the ballpark I remembered reading an article about Bobby Aspromonte in the Atlanta paper. I knew Bobby and liked him a lot as a person and a player. Now, he was a member of the Braves. In the article he said that he had called home to speak to his father Charles, who originally came from Italy and was living in Brooklyn where Bobby had grown up. His father said to him, "We'll win it." Bobby related, "I told him 'Not yet pop, we still have to play the games,' but my dad said, 'Not you, the Mets. You guys can hit, but not Seaver and Koosman. They are tough.'" I really got a chuckle out of that and thought maybe it was some sort of prophecy.

When the game was about to start, I did feel a little more nervous than the normal pregame jitters. All of us knew this was a "different ball game." I'm sure everyone on both teams felt it.

The first game pitchers were Phil Niekro against Tom Seaver. All signs pointed to a pitchers' duel. All year long, Gil Hodges had platooned players at first, second, third, and right field. It wasn't a great situation, but it had worked well for us all year. Since the Braves' starters were right-handed it gave an opportunity for our heavily left-handed batting order to show what they could do. And, that didn't take very long to do. In front of more than 50,000 fans the anticipated pitching contest never materialized. Niekro gave up nine runs on nine hits and the Braves made some awful fielding plays to help the Mets' cause. On our side, Tom Seaver pitched seven innings and gave up five runs on eight hits as we won 9–5. So much for the pitching duel. The Met hitters rose to the occasion and carried the team to victory. I got three hits, Wayne Garrett two, and Jones, Harrelson, and J. C. Martin all drove in key runs.

After the game Seaver was interviewed by Joe Durso of the *New York Times* and said, "I just couldn't find the groove." It really didn't matter. As happened so often during the regular season, one part of the team picked up the slack when the other was having a bad time of it. In this case, the hitters came through. The locker room afterward was noisy, but we were apprehensive. Our ace pitcher had been hit hard. Still, we had won the game and felt the worst that could happen was a split here in Atlanta with us going home in good shape. Seaver yelled in the locker room, "I gave up five runs and still won the game. God truly is a Met." The lone bright spot for the Braves was Hank Aaron. He hit a home run, had two hits, and drove in two runs. Like I said, Aaron, two hits every game.

The second game of the series had right-hander Ron Reed pitching for the Braves against lefty Jerry Koosman. Another supposed pitching duel on tap. Reed had been very reliable all year and Koosman was as strong and tough a pitcher as you could find. But, in front of another 50,000 plus fans, the second game turned into almost a mirror image of the first. The final score was 11–6 as both starting pitchers were gone by the fifth inning. The Braves again displayed shoddy fielding with three costly errors. On top of that, they made a slew of mental mistakes such as missing cut-off throws and throwing to the wrong base. Once again, it was the hitters who carried us, this time with three home runs. Ron Taylor, a pitcher who I felt never got due credit for his contribution in 1969, picked up the win in relief.

One of the strangest plays I ever saw in all my years of playing baseball occurred in this game. In the seventh inning we were leading 9–6, Tommie Agee was on third base and Cleon Jones was batting. With Cecil Upshaw, a side-arm right-hander and the fifth Brave pitcher of the game on the mound, Agee tried to steal home. He got a terrific jump on Upshaw and it looked like he was going to make it, except Cleon swung at the pitch and lined the ball hard, but foul, right by Agee's head down the left-field line. As Agee pulled up, the two friends stared long and hard at each other. Slowly, Tommie walked back to third base and Cleon just sort of glared at him. Cleon then stepped out of the batter's box, took a deep breath, stepped back in, and hit the next pitch for a home run. Strange, and scary, to say the least. After the game Cleon explained, "I didn't want to hit the ball, I just swung to keep the catcher occupied." Agee said, "There was no sign and I was stealing on my own. He wasn't supposed to swing." This must be the Mets' year! The only bright spot for the Braves this game was, you guessed it, Hank Aaron. Only one base hit—another home run, and three runs batted in.

After the game, there was much more noise and excitement in the clubhouse. We were coming back to New York leading the series 2–0, and I would venture to say, some of us were quietly thinking about a possible sweep. One more win and we were in the World Series! Luman Harris, the Braves' manager, put it frankly, "We've got one foot in the grave and the gravediggers are going for their shovels." Clete Boyer gave his perspective, "The Mets are unconscious. They don't know where they are. They don't understand the pressure." Someone, after hearing this quote from one of the sportswriters in the clubhouse, yelled out what Boyer had said and everyone just laughed. How wrong Clete was!

The flight home from Atlanta on Sunday was as sweet as any I've ever had. Sitting there my mind flashed back to a sign I spotted in the stands in Atlanta. Obviously held by a Met fan, the sign read, "The Mets are going to Baltropolis." It didn't matter to him who won the American League pennant, Baltimore or Minnesota. In his mind, the Mets were going to be in the World Series. I asked myself if he could be right? Thoughts of impossible things were starting to creep into everyone's head.

I was looking forward to coming home for the third game of the play-offs the next day. The fact that we came out of Atlanta ahead two games to none added to the already incredible media coverage. All the players and coaches were very careful in their comments to the press. We were a bit more self-assured, yet still well aware of the Braves' prowess. Not wanting to sound over-confident, we sidestepped talk about a sweep. Even so, the team had a feeling of something special on the way.

The entire city was abuzz with excitement. Even non-sports programs on radio and television were talking about the series. Everywhere in Manhattan people talked about the Mets. Doormen, cabbies, vendors, everyone I came across! It felt great because for so long we were viewed as a losing team and had received little or no respect. The "lovable losers" were on the move—way up. Now, I was afraid to answer my home telephone, not due to the media, but because there was no way I could get enough tickets for everyone who thought a whole section of complimentary tickets were mine to give away.

I arrived at the ballpark on Monday morning earlier than usual for the 1 P.M. start. I normally got there two and one half hours before a game, but even as early as I got there, it was a shocking sight to encounter the hoard of people lined up to greet myself and the other players as we drove our cars into the parking area behind right field. There must have been two thousand screaming fans. They were ready to celebrate. The media blitz also started earlier than usual. Most of the press was there before we even put our uniforms on.

The clubhouse was upbeat with the usual barbs and degrading comments between the players beginning right on time. Clendenon was the worst. As he had done many times before, Donn yelled across the room at Kenny Boswell and myself. This time it was about our uniforms not looking good on us, and that we were embarrassing the team. We then complained to Nick Torman, our clubhouse attendant, and he got angry. That started problems. It became a never-ending cycle of clubhouse needling. Nick recently passed away, but his brother Steve, who worked with him remembered, "Nick was always touchy about the uniforms. Clendenon used to agitate the other players and then they would agitate Nick. Nick always would say, 'I didn't take the measurements for these uniforms. You guys were measured by a tailor.' It didn't make a difference. The players just started up again." I was always glad when Donn got on me first, because I figured it was over and done, and he would move onto somebody else. That wasn't always the case, but I liked it that way. After a while, I learned that once he started getting on me, I would try and divert his attention to someone else. That also worked on occasions, but the truth was, you knew everyday he was going to get on you about something.

This type of good-natured banter is fairly common on all teams. For us, it had been going on all season this way; but realizing today was no typical situation, it really helped to take edge off the tension. I have to admit that to this day I miss the clubhouse, the ball-busting, all of it. I actually miss Donn getting on me.

As we were getting ready to run out onto the field for the start of the game I saw Mrs. Payson again. She was sitting in her usual box on the right, next to our dugout. She looked excited. More important, she appeared happy and it made me feel good. And, suddenly a thought struck me. This is the stadium where the Jets played. They won the AFL Championship right here, right on this field. And, they made history by winning the Super Bowl this past January. Wouldn't it be something if we won today and then went on to win the World Series? The Jets and the Mets, "Champions of the World." At the time it seemed a little farfetched since we had a long way to go, but then again, maybe it wasn't. Perhaps, it was merely wishful thinking on my part. Just a little something to dream about.

The starting pitchers that afternoon were Pat Jarvis for the Braves against Gary Gentry. Would this finally be the pitching duel of the series? All of us were surprised that the playoffs so far had turned into a hitting contest with the Mets winning it. With over 53,000 frenzied fans at Shea, once again, good pitching didn't materialize. This game followed the same pattern as the first two. The lead changed hands three times on home runs in the first five innings. Hank Aaron hit a two-run homer (his third home run in three games) in the first inning, and we were held scoreless in the first and second innings. Tommie Agee hit a solo home run in our half of the third. In the bottom of the fourth I led off with a single and Kenny Boswell followed with a home run to put us in front 3–2. Standing at home plate waiting to congratulate my friend and roommate was a thrill. (Ken would end the day with three hits and three RBIs.)

In the top of the fifth the lead changed again. Orlando Cepeda hit a two-run shot to put the Braves back in front. That was short-lived because, in the bottom of the fifth, Nolan Ryan, who had come in to pitch in the third inning, bounced a single up the middle, only his third hit all year. Wayne Garrett then came up to bat and homered into the stands just inside the right-field foul pole. That shot put us back in the lead for good. It was Wayne's first round-tripper in five months. Ryan pitched the final seven innings giving up only two runs on three hits and striking out seven, to get the win in the 7–4 game. When first baseman Ed Kranepool caught the throw from Wayne Garrett for the final out, suddenly, the Amazin' Mets became . . . *The National League Champions!*

And, then it was pandemonium again. For the second time thousands of fans ran on to the field. Whoever was in charge of crowd control must have been caught up in the emotion like everyone else. When we won the division title, I thought the fans reacted wildly, but this was worse. And this crowd appeared twice as big. It seemed "like déjà vu all over again," to quote a famous orator. Even with all that going on it was another opportunity to relish the moment.

We had swept the powerful Atlanta Braves. Not by superior pitching as most experts thought, but by power and clutch hitting. Afterward I think all the hitters on the club felt a little vindicated since our pitchers were given so much credit for the success of the team during the regular season.

It was crazy in the clubhouse. Everyone got the traditional champagne dousing. You couldn't move there were so many people; press, dignitaries, friends, even some fans managed their way in. I noticed Mayor John Lindsay walk in with a small entourage. He was dressed impeccably, as always. That didn't last long. P. P. Gaspar and Jerry Grote got him good. "He loved it," said Gaspar recently. "I poured the champagne on him and Grote was scrubbing his head. I got in the limelight doing it, and it helped get him reelected." Everyone who came into the locker room was showered with champagne. Mrs. Payson tiptoed in, smiled, turned around, and left. She decided discretion was the most prudent course under the circumstances.

Everyone was being interviewed. Even players who hadn't appeared in the game rightfully got well-deserved attention. Because the Mets hadn't ever been remotely close to this kind of situation before, the press was anxious to get everyone's reaction. I thought about that sign in Atlanta again, "Bring on Baltropolis." Whoever made that sign had vision! Who would we play in the World Series? Who really cared at that moment? The Mets were the champions of the National League. I wondered once more about the Jets and this stadium. Could it happen again? Could there be two world championship teams in New York City in the same year?

The celebration in the clubhouse seemed to last forever. Three hours after the game ended, I finally left the ballpark. There were at least 5,000 fans outside the right-field parking area. It was their party and they were going to make it last. And, in Manhattan, it was mass hysteria. It seemed incredible to me, infinitely more than when we clinched the Eastern Division. There was nothing else anyone was talking about. We had brightened the lights of a dark city. How could it be possible that the Mets, the lowly Mets, would be playing in the World Series? There were many more people believing in miracles now than before.

The next morning local newspapers had front-page pictures showing Mayor Lindsay being doused with champagne by Grote and Gaspar. Weeks later it turned out that attaching himself to the Mets and prominently participating in every public celebration of the team's postseason victories was one of his most successful campaign tactics for the upcoming November mayoral election. Just like in the rest of the country, but much more so in New York, the city had been going through Vietnam War trauma, antiwar unrest, racial strife, and generally low morale. New York also had major economic and social problems and city labor issues. All of this resulted in everyone predicting John Lindsay would lose his bid for reelection. In the primary, Lindsay lost the Republican Party nomination for another term and was now running on the Liberal ticket. Many people have come to believe that our playoff and subsequent World Series victories were key factors in John Lindsay's reelection.

Players and managers from both teams were quoted in all the New York City papers. Luman Harris, the Braves' manager, put it bluntly. "They beat the hell out of us." Yogi Berra, our first base coach said, "Now I've done it all. I've played, managed, and now will coach in a World Series. That is all, isn't it?" Ed Sudol, an umpire who worked the playoff series said, "I had them (the Mets) a lot of times this year, but this was the greatest thrill. They're appropriately named the Amazin' Mets. They've come from the depths of despair to the celestial. I studied literature and made that up myself." Casey Stengel put it in his usual profound way. Asked about the Mets turnaround from the bottom rung to pennant winners he said, "The team has come along slow, but fast." Gil Hodges, as always, put it in proper perspective. "This meant more to me because it's the championship of the whole league. We just have to go another step further." Most of the players felt the same that day.

Cleon Jones, while soaking wet from champagne, flatly stated, "We're gonna beat Baltimore and then I'm going fishin'." Bud Harrelson wisecracked, "We've gone this far, we might as well fool the whole world, including Baltimore." I even got into the quote thing. The New York *Daily News* caught me saying, "I'll walk down the street in New York now and people will say, there's Art Shamsky of the Mets. People used to laugh. They won't anymore." I don't remember saying that, but after the champagne I could have said anything.

Ron Taylor recalled, "For me, personally, the playoff series was special. I got a save and a win in the first two games in Atlanta. To have affected two out of the three games was great." Ralph Kiner recalled his thoughts at the time. "I was hoping the team would get past the Braves. After beating Atlanta, I think the Mets had a feeling they could beat anybody."

Larry Merchant, in his column in the *New York Post*, wrote something that I later came to believe as being one of the most profound statements about our incredible season: "The Mets made people care again. They hadn't for so long, they had forgotten they once did." Yes, we made people care. They were starting to believe again. The Jets had done it earlier in the year and we carried it a giant step further even though the job hadn't been completed yet. We all hoped we could keep people caring and believing for another week and a half. One fan quoted in the *New York Times* wrapped it up succinctly. "Man, this is the day."

It took twenty-five groundskeepers to fix the playing field at Shea the day after we won the pennant. "It wasn't as bad as the last time," (the game clinching the Eastern Division) chief of the grounds crew, John McCarthy said. "They got home plate and second base, but they couldn't get the pitching slab." He didn't mention the myriad of holes in the infield and outfield turf that had to be replaced because the fans dug it up for souvenirs.

There were some interesting footnotes that occurred right after we won the pennant. First, because of the impending World Series, the Super Bowl champion Jets had to move a home game at Shea Stadium against the Oilers to the Astrodome in Houston. Second, a few short articles appeared in the New York City papers about the New York Knicks winning their fifth exhibition game prior to the start of the regular 1969–70 NBA season. For the Knicks, it was just the beginning.

And ironically, less than two minutes after the New York Mets won the National League Pennant, not far away, a horse by the name of "The University," with jockey Angel Cordero on board, wearing the colors of Greentree Stables, won the Long Island Handicap at Aqueduct Race Track. Joan Payson owned Greentree Stables.

Not all was quiet outside the celebration at Shea Stadium. Around the same time we were winning the National League Pennant an explosion rocked the Army Induction center in lower Manhattan. It was the second bomb in recent months at the center that had become a magnet for pacifist demonstrations. Also, that same day, the government announced that unemployment in the country had increased significantly, the biggest rise since the Eisenhower administration.

No doubt, it was unsettling times in the city and country. But, for the 1969 Mets, it was time to get ready for the last hurdle and make history.

12. Truly Amazing—The Mets Are in the World Series!

"The whole thing was probably the best in the history of baseball."
—Ralph Kiner

It didn't take long for us to find out what team we were going to play in the World Series. That's right, the World Series. It was still hard for us to believe. Soon after the end of our final game with the Braves, the Baltimore Orioles beat the Minnesota Twins in three straight to win the American League Pennant. I wasn't in their locker room, but would be surprised if most of the Oriole players weren't already counting their World Series money and thinking about the championship rings they would get next spring. One can only imagine what they were thinking. "Us against the Mets, pleeeease. No contest. The Mets have great pitching, but so do we. We've got two twenty-game winners and a sixteen-game winner. And, the rest of the Mets team—forget about it. They can't compare to us. It will be over quick. No problem." That had to be the typical conversation in the Oriole locker room in Minneapolis. Actually, they had every right to be confident. A superpower, the Orioles won one hundred and nine games during the regular season.

With the Orioles ahead by a big score in Minneapolis some players got a chance to watch part of our celebration on television in their clubhouse. Sometimes people say things in the heat of battle, or in this case the dousing of champagne. The Orioles saw an interview with Rod Gaspar, aka "P. P." Now "P," as I used to call him, was a little bit of a clubhouse philosopher. Not in the mold of Curly Johnson, but a philosopher nevertheless. When asked a question about the Mets chances, he answered bluntly in a very loud voice, "The Mets are going to win four in a row." Needless to say, Rod became "Rod Expletive" in the Oriole clubhouse. "Typical Gaspar. Mouthing off before thinking," said Rod. "I just said we would win in four straight. In the Oriole clubhouse Frank Robinson got hold of it and said, 'Who the hell is Rod Gaspar?'"

Back in our clubhouse after the series against Atlanta was over, most of us were still relishing the victory. It was only Monday. The World Series wasn't going to start until Saturday in Baltimore. Right now we could only think of how far we'd come. The year before, we languished near the bottom of the National League. All the other years had been disasters. "Losing was contagious," said Ed Kranepool. "Now winning is contagious." This year we came full circle. Well, almost full circle. We needed another arc in the orb to complete it.

In contemplating the upcoming World Series, sportswriter Maury Allen remembered this: "The thought most of the writers covering the 1969 World Series had was that we were happy to be covering the Mets in the World Series, but if it's a four-game sweep by Baltimore we're not going to be shocked, and we're not going to be disappointed. We all knew that the 1969 Baltimore team was considered the best in baseball that year. They had great pitching, hitting, and defense. I remember a bit of a smirk on Earl Weaver's face when he said the Mets' win in the playoffs was a kind of freak thing."

We planned to leave for Baltimore right after a short workout at Shea on Thursday, October 9th. That day, lines of people waited all night for the ticket windows to open at 8 A.M. to buy tickets for the World Series games at Shea. The Mets put 7,000 general admission seats on sale and by 10:30 A.M. they were all gone for game three, the first to be played at Shea. By 1 P.M. they were all gone for game four. Soon after that, all seats plus standing room for all games were sold out.

As a reminder of other events rocking the rest of the country, on October 9th, we learned the National Guard was called into Chicago for crowd control as large demonstrations were occuring in connection with the trial of the "Chicago Eight."

New York City, on the other hand, became our kingdom. Everyone was into the Mets. Newspapers, television, and radio were covering our every move. Feature stories on the manager, coaches, and players were everywhere in every medium. Governor Rockefeller invited the players and their families to his "apartment" on Fifth Avenue for a cocktail party the night before we left for Baltimore. Now that was someone who was rich. With famous paintings galore and an apartment as big as an estate, the governor and his wife were great hosts. To my best recollection, I didn't remember the team being invited to the governor's apartment the year before when we finished near the bottom of the standings.

Mayor John Lindsay didn't lose out on any of this. Now he became a true New York Met baseball fan. With the World Series starting in a couple of days, the mayor was in the middle of his re-election campaign. Because he lost the Republican nomination, his problem was he had to run as a Liberal-Independent. This party had no clout, presence, or money to push a candidate. So, he needed a boost from somewhere. Political advisor David Garth said, "At that point we were so desperate we would have supported any winning team."

The mayor was no fool, he was right there at LaGuardia Airport to see us off when we left for Baltimore. There was also an eight-piece band to serenade us. Before we took off, the mayor read the following poem that Jeff Greenfield wrote for him:

Ode to the New York Mets

Oh, the outlook isn't pretty for the Orioles today,
They may have won the pennant, but the Mets are on the way.
And when Gil Hodges' supermen get through with Baltimore,
They'll be the Champions of the World—they'll win it in four.
The experts say they cannot win, but they'll just eat their words.
When Jones and Koos and Agee pluck the feathers off those Birds,
When Gentry shuts out Robinson and Ryan does the same,
The world will know the Mets have come to dominate the game,
With Harrelson and Kranepool, with Gaspar and with Weis,
With Grote, Shamsky, Boswell—we've got the games on ice,

And when we've got a manager like Gilbert Raymond Hodges
We've got a team that makes up for the Giants and the Dodgers.
So good luck down in Baltimore, New Yorkers place your bets,
We know we've got a winner—with our Amazin' Mets.

It wasn't the most beautiful poem, but the Mayor did have good intentions.

The plane ride to Baltimore was quick even though we left about an hour late due to the festivities. Again, because we were a good road team, opening in Baltimore was fine with all of us. One of the players really happy to be going to Baltimore was Ron Swoboda. Not only was he getting an opportunity to play because the Orioles had two left-handed starters, he had the chance to play in his hometown. He would need to buy some extra tickets. "I needed 20 to 30 tickets for all the games in Baltimore," Swoboda said. "That's when I really started not liking my relatives and friends."

We arrived at our hotel in Baltimore and thought it had to be a mistake. The Sheraton-Belvedere was one of the oldest and shabbiest hotels I ever saw. Once again, Lou Niss, our traveling secretary, bore the brunt of players' frustrations. Lou, who was partially deaf and had selective hearing when he did hear, just shrugged it off like he always did. As it turned out, the hotel was bad, the food so-so, and the service awful. Three nights in that place was more than enough. We all hoped we wouldn't have to come back.

A 1:30 P.M. workout was scheduled for us at Memorial Stadium for Friday. The Orioles had to work out at 10:30 in the morning so they could be finished early enough to get to a downtown motorcade and civic reception. It appeared as if the Orioles and their fans were already celebrating a victory most people thought inevitable.

Looking at the 1969 Baltimore Orioles you could see why they won 109 games during the regular season. They breezed through the difficult Eastern Division of the American League, winning by nineteen games. Then they swept the Western Division Champion Minnesota Twins in three games to win the American League Pennant. Their lineup was terrific, pitching outstanding, and defense simply one of the best. In other words, the Oriole team we were facing in the World Series could be classified as one of the best of all time.

The Orioles had some of the game's premier stars, the foremost of which was rightfielder Frank Robinson, my former teammate at Cincinnati. Frank and I played together in 1965. He had a good year then, but Bill DeWitt traded him to the Orioles because he thought Frank was an "old" thirty. Of course, no one believed that except Bill DeWitt. When Frank came over to the Orioles all he did was lead them to the 1966 world championship. Robby was one of those players who was all business, all the time, once the game started. He played hard and the opposition knew it. If he didn't like a player on the other team, particularly a pitcher, he would get on his case, usually from the dugout. He was tough.

I remember one experience I had when we were both with the Reds in 1965. Ironically, we were playing the Mets in an afternoon game. The night before, Robby was hit by a pitch on his left forearm. Frank stood right on top of the plate and often got hit by pitches. Sometimes, it was accidental, most of the time intentional. We were ahead by a big score and Robby was in the on-deck circle. The Mets decided to bring in Tom Parsons, a side-arm, right-handed relief pitcher. During the pitching change, our manager Dick Sisler, who had a slight stutter, decided to pinch-hit for Frank. He wanted to avoid the possibility of another hit-by-pitch scenario. I was minding my own business when Sisler, in his stuttering voice, called my name to pinch-hit for Robinson. This was like a scene right out of the movie *Taxi Driver.* I said, "You talking to me?" He nodded yes. Reluctantly, I started toward the bat rack when someone said "Good luck." I knew exactly what that meant. Grabbing a bat, I walked toward the on-deck circle. Now, it's important to understand something. At that time I was a rookie, and always addressed Frank as "Mr. Robinson." I barely ever talked to him. He was a star, I was an extra outfielder. He hadn't been paying attention to anything going on in the dugout, so when I got next to him at the on-deck circle he looked at me and bluntly said, "What the fuck are you doing here?" I said, "Dick wants me to hit for you." Frank said, "You can't be serious. Get out of here!" I turned around and did a slow amble back to the dugout. Sisler looked at me and said with a stutter, "G-G-Go back out there and hit." I said, "He doesn't want me to hit for him." Sisler said, "J-J-Just go back there and hit." So, I turned around and walked back toward the on-deck circle. When I got there Frank looked at me again and said, "Get out of here." I replied, "But Mr. Robinson, he wants me to hit for you." I didn't know what to do. At that moment we both heard Dick Sisler's stuttering voice calling out. We looked toward the dugout and saw Sisler touching his forearm to show Robby what he meant by all this. I heard Frank say, "Shit," and as he started to walk back to the dugout he paused for a second, turned back to me, and said flatly, "You better not embarrass me." Talk about pressure. I didn't know what to think. Maybe Sisler would see how nervous I was and pinch-hit for me! It didn't happen. With a lot of trepidation I went up to home plate and got into the batter's box. I'm thinking, "let this be over quick." It turned out it was. I hit the first pitch over the center-field fence for a pinch-hit home run. Running around the bases, I couldn't believe what had just happened. My only thought was that my big-league career was going to be a strange one. When I got back to the dugout all my teammates were congratulating me, except Frank Robinson. When all the handshaking was done, Frank casually walked over, stuck out his hand, looked me in the eye, and said, "OK. Now you can call me Frank." It's a day I will never forget.

Along with Frank Robinson, who hit .308 with 32 home runs and 100 RBIs that season, there was another Robinson—Brooks at third base. Brooks didn't hit for average that year, but had 23 home runs and drove in 84 runs. Better than his hitting, Brooks Robinson was unquestionably the best third baseman in the game. When third basemen are talked about in the history of baseball, Brooks Robinson's name will always be mentioned as one of the tops of all-time.

At first base was big Boog Powell. Boog was coming off a super year. He hit .304 with 37 home runs and 120 RBIs. That's a pretty good year in anybody's book! At shortstop the Orioles had steady Mark Belanger who hit .287 for the season, but was better known for being an outstanding fielder. Davey Johnson played second base. He hit .280 with 7 home runs and 57 RBIs. In the outfield, besides Frank Robinson, the Orioles had two good players. Paul Blair played center field. A great defensive center-fielder, he was coming off a good year at the plate hitting .284 with 26 home runs and 76 RBIs. Don Buford was the left fielder. Don wasn't a big guy, but quite a capable hitter. He batted .291 with 11 home runs and 64 RBIs. Behind the plate was the one position the Orioles platooned. It was either Andy Etchebarren or Elrod Hendricks. Together, they combined for 15 home runs and 63 RBIs. The Orioles' bench was so-so, but with their stellar regular line-up and star pitching, they didn't factor in too much during the season. There was little comparison between the Orioles' hitting and ours. As a team the Orioles' batting average was twenty-three points higher, .265 to .242, a big difference. They hit 66 more home runs during the regular season than we did, 175–109. Their hitting, at least on paper, was superior.

Regarding pitching, the Orioles had two twenty-game winners in

Mike Cuellar and Dave McNally. Cuellar's record for the regular season was 23–11 and McNally's 20–7. Jim Palmer, the third starter, who had arm problems the year before, won sixteen while losing only four games during the season. Their fourth starter, Tom Phoebus, also had a good year with a 14–7 record. Plus, the Orioles' bullpen had good names certainly capable of doing the job. The total team pitching earned run average was less than three runs a game at 2.83. You don't win 109 games during a season without outstanding pitching. Even though we had many quality pitchers, from an earned run average standpoint the Orioles had the edge. Our team ERA was 2.99.

The other factor that could come into play was the Orioles' defense. With Brooks at third and great strength up the middle, they were outstanding. The series might just come down to both pitching and defense.

The Orioles' manager was Earl Weaver. I had played against Earl when he was managing a minor league team in Wisconsin back in 1961. He managed Fox Cities and I was playing for the Topeka Reds in what was then called the Class B Three I League. Earl was a fiery little guy with sort of a gravelly voice, the complete opposite of Gil Hodges. Gil would sit back, take the game in, and make moves along the way. If he had something to say to you it was usually behind closed doors, either after the game or the next day. Also, he was mild-mannered when it came to the umpires. Weaver, on the other hand, seemed to be much more boisterous and inclined to be on the first step of the dugout, always looking for something to argue about. Both styles worked for the individuals. I know it worked for Earl Weaver because he was a success as a manager wherever he went. He had just managed a team to 109 victories in a season. Gil Hodges also did a remarkable job with his team winning 100 games during the regular season.

The bottom line seemed to be that the Orioles had everything a team needed in order to be world champions. Most of the current players on their team had played in a World Series and won, as recently as 1966. The Mets, on the other hand, had only the recent experience of once being the laughingstock of baseball.

Friday night, the night before the series started, was relatively quiet. Both my roommate and I had relatives and friends come to Baltimore so we spent time with them and got back to our hotel early. Kenny and I were still trying to buy tickets for the first game. People came out of the woodwork asking for tickets.

Sleep didn't come easy for Boswell or myself. This was our first experience of this magnitude. Yes, we did play in the playoffs, but this was the World Series.

When we came down for breakfast the next morning we couldn't believe the crowd of people at the hotel. Of course we couldn't get a table in the restaurant. We would have to grab something at the clubhouse, like a cup of coffee.

The ride over to the game was unnaturally quiet. We needed someone to fire out, "a chicken ain't nothing but a bird." No one did. The Glider, Ed Charles, kept telling everyone, "It's just another game. Relax, don't worry, we got Tom Terrific on the mound." The Glider was usually right, but today was different for all of us. No matter how you sugar-coated it, for almost all of us today's game was going to be unlike any other we ever played. The butterflies started as soon as we woke up and continued for what seemed like forever.

I had bought a *New York Times* and a local paper at the hotel. On the bus ride to Memorial Stadium I remember reading an article in the *Times* where Earl Weaver was asked to describe our team. I said to the guys around me that Earl Weaver described us as, "Two pitchers, some slap hitters, and a little speed." A lot of expletives were then voiced. In the local paper the articles were about the Orioles and the mismatch. A headline read, "Mets' Miracle Story Nearing End." There was one interesting footnote in the *New York Times*. It was about a national survey that asked for people's preference for a World Series champion. The results from a poll of 1,200 adults showed that 52.3 percent wanted the Mets to win, 7.4 percent preferred the Orioles. The rest had no opinion. By far the people's favorite. How about that?

For the left-handed platoon like Boswell, Kranepool, Garrett, and myself, it was tough. We had played the whole Atlanta series and done well. Obviously, given a choice, I would like to start the first game of the World Series and get the nervous anxiety over with. But, it was not to be. We had to make the best of it.

Pre-game batting practice and warm-ups were pretty much the same routine, except, in reality, nothing was routine today. So many press people in the clubhouse and on the field made it at times impossible to move around. One interesting thing did happen. Before we took the field for batting practice and as the Orioles were leaving to go to their clubhouse, Frank Robinson was near the batting cage. Donn Clendenon called him over to meet Rod Gaspar. Rod, who by now was noted for his, "We'll win in four straight" quote, was a bit apprehensive. He recently recalled this little meeting. "Yeah, before the first game in Baltimore our buddy Clendenon grabs me and says, 'Come over here Rodney.' He calls Frank Robinson over to introduce me to him. Clendenon liked to stir things up. When Robinson met me, he still didn't know who I was. We just looked at each other and walked away."

I was happy when I was in the outfield during batting practice, away from the batting cage and out of the clubhouse. It was just plain annoying.

Shortly before the game, reporters finally had to leave the clubhouse. It gave all of us a time to sit back for a minute. We needed to catch our breath and take a few moments to savor the situation before the pregame ceremonies. There was some light chatter, but Donn Clendenon was un-usually quiet. Boswell and I waited for his usual derogatory comments about anything, the clothes we wore to the ballpark, our uniforms, or even how we hit in batting practice, but not today. Even Donn was caught up in this significant moment.

When we went out on the field everyone was nervous as the introduc-tions started. It is difficult to describe the feeling when your name is an-nounced and you run out to the foul line. Besides, many more people knowing your name now, you realize where you are. Not so much the par-ticular place, but your life at that moment. More important, you just reached the one place every young kid dreams about. How many times have you watched the World Series and said to yourself, "I wish I got a chance to play in one."

Finally the pregame festivities ended. By this time all of us had enough hype, and it was time to play.

The pitching matchup for the first game had Mike Cuellar going against Tom Seaver. Both of them were coming off great seasons, al-though Tom did not pitch well in his lone playoff appearance against the Braves. The right-handed platoon was set for us.

We did not score in the top of the first inning. The first batter for the Orioles in the bottom half of the inning was Don Buford. On Seaver's second pitch Buford hit a high lazy fly ball to deep right field. Ron Swo-boda went back for it and it looked like he would make the catch. When he got to the right-field fence he jumped up. The ball nicked the webbing of his glove and went over the fence for a home run. "I let the ball get over my head," said Swoboda recently. "When I went out on that field I was petrified. When Buford hit the pitch off Seaver, I think I turned the wrong way and too slow, and got back to the fence late. It was catchable, but when I put my glove up the ball was off to the side. It didn't go over my glove; it went off to the side. I just missed it."

We got out of the inning with just the one run being scored. Swoboda remembered when he came off the field, "I was pretty upset with myself. We were down one nothing and I was ranting and raving when I came into the dugout. Ed Kranepool said in his normal sympathetic way, 'Shut the fuck up and get the next one.'"

There was no further scoring until the bottom of the fourth. With two runners on, Mark Belanger singled to right field for one run and then pitcher Mike Cuellar blooped a single to center to make the score 4–0. Seaver just didn't seem to have the sharpness he usually had during the season. Tom left the game for a pinch hitter in the sixth and Don Cardwell and Ron Taylor didn't allow a hit in the final three innings. "I ran out of gas in the fourth inning," Seaver said. "Until then I thought I had good stuff." Tom confessed he had strained a calf muscle the day after pitching in Atlanta during the playoffs. He was running in the outfield during batting practice and felt something strange in his calf. He wasn't able to run for four days. "I thought I would run out of gas pitching the first game of the World Series, but I figured it would be later in the game."

Meanwhile, Mike Cuellar wasn't having much trouble against us. In the first six innings he gave up two hits and two walks. In the top of the seventh, Donn Clendenon led off with a single and Ron Swoboda walked. Jerry Grote singled to load the bases and we scored a run on an Al Weis sacrifice fly. With two out and two men on, Rod Gaspar, batting for reliever Don Cardwell, topped a ball down the third base line. It looked like a base hit, but Brooks Robinson did what he had done so many times. He turned a base hit into an out. Brooks charged the ball, picked it up, and fired a strike to Boog Powell at first for the last out of the inning. It was a magnificent play by a magnificent third baseman. It got the Orioles and Mike Cuellar out of a jam.

With the score 4–1 in the top of the ninth our pitcher was due up if any runners got on base. When Gil called my name I was somewhat surprised. Pinch-hitting is one of the most difficult jobs in baseball. You sit around most of the game not knowing if you are going to get a chance to hit. It's hard to get loose and you are usually going against a pitcher who is throwing a good game or a top reliever trying to save the game. But, pinch-hitting in the World Series is another story altogether. Ironically, I didn't start the game because it was a left-handed pitcher pitching against us. But, here I am pinch-hitting versus the same guy I couldn't start against.

In the on-deck circle my life literally flashed in front of me for about thirty seconds. I thought about all those days with my friends in St. Louis playing ball in the park and the many years playing amateur baseball. I thought about my minor league days when I rode buses and talked baseball all the time. I thought about the constant dreams I had of wanting to play professional baseball and then wanting to make it to the big leagues. Here I was in front of over 50,000 fans at Memorial Stadium in Baltimore and maybe one hundred million people watching on television. This was the moment all those days of practice and working out finally paid off. This was the World Series.

We got a base hit and a walk and now with two out I was the pinch hitter. I would be lying if I didn't say my heart was beating as fast as it could. Even though I had hit over .500 in the playoffs and was swinging the bat well, I was nervous. I don't believe anyone can be thrown into a more difficult situation. I was the tying run with two outs in the top of the ninth inning in the first game of the 1969 World Series against a left-handed pitcher who had only given up six hits while trying to pitch a complete game.

After being announced as the pinch hitter I finally made it into the batter's box. I actually felt better there. Maybe, I was in my comfort zone. Who knows? I've always enjoyed that one-on-one confrontation. I don't think there's anything like it in sports. I knew the situation and, I must confess, thoughts of being a hero did enter my mind. The first pitch that Mike Cuellar threw was a slider low and away that I swung wildly at and missed. Actually, I felt better after the pitch because even though I swung and missed, I just knew that he wasn't going to strike me out. The next pitch was another little slider right down the heart of the plate. I swung and hit a one-hopper to Davey Johnson at second base who threw me out at first to end the game. I had a chance to be a hero but it was not meant to be. To this day, whenever I see Mike Cuellar we joke about that pitch being right down the middle of the plate. I could have just as easily hit it out of the ballpark, but I didn't.

Going into the clubhouse I felt bad for my teammates and more than a little sorry for myself. Everyone wants to be a hero. I wanted another swing at that same pitch. To this day, I still think about that pitch.

It was not a silent clubhouse. Even though we lost the game most everyone felt we had been competitive. And it was only one game. There still was a long way to go. "I felt like we had gotten over our first game jitters," recalled Ed Charles. "At the end of the game as we were walking off the field I remember telling George Bamberger, who was a coach for the Orioles, 'That's the last game you guys are going to win.' He looked at me and said, 'You've got to be kidding.' We had been teammates in the minor leagues. I had confidence our team was going to respond because we had done that all year."

Yogi recalled his feelings: "I still thought we had a chance after the first game we lost. Doesn't four out of seven mean that you have to win four games?"

"I was a little worried," Ralph Kiner told me not long ago. "I thought you could lose in four. You guys always bounced back that year, but the Orioles had a great team with great players and a lot of us thought the Mets had gone further than anyone expected." Donn Clendenon said, "I remembered some of us talked after we lost the first game of the World Series. "Seaver couldn't blacken your eye with his fastball that day, but we had Koosman starting the next afternoon."

"Baltimore wasn't intimidating," said Cleon Jones. "After we lost the first game it didn't change my opinion. When I saw them on paper I felt like we could beat them. Besides, it was only one game. I remember going out to dinner after the first game with my wife and some other people. A few of the people wanted to bet the Orioles would win the series. I wanted to bet them because I had so much confidence."

Ron Swoboda had a bleaker outlook. "I thought maybe this series wouldn't take long. I was thinking, 'These are the Orioles with all the future Hall of Famers.' I thought the Orioles were probably happy to see us."

"Two things came to my mind after the first game," said Tom Seaver. "We were this group of so-called brash individuals that had no right to be in the World Series against the big, bad Baltimore Orioles with all the big names on that team. After we lost the first game I remembered here were these big, bad Orioles and they were jumping up and down in celebration. For some reason I expected them to be much more serene in victory. I was thinking, 'Why are they so jubilant?' Donn Clendenon came walking toward me, put his arm around me walking toward the clubhouse and said, 'We're going to beat these guys.' It was the same thought I had in my mind. I pitched lousy relative to how I pitched during the season, yet Clendenon was feeling the same thing I was."

"I didn't think we were in trouble," said Ed Kranepool. "We were close and competitive in the first game. I had tremendous confidence in Jerry Koosman. He was a fighter and a terrific pitcher. I knew he was going to give everything he had."

Kenny Boswell was calmer about the situation. "There was no reason to panic after the first game of the series. We all felt we had a good team. We had scored runs against Atlanta and we had good pitching. I knew we would come back."

"One game doesn't make a series, I wasn't worried at all," added Ron Taylor. "I pitched in the 1964 World Series for the Cardinals and we were underdogs to the Yankees. That series went seven games and we won. You just can't get discouraged after one game. With the Mets we had a team that came back all the time during the season. And with Jerry Koosman pitching the next day, we knew we would have a chance."

Sportswriter Maury Allen had the same thought. "I wasn't worried because you played so well in the first game, and I had so much confidence in Jerry Koosman who was pitching the next day."

The following morning the Baltimore papers had the World Series all but over. Another three games and the real celebration would begin in Baltimore. The superlatives for the Orioles were flowing, and questions about our ability were the topic of the day. There was an interesting comment in the *New York Times* from Frank Robinson. He said he thought the Mets lacked spark during the game. "I thought it was very strange," Robinson said, "that they didn't show any enthusiasm when they loaded the bases in the seventh inning. I took a good look at their bench and it was very quiet." I didn't know what he was talking about because I was right there and all of the players on our bench were chattering for a rally. In response to Robinson's remark the *Times* reported Gil Hodges had this to say: "I'm glad to see that Frank is watching our bench and not paying attention in right field. But I'm not concerned with what he says." To which Robinson replied, "Tell Hodges to manage his ball club and I'll play right field." All this after just one game!

Jerry Koosman is the type of person you can't help but like. A big guy with a big heart, Jerry grew up in Appleton, Minnesota. That's about as middle America as you can get. Jerry always had a joke to tell or a funny story to relate. Some of his jokes were downright stupid, but you found yourself laughing at them just because Jerry would tell them in his own strange way. On the other hand, we were all aware how well he could pitch. Although Jerry didn't win as many games as Tom Seaver during the season, you knew he was going to battle the opposition and give it his all.

Everyone on our team thought he could beat the Orioles in the second game of the World Series.

Opposing Koosman on Sunday, October 12th, was Dave McNally, another left-hander and twenty-game winner. The Orioles stayed with the same line-up except for the catcher. Elrod Hendricks caught the first game and Andy Etchebarren would catch the second. After the usual pregame festivities it was time to get to work.

For three innings it was a good pitchers' duel. Two excellent left-handers in control with no runs scored. In the top of the fourth things changed. Donn Clendenon hit a home run to right field to give us a 1–0 lead. It was the first run McNally had given up in twenty-four postseason innings going back to the 1966 World Series. Meanwhile, Koosman was pitching a no-hitter through six innings. You couldn't ask for a better game from him. In the seventh, Paul Blair broke up the string. He singled, stole second, and scored on a base hit by Brooks Robinson to tie the score.

The pressure was mounting. We needed a win in Baltimore; otherwise we would be in an awful predicament being down two games to zip in the best-of-seven series. But Koosman got back in control. McNally was hanging tough, too, only allowing three hits through eight innings.

In the top of the ninth we came to bat badly needing to score. McNally quickly got two outs. Ed Charles, our senior citizen, came to the plate. The Glider promptly singled for his second base hit of the game. Jerry Grote followed with another base hit on a hit and run that got Ed to third base. That brought up Al Weis, known more for his fielding than his hitting. Little Al came up big, lining a single into left field for the go-ahead run, giving us a 2–1 lead. Al's hit also kept Koosman in the game because he was the next hitter and most likely, Hodges would have pinch-hit for him if Weis hadn't gotten a run-scoring hit.

In the bottom of the ninth, Koos got the first two batters. Then came some excitement. With Frank Robinson coming up as the tying run, Hodges decided to move Al Weis from second base into the outfield as a fourth outfielder. This was the first time in World Series history that four outfielders had been used in a game. Gil had done this before in a few games when a big hitter was coming up to prevent a ball being hit in the gaps in the outfield. Robinson ended up walking and a pinch-runner was sent in for him. Koos then walked big Boog Powell and it was nail-biting time. Hodges decided to bring in a right-handed pitcher to face Brooks Robinson. In came Ron Taylor. Koosman had pitched a tremendous game, one to be proud of. But now we needed Taylor. When Hodges gave Taylor the ball he simply said, "You've got to get one man out."

Taylor finished his warm-ups. The good thing was that he was in a familiar situation. The only Met with previous World Series experience, he could handle the pressure. Brooks Robinson worked the count to 3–2 and, with the runners running, hit a hard smash right at The Glider at third base. Charles's first inclination was to tag third but he changed his mind and threw that beautiful rainbow he was noted for over to first base and got the last out of the game. It was going to be a real series.

"I knew I had to get Brooks Robinson out," recalled Ron Taylor. "I wanted to keep the ball down and not go to a three and two count. Unfortunately, I did get to three and two and with the runners going Brooks Robinson hit the ball right to Ed Charles." That would be the last time Ron pitched in the series. He had pitched brilliantly in postseason play all during his career. Between the Cardinals in 1964 and the Mets in 1969, he hurled eleven innings not giving up a run and ending with three saves and a win. In World Series play he pitched seven innings with no hits, no runs, and one save. Terrific. Ron Taylor never got the recognition that he deserved for his heroics with our club.

The clubhouse was much noiser than the day before. We had a new sense of accomplishment. The whole team was now much more confident.

I always thought the second game was the pivotal and most important of the World Series. If we lost and came back to New York 0–2 who knows what would have happened, we might have lost four in a row. Not that we couldn't have pulled it out, but it would have been difficult. The fact we gained a split in Baltimore and knew we could compete with the Orioles gave us much more confidence. Ken Boswell had a similar reaction: "I think the second game put a punctuation mark on the series. It proved we could play with the Orioles and win."

When I asked Brooks Robinson if that game was the most important he said, "You're right. The second game gave you (the Mets) confidence. It was a close game, and if we could have beaten Koosman it would have been a different story in the series."

"After the second game, I walked up to Tommie and just said, 'We're not going to have to come back here,'" Cleon Jones remembered.

Jerry Koosman recently gave me a personal take on his performance. "I knew we had to win a game in Baltimore. I certainly felt the weight on my shoulders about going out and doing my bit without screwing up. Going into the seventh inning I had a no-hitter. I threw a curve ball to Paul Blair and he grounded it between short and third for a base hit. Then he stole second. Brooks Robinson then hit a fastball up the middle for a base hit and drove in the run to tie the game. I was upset with the two walks in the ninth inning, but I had a lot of confidence in Ron Taylor."

"Me, one of the heroes of the game. How sweet is that?" recalled Al Weis. "It was important that we won at least one game in Baltimore. To be a factor in that was very special."

When asked later after the game why he didn't walk Weis to force Gil Hodges to make a decision to leave Koosman in or pinch-hit for him, Earl Weaver told the *New York Times*, "I figured if I walked Weis to get to Koosman then Hodges would have pinch-hit for Koosman and whoever he sent up there would be a better hitter than Weis."

It was a good flight home. With a light workout scheduled for Shea on Monday, there was a little time to enjoy the World Series so far.

Monday October 13th, New York City was in a frenzy. The commotion about the Mets and the World Series was the number one subject of the day. That's all anyone talked about. I was getting calls from all over for World Series tickets. I figured most people thought I had an unlimited supply, and on top of everything the tickets would be free. Everyone probably thought I asked the Mets for tickets and they said, "Sure Art, what do you need? How about a whole section for your family and friends? And, don't worry about the cost. Just tell the people to have a good time and enjoy themselves." It just didn't work that way. The Mets allotted two World Series tickets each game for each player, and we had to pay for them.

The workout for us Monday started at 11:00 in the morning and lasted ninety minutes. The Orioles worked out at Shea at 2:30 for a little more than an hour. The grounds crew worked hard to transform the field into playable condition. It had taken a beating from the fans in two celebrations. You could see the patchwork, but in all honesty the crew did a great job in a short time to get it to look even that good.

"Shea Stadium was built on top of a dump which sank all the time," explained groundskeeper Pete Flynn. "Besides the poor drainage we dealt with, we had to replace all the holes dug up by the fans. Most of us slept at the ballpark to get it ready for the World Series. Besides the turf being torn up, we had to replace bases, home plate, and signs. We were lucky the World Series didn't start at Shea."

The third game pitchers were Gary Gentry and Jim Palmer. Palmer, another future Hall of Famer, won sixteen games during the season and even pitched a no-hitter. Jim was bothered the last three seasons by shoulder problems. In fact, he spent forty-two days on the disabled list during the regular season in 1969. The third game of the series was also a chance for the lefty-platoon guys to get a chance to start. The only change for the Orioles would be at catcher, where Elrod Hendricks would be back behind the plate.

It was also time for the Orioles to play in front of the Met fanatics. They weren't used to the antics of our fans who had no qualms about being obnoxious or boisterous, and in some instances demented, but always pulling for their beloved New York Mets.

Gentry had not pitched well in the playoffs against Atlanta. Although, he wasn't alone in that department, he blamed his outing in the third game of the playoffs on being "over relaxed." He told the *New York Times*, "I wasn't psyched up enough against the Braves. I should have been a little nervous, but I wasn't because we won the first two games and all we had to do was win one of the next three games."

Jim Palmer told me, "I didn't feel a lot of pressure starting game three, but anytime you pitch in the World Series its pressure. I was aware that it was Shea Stadium and not like you're pitching at home."

The one other thing Gentry had to worry about was the Orioles' big three: Frank Robinson, Boog Powell, and Brooks Robinson. They combined for only two hits in twenty-two at-bats, both singles, for the first two games of the series. They were due to break out.

It was a test of two good, young right-handed pitchers; one of which, Palmer, already proved he could pitch in big games based on his effort in the 1966 World Series when he bested Sandy Koufax.

Once again there were the usual pregame festivities. Things were a little different for me as I was introduced in the starting lineup. There is something about hearing, "And playing right field for the Mets . . ." on the loudspeaker at Shea Stadium before the start of a World Series game. Plus, it was my birthday.

The Orioles didn't score in the first inning off Gentry. In the bottom of the first Tommie Agee, ahead in the count two balls and one strike, homered over the fence in center field. This was the fifth time this year Tommie had hit a home run as a leadoff batter. In the bottom of the third inning, after Jerry Grote walked and Bud Harrelson singled, Gentry, of all people, drove a Jim Palmer fastball toward right center for a double that drove home two more runs. Gary's first base hit since August 3rd made the score 3–0 in favor of the Mets. He had been 0–28 since then and only drove home one run all season.

In the top of the fourth inning Frank Robinson hit a line drive to left field that was ruled a trap ball when Cleon Jones made a play at his shoe-strings. Boog Powell followed with a single to right field. With one out and two men on Gentry blew a third strike past Brooks Robinson for the second out of the inning. That brought up the lefty swinging Elrod Hendricks. Elrod, who was a teammate of mine in the winter of 1965 when we both played for Santurce in the Puerto Rican winter league, was a pretty good pull and fastball hitter. With the outfield shifted toward right field Hendricks hit a ball toward left center. With two outs both runners took off with the crack of the bat. The only outfielder that had a chance to make a play was Tommie Agee. As soon as the ball was hit Tommie took off. He needed to go about forty yards and caught up with the ball near the warning track in left center. Reaching up backhanded, he caught the ball in the very edge of the webbing in his glove. It was a great play, one of the best ever in World Series play. It saved two runs and got Gary Gentry out of a difficult jam.

"When the ball was hit I looked over at Tommie," recalled Cleon. "I knew right away that he could get to it. He had a habit of pounding his glove when he thought he could make a play. He learned that when attending Grambling. They taught him that to make sure the crease in the glove was not up so the ball wouldn't pop out of his glove. When I saw Tommie pound his glove I started to let up in order to play the ball off the wall just in case he didn't get to it. But, I had a feeling he was going to make the play. I kept yelling to him that he had lots of room."

As Tommie ran in from the outfield the crowd gave him a well-deserved standing ovation. A home run and a great catch in the same World Series game—wow.

After the game Agee said, "I almost didn't make the play. The ball nearly went through the webbing of my glove."

In the bottom of the sixth inning Ken Boswell singled and moved over to second base on a groundout. Jerry Grote then doubled driving in Kenny. In the top of the seventh inning with the score 4–0 in our favor, Gentry started to lose his fastball and his control. He walked three batters and had two outs. With the ever-dangerous Paul Blair coming up to bat, Gil Hodges decided to make a pitching change. To everybody's surprise he brought in Nolan Ryan. Nolan pitched well in the playoff series against the Braves, but still had control problems. To bring him in this situation seemed a little strange. "When Gil brought in Nolan I thought, 'Oh my Lord,'" said Jerry Grote. "Maybe Gil knows something I don't know. Gil must have had the confidence that Nolan was going to throw strikes."

Ken Boswell recalled his own similar thoughts. He told me, "When Gil brought Nolan in to pitch to Paul Blair, I was wondering what he was thinking. I was just hoping that Nolan would throw strikes. I remember one time during the 1969 season Nolan was struggling to throw strikes so I went in from second base to talk to him. I told him I was falling asleep at second base. He told me, 'I'll pitch and you go try to play second base.' I knew if he threw strikes he would strike the batter out or we could make a play in the field."

"As a player I never questioned Gil Hodges' judgment," said Cleon Jones. "He made all the right decisions that year. I just thought he was looking for a strikeout."

Nolan did get two strikes to Blair who then hit a shot to deep right center field. It looked like a sure triple. Both Agee and I started after it. Tommie, as usual, got a good jump on the ball, this time running to his left. As the ball was about to drop in, Tommie dove toward the ground and caught the ball. He skidded for a few feet, but held onto the ball. Another spectacular catch by Tommie Agee! This time he saved three runs. After the game the *Daily News* quoted Tommie as saying, "I thought I might get it without diving, but the wind dropped the ball straight down and I had to hit the dirt." Cleon Jones remarked, "I thought he would make the play."

Once again as Tommie trotted into the dugout, the huge crowd, hysterical now, gave him another standing ovation. What a game Tommie was having. A home run and two spectacular run-saving catches. The crowd was going wild. This was indeed retribution for the struggles Tommie experienced the year before. For many years I kidded Tommie about that play to right center. I used to tell him he made an easy play look hard, and he's been fooling people for a long time. In reality, it was a fantastic catch and I got a chance to see it real close.

In the bottom of the eighth inning we got one more run as Ed Kranepool hit a home run off Dave Leonard who came on in relief of Jim Palmer in the seventh. The home run made the score 5–0. In the ninth inning with the crowd on its feet looking for the shutout, Nolan lost a bit of his control, walked two batters, and gave up a pinch single to Clay Dalrymple. Hodges came to the mound to talk to Ryan, but decided to give him the chance to finish the game. Whatever he said worked. Paul Blair, who had hit the ball off Ryan to right center field when Agee made the great catch, had another chance with the bases loaded. This time with two strikes and Blair looking for a fastball, Nolan threw him a curve that had Paul's knees buckling. It froze Blair and broke over the plate for a called strike three.

"In his previous at bat in the third game of the series, Blair hit the ball to right center and Agee made the great catch," recalled Jerry Grote. "This time Nolan was ahead in the count and I called for a curveball. Nolan didn't shake me off. He threw the curveball right at Blair's head. Everything in his body buckled. The ball broke right across the middle of the plate. Nolan had the great fastball, but he also had a great curve. I don't think Blair was looking for the curve. I had enough confidence in the way Nolan was pitching that day to call for it." He was right, and the Mets had won game three. We were two games into a "miracle."

In our jubilant clubhouse the talk was about Tommie's two catches and Nolan's pitching. Kenny Boswell and I talked about all those times we had to hit off Nolan in batting practice when he couldn't throw a strike, and everything coming in at 100 miles per hour in an effort to impress Gil and Rube Walker. It wasn't much fun then. However, today he proved how well he could pitch. The press besieged Tommie. What a game he had played. It gave credence to Cleon's opinion. "The third game of the World Series just proved to me what I thought about Tommie," said Cleon. "To me, he was our MVP. The way he hit in 1969 and the way he played center field, particularly at Shea Stadium."

Discussing those two catches, Tommie was quoted in the *Daily News* as saying, "I thought the first catch was harder because I had to run farther." The paper related Gil Hodges' comment, "I thought the second catch was harder. In my opinion, I believe it was the greatest I've ever seen in the World Series." Pretty strong praise from a guy who had seen a lot of World Series games.

In talking to Jim Palmer recently, he thought the Orioles' scouting on Gary Gentry for the World Series was incorrect. "Our scouting report said that Gentry was an average pitcher, and he didn't have outstanding stuff," he said. "Well, he beat us pretty good. I had seen him pitch and knew he was a good pitcher. I told our guys before the third game of the series that they shouldn't go up to the plate thinking he is an average pitcher." On Gentry's base hit off of him, Palmer said, "Our scouting report also said Gentry just swings the bat and wasn't a good hitter. I've always thought that Paul Blair was in the wrong position because he was playing Gentry to pull the ball. After that base hit I began paying more attention to where the outfielders were and started moving them around when I was pitching." And on Tommie Agee's first inning home run, Palmer commented, "I gave up one lead-off home run in my career and that was the one to Tommie Agee."

Frank Robinson recalled, "I thought the third game of the series was the most important. We had Palmer going against Gentry. I didn't even think about losing. It was a perfect matchup for us." The Orioles' Davey Johnson concurred, "Most of us thought the third game was the key game because we thought our starter, Jim Palmer, was better than your starter, Gary Gentry. We were all surprised when Gentry pitched so well. I definitely think that was the key game."

Up two games to one the odds makers suddenly made us 3–2 favorites to win the series. From 100–1 before the season to 3–2—Amazin', simply Amazin'.

Across the East River in Manhattan later that evening the New York Knicks basketball team opened their 1969–70 regular season by beating the Seattle Sonics 126–101. That game marked the coaching debut of Lenny Wilkens as a player-coach for the Sonics that season.

The next day, Wednesday October 15th, saw the fourth game of the World Series. It also marked National Moratorium Day when all over the country hundreds of thousands of people took part in anti-war demonstrations.

The game saw the return of the opening game pitchers, Mike Cuellar and Tom Seaver. It also got our righty platoon back into play. Tuesday's game drew over 56,000, and there would be another huge crowd today. New York City was aglow over the Mets. If you didn't know any better you would think things outside of Shea Stadium weren't as bad as they actually were. But now baseball had become the number one topic for everyone. The Amazin' Mets were indeed for real.

The game started with a scoreless first inning. In the bottom of the second Donn Clendenon hit his second home run of the series to give the Mets a 1–0 lead. In the top of the third there was a little, out of the ordinary, excitement. With Mark Belanger at bat, Oriole manager Earl Weaver took exception to a pitch called for a strike. On the next pitch to Belanger, home plate umpire Shag Crawford called another strike that brought some unkindly remarks from the Oriole dugout. Crawford then made a move toward the dugout and said something to the Oriole bench.

Weaver then jumped out of the dugout to "discuss" the matter with Crawford. One thing led to another and moments later Crawford gave the
thumb to Weaver. It was the first time a manager had been thrown out of
a World Series game in thirty-four years. "I wasn't arguing balls and
strikes with him, which I know is taboo," said Earl Weaver. "I was just trying to protect my player who was batting. The umpire politely asked me
to leave." Oriole coach Billy Hunter took over the managerial duties.

A tremendous pitching duel developed and the 1-0 score lasted until
the top of the ninth inning. Until this point the Orioles were shut out for
nineteen consecutive innings and only scored one run in their last thirty
innings in the series. With the Orioles at bat, both Frank Robinson and
Boog Powell singled. Brooks Robinson was the hitter with runners on
first and third base and one out. On Seaver's first pitch, Brooks hit a sink-
ing line drive toward right field. It looked like a sure base hit to score the
tying run. Ron Swoboda went after the ball at full tilt and dove at the last
second. He made a spectacular catch and came up throwing toward home
plate. Frank Robinson, playing heads-up baseball, had the presence of
mind to tag up and barely beat the throw to score. Rocky's remarkable
catch got an important out and probably saved the runner on first from
scoring and the Orioles from taking the lead. It was a remarkable play, but
there were some who thought Ron shouldn't have tried to even make the
catch.

"At first I thought he shouldn't have gone after it in that situation and
played it safe instead," said Ed Kranepool. "Knowing Swoboda anything
could have happened. The ball could have hit him in the head and gone
over the fence. He was the last guy in the world I would have thought
could make that play. I was more surprised that he got up and threw a
strike to home plate even though a run scored. He was unpredictable."

Maury Allen remarked, "I'm not sure he should have gone after the
ball the way he did. But when it happened you knew the Mets were going
to win. No question about it. It was one of those destiny, miracle things.
The catch was better than any I had seen. Everyone jumped up in the
press box screaming, which was something you weren't supposed to do."

Swoboda had his own take on the play. "Frank Robinson was on third
and Boog Powell was on first," Rocky recalled. "We're up a run with the
tying run on third base. I'm hoping I get a fly ball with the chance to
throw out the runner at home. Brooks Robinson hit Seaver's first pitch on
a line a little toward right center. I was pretty deep in right field. I just

broke and thought, 'if I don't get there I don't get there.' It was a bang-bang play. I dove for it just to give it a try. I didn't think I was going to get there."

When I mentioned to Ron that some people thought it might have been the greatest catch in World Series history he remarked, "Well, Mickey Mantle said it. God bless him. You know, I was not regarded as an outfielder of any merit. But I worked on my fielding. The bottom line is, some guys had a career—I had a catch."

"I didn't think a whole lot about the catch because it ended up being a sacrifice fly," said Brooks Robinson. "Every time I see Swoboda I tell him nobody would have ever heard of your ass if I didn't hit that ball."

When asked about Swoboda's great catch, Mets broadcaster Ralph Kiner said, "He had the presence of mind to throw home with the runner on third. By that time I had a feeling destiny was happening. Everything was going the Mets' way."

With the score tied in the bottom of the ninth we made a little noise as Jones and Swoboda singled. Once again Hodges sent me up to hit, this time for Ed Charles. With another chance to be a hero, I grounded out again to second base. Another huge disappointment for me.

In the bottom of the tenth inning, with the score still 1–1, Jerry Grote hit a pop fly double to left field. With Rod Gaspar (Frank Robinson's good friend) running for Grote, Al Weis this time was walked intentionally. With no outs Hodges sent up J. C. Martin to pinch-hit for Tom Seaver. Seaver had pitched magnificently; 10 innings, six hits, one run, and six strikeouts. When Martin was announced, as officially in the game, the Orioles brought in lefthander Peter Richert to pitch to J. C.

"When Gil sent in Gaspar to run for Grote, I knew I would stay in the game and catch if we didn't score," said J. C. "I initially was going to try and pull the ball to get the runners over to third base, but the Orioles changed pitchers and brought in a left-hander to pitch to me. When they did that, Gil called me back from the on-deck circle and said, 'What do you think about bunting the ball down the first base line to keep it away from Brooks Robinson?' That's how Gil was. He had such a dry sense of humor. I said, 'You're the boss.' He laughed and said, 'OK, let's do that.' So, that's what we did."

J. C. bunted the first pitch from Pete Richert perfectly toward first base. Richert picked the ball up and fired toward the first baseman. The ball hit J. C. on the left wrist and ended up going between first and second base. While this was going on, Rod Gaspar was running nonstop past third toward home. With a full head of steam and a giant leap on the plate, Gaspar scored the winning run.

"It was a pretty good bunt," J. C. Martin remembered. "The catcher and pitcher didn't know who was going to field it. Finally, the pitcher fielded it and, because he was left-handed, had to turn around and throw to first base. By that time I was pretty close to the bag and the ball hit me on the left wrist. It ricocheted between first and second and Gaspar scored the winning run."

"I was watching the play as I was running toward third base," recalled Gaspar. Then I looked at our third base coach Eddie Yost who started yelling. The crowd noise was so loud that I didn't hear what Eddie said. As I rounded third base Yost was no more than two feet from me. I looked at first base and saw the ball rolling toward second. I was running as hard as I could and when I touched home plate the first person I remember greeting me was Tom Seaver." At that moment every Baltimore Oriole knew who Rod Gaspar was.

To many peoples' surprise the Orioles did not argue the play very much. There was a little question about Martin running inside the base path but not until the next day was there any controversy.

"There was no question. There was no controversy at all. None," said J. C. "The ball hit me and nobody said a word. Everybody went off the field and the game was over. Shag Crawford was the umpire behind the plate and he made the call. The controversy started the next day when the picture came out in the paper. That's when the Orioles started to complain. As far as I'm concerned, it was a perfectly legal play and the photo proves it." What the photos show was that it was a close play. Any controversy was quickly squashed when Commissioner Bowie Kuhn stated it was a judgment call made by a veteran umpire. We were one game away from winning the World Series.

There are few words to describe the anticipation knowing that I was part of a team that, with one more victory, would win the World Series. Having never been in that position before, I can only relate what I was feeling on the morning of October 16, 1969. To wake up and know that later in that afternoon there could be a chance I might be part of history is a feeling of complete exhilaration. It wasn't going to be easy, but I also knew it was possible. While your mind thinks about all different types of scenarios, it always comes back to the big one. The year had already been a success for me just by coming back from the injury. Then to be part of this Mets team that no one thought would go anywhere followed by the division win, then the playoffs, and now, up three games to one in the World Series was just fantastic. "Miracles do happen and dreams come true," I thought.

In the clubhouse before Game Five and on the field during batting practice there was a sense it was going to happen today. Our confidence was as high as it could go. We had Koosman pitching, and if necessary Gentry, Seaver, and Koosman available the ensuing weekend in Baltimore. Not that anyone was thinking about going back to Baltimore. No one wanted to go back there to play any more games. And, no one wanted to go back to that hotel. I'm sure Lou Niss, our traveling secretary, didn't want to go back there, either.

The crowd was into the excitement as soon as the gates opened. Shea was buzzing and as the crowd filled the stadium it became electric. Even though this was a day that no sane Met fan ever thought would happen, it was for real and the fans were up for it.

Like the second game of the series, it was Koosman against McNally. The first two innings passed without any score. Met fans started to worry a little bit in the top of the third inning when Orioles' pitcher Dave McNally hit a two-run home run and Frank Robinson hit a solo shot off of Koosman to give the Orioles a 3–0 lead. In most circumstances being down 3–0 to the Orioles and Dave McNally might be insurmountable, but we were on a roll and everyone in the dugout expected something positive to happen. We had won fifteen out of our last seventeen games going back to the regular season. We prayed for just one more.

In the top of the sixth inning with Frank Robinson at bat it appeared Koosman hit him with a pitch. Plate umpire Lou DiMuro ruled the ball didn't hit the batter and a big argument followed. Robby then struck out. It was another break that went our way.

The score was 3–0 in the bottom of the sixth inning and Cleon Jones was at bat. Things started to happen. McNally threw a pitch down and inside to the right-handed hitter. The ball appeared to hit Cleon and then it rolled into the Met dugout. Again, plate umpire Lou DiMuro ruled the batter wasn't hit by the pitch. Donn Clendenon who was in the on-deck circle, walked toward DiMuro, said something and pointed to the dugout. Seconds later, out of the Met dugout came Gil Hodges with a ball and showed it to the umpire. The ball appeared to have a dark spot on it. After checking out the ball, DiMuro awarded Cleon first base, to the obvious displeasure of the Orioles. The next batter was Donn Clendenon. True to the Mets' postseason karma, Donn hit a 2–2 pitch into the second deck in left field for a two-run home run, his third homer of the series.

"Dave McNally threw me a slider down and in," remembered Cleon. "The ball hit my foot and rolled into our dugout. The umpire didn't say anything, and I didn't say anything because I wanted to hit off this guy. Clendenon was the one who was hollering it hit me from the on-deck circle. I guess he wanted me to get on base so he could hit with a runner on. Then Hodges walked out of the dugout with the ball and showed it to the umpire. I said to myself, 'Why are they raising hell, just let me hit?' But, Clendenon is yelling it hit me, and Hodges shows this ball to the umpire with a mark on it. The rest is history. I got on first base and Clendenon hit a home run."

"I told Cleon to go on down to first base," Clendenon said. "He wanted to hit. I told him we needed base runners. I don't know if Hodges heard me or not, but out he came with the ball."

"That was just one of the many breaks for the Mets in the series," said Jim Palmer. "One funny thing happened the next year. We were playing in Chicago and Lou DiMuro was behind the plate in this game, too. Earl Weaver went out to argue a call at home plate, but before he walked out he put a ball in his back pocket. He ran out to home plate, argued the play, lost the argument, then took a ball from his pocket, rubbed it on his shoe, and left it at home plate. He ran back to the dugout and DiMuro saw the ball with shoe polish. Obviously, he knew what Weaver was alluding to and threw the ball at Weaver but missed him and hit our third base coach, Billy Hunter. Billy picked up the ball and threw it back at DiMuro. It was hysterical."

"After the ball hit the dirt it somehow rolled into the Met dugout," remembered Earl Weaver. "Then Hodges came out of the dugout with a ball that he showed the umpire and all of a sudden the umpire signals for Jones to go to first base. How did that happen? It was just another thing going against us."

In the bottom of the seventh inning, with the score now 3–2 in favor of the Orioles, Al Weis came to the plate. Little Al Weis, the good-field, no-hit Al Weis who was one of the heroes in Game Two. This is the same Al Weis who drove in only twenty-three runs all during the 1969 season and had never hit a home run at Shea Stadium. Of course, Al promptly hit a home run into the left-field bleachers to tie the score at 3–3. There were no more doubters at that moment. The Orioles must have known it was inevitable.

Not only did Weis's home run tie the score, it kept Jerry Koosman in the game. A determined Koosman was not going to screw up this opportunity. Koos got the Orioles 1–2–3 in the top of the eighth. Eddie Watt came in to relieve for the Orioles. Cleon greeted him with a double over Paul Blair's head in center field. Donn Clendenon tried to bunt Cleon over to third, but failed. He ended up grounding out to third as Cleon remained at second base. That brought up Ron Swoboda. Rocky hit a semi-line drive down the left-field line that Oriole leftfielder Don Buford trapped in his glove. That scored Cleon from second base with the go-ahead run and Swoboda took second on the throw.

There was bedlam in the stands. The noise was deafening. A final run scored when Jerry Grote hit a ground ball to Boog Powell at first base that was bobbled. Boog tossed the ball too late to the pitcher, Eddie Watt, who was covering first base. Watt then dropped the throw and Swoboda, with some heads-up baserunning, scored from second on the play. When the inning was over the crowd was on their feet in a state of mass hysteria. Nobody was sitting down.

It was now the top of the ninth inning. Koosman recalled the moment: "I was thinking," he remembered, "what a place to be. On the mound at Shea Stadium, in the top of the ninth inning, ahead in the game 5–3, and ahead in the World Series, 3–1. Could you ever pick a better spot?"

Frank Robinson opened the ninth with a walk. A little of the buzz was taken out of the crowd. Everyone in the dugout was on his feet. The next batter, the dangerous power hitter Boog Powell, hit a grounder to second that turned into a force out of Frank Robinson at second. Brooks Robinson then flied out to right field. One more out and it would be over. People in the stands were chanting "World Champions, World Champions." It was an incredible moment in all of our lives. With two out and a runner on first, Davey Johnson, representing the tying run, stood at bat. What a moment for him. With everyone in the stadium on their feet, Johnson hit a deep drive that seemed like it took forever to come down. When it did come down Cleon Jones was there. As the ball came into his glove, Cleon went down to one knee. It was over! Incredibly, unbelievably, miraculously: *The Mets Were World Champions!*

And then there was chaos. Thousands of people ran onto the field; the third such exuberant celebration at Shea that season. The grounds crew would have the difficult job of getting the field ready for the next Jets home game, which was the following Monday night. At that moment they certainly weren't thinking about it. Everybody was running around. There was a big pile of Mets in the middle of the infield where all of us jumped on Koosman and Grote who had picked Jerry up. Fans were tearing up the field again. They were grabbing our hats and gloves. Everyone wanted a souvenir from this wondrous occasion.

Groundskeeper Pete Flynn remembered getting ready for mass hysteria. "When we got to the eighth inning," Pete said, "people were moving down the aisles toward the field level boxes. Everyone was getting ready for the charge onto the field. The excitement was unbelievable. At that point, all of us on the crew just threw up our hands and sort of said, 'whatever happens, happens.' We got caught up in it, too. Actually, I was supposed to go get second base. I didn't get within fifty feet of it. There were people all over me."

It was the most incredible scene any of us ever imagined. We had conquered the world and these fans were part of it. They had suffered through embarrassment and frustration and were now part of one of the most unbelievable sports seasons ever. First the Jets, and now the Mets.

"I was under the ball waiting for it to come down," recalled Cleon. "I went down to one knee because it was such a great moment. Later, when we worked for the Mets, Davey Johnson and I were roommates as coaches. He maintains that it was the hardest ball he ever hit in his life. I told him it was a weak fly ball. When it was coming down I said to myself, 'Come on down baby, come on down.'" Cleon also remembered trying to get off of the field after the last out. "I planned to go through the right-field bullpen," he said. "They were supposed to have the gate open. When I got halfway, I saw it was closed. I made a u-turn back to the other bullpen in left field. It was also closed so I just climbed over the fence."

Davey Johnson remembered what happened after making the last out. "I was running toward second base when the ball was caught," he said. When I turned to cut across the infield to get back to our dugout it was absolute bedlam. Thousands of people were running onto the field. It was unbelievable. I was hoping they weren't coming after me."

"The happiest moment for me," said Donn Clendenon, "was the last out caught by Cleon. When he settled under it, I just said, 'catch it.' I never thought I would be with a World Series winner." When asked how he felt about the ball hit by Davey Johnson, Jerry Koosman said, "I can't tell you how the goose bumps went down my back. You imagine all kinds of things when the ball is in the air."

Veteran sportswriter Maury Allen told me, "My personal thoughts after the last out of the 1969 World Series were, 'If you live long enough you can see everything. Thinking back, there maybe were a half a dozen of us who had been there since the beginning. And, to go through it from the beginning and to see you guys win was truly a miracle. A lot of the writers said that no matter what happens in baseball, or our own careers, we'll never have as much fun or as much excitement as we had watching the 1969 Mets. And, the sense of what you did not only for yourselves but also for New York City was absolutely astounding. One thing of significance was the emotion of the fans. It made them much more a part of what the Mets did than any other fans in any other city. It was an 'us against them' kind of psychology. When the 1969 Mets won, we the non-players, felt like we won, too. That's what the Mets accomplished for us. The city was taking a horrible beating with everything that was going on so the Mets victory was an incredible unifying event. All our lives were affected."

Inside, our clubhouse was madness. Everybody was getting soaked with champagne. There were hordes of cameras and press people. They were getting doused, too. Multiply everything that happened when we won the division and the pennant by ten. That's how much more intense the excitement and celebration seemed. I was able to bring my dad in our clubhouse when things settled down a bit. I was glad he got a chance to share those moments with me.

Tom Seaver took the opportunity with a microphone in his face to say, "If the Mets can win the World Series, we can get out of Vietnam." Tom recently told me, "I just decided to say it. History proved that they couldn't figure a way politically to get out."

One of the questions that has come up over the years is who got the last ball of the game, the one Cleon caught. "I gave the ball to Koosman when I got into the clubhouse. But, if I knew then what I know now about memorabilia, Koosman would have never seen that ball," Cleon said.

Besides champagne being poured over everyone, somehow shaving cream got into the mix. Everyone was being interviewed. Rod Gaspar was going around the clubhouse saying, "Who's stupid now? I told everyone we would win four straight. The Orioles thought I was an idiot. Didn't we win four straight?" I told him to go ask Yogi if we won four straight.

The celebration was unlike any we had seen before. "I thought the World Series celebration in the Mets' clubhouse was the most spontaneous celebration I ever saw," recalled Ralph Kiner. "The happiness and true spontaneity of the whole thing was probably the best in the history of baseball, and probably will never be duplicated."

Of course, Mayor John Lindsay was there. The mayor was getting doused for the umpteenth time, and he loved it. His cleaning bills were well worth the amount of positive publicity he was getting. Most New Yorkers liked him right at that moment. Myriads of people not lucky enough to be at Shea Stadium for the miracle reaped pleasure out of watching the Mets win the World Series. "I remember that day I was interviewing McGeorge Bundy," said author David Halberstam. "He was one of the architects of the Vietnam War. It had been a very unpleasant interview. It was for my book, *The Best and the Brightest*. It was an interview that was quite combative. I had gone to Harvard and he had been dean there. I knew he didn't believe in the war anymore and I said, 'Why are you silent, you were the dean of our college? We looked up to you as a great figure and here's the most pressing issue of our time and you're silent on it.' He said to me, 'You're very arrogant and that's a very arrogant thing to say.' I said, 'No, you're the arrogant one because you are sitting on the sideline at a terrible moment and you're remaining silent.' So, it was pretty hostile. When I left his office I was feeling terrible. I came out of the interview and went by a store window and the World Series was on. A lot of people were gathered around watching. The Mets were winning. I went from sort of a dark interview that wasn't fun, a dark moment for me, to where my whole attitude changed from dark to smiling. Maybe it affected a lot of people like that."

I asked Yogi during the celebration, "How many World Series rings will you have now?" He said as honestly as he could, "I don't know. Too many for my fingers."

The celebration in the clubhouse seemed to go on forever. Sal Marciano, a top sportscaster in New York, remembers an interview he did with Kenny Boswell. "The day the Mets won the World Series I interviewed Boswell after the game on film. At the end of the interview he said, 'All you Mets fans meet us tonight at Mr. Laffs (a well-known bar on First Avenue in Manhattan at the time), we're going to have a great party.' So, we left it in the sports segment for the early news show and also for the eleven o'clock show. When I got to Mr. Laffs at midnight there were a couple of thousand people trying to get in. The place held about one hundred. The crowd blocked most of First Avenue. Only one lane could go north at Sixty-fourth and First."

While we celebrated, the Oriole clubhouse was in shock. They had just witnessed a Met miracle right in front of their eyes. A team that won 109 games during the regular season and rolled over the Twins in the playoffs, had just had their marvelous season turned around. I got the opportunity to talk to many of them recently. They were open and gracious about that hard loss.

Brooks Robinson reflected, "I thought we had the better team. But, people failed to realize that you guys won one hundred games during the regular season and beat a very good Braves team in the playoffs. I tell people when you run a Seaver, Koosman, Gentry, and Ryan out there you are going to win a lot of games. There were a lot of crazy things that happened in that series—the shoe polish incident, Swoboda's catch, J. C. Martin running down to first base, and Agee making some spectacular catches in the outfield. You know, one or two of those things could have turned everything around. Actually, if you lose in the playoffs, that's more disappointing. When you get to the World Series you just say this is it, we'll see what we can do. If you're around long enough you'll see a lot of things. You win sometimes when you're not supposed to and lose sometimes when you're not supposed to. That's what makes baseball such a great game."

"Looking back on the Orioles' ball club," said Jim Palmer, "we had a terrific year. In a short series like that anything can happen. The Mets were confident and had great pitching. I didn't think because we won the first game that it was going to be easy. But, it was very disappointing for all of us."

"It took me a while to get over that World Series," said Frank Robinson. "I don't talk about it—just kidding. But, it took until we won the next year. Overall, the 1969 Orioles were the best team I played on in the six years I was there. Going into the World Series we didn't take the Mets lightly. I think the key to that series, other than the fantastic plays the Mets made defensively and the offense they got from unexpected people, was the third game when Gentry pitched. We knew about Seaver and Koosman, but the scouting report didn't give us real good information on Gentry and how good his stuff was." I asked Frank if he thought we got all the breaks? "When you play good baseball you make your own breaks," he said. "You guys played hard and deserved the breaks. You played aggressive, played great defense, and, true, got some breaks. I remember when Cleon was batting and the ball supposedly hit him and went into your dugout. It seemed like it was there for twenty seconds before Hodges brought it out with a smudge on it. In a short series you just don't know what's going to happen." I then asked Frank one more question. I asked, "Do you remember that little spat with Rod Gaspar who made the statement, 'The Mets are going to win four straight?" Robby replied, "I don't remember anything like that. The name sounds familiar; did he play on the Mets that year?"

Davey Johnson had this to say about the series: "I was very disappointed. We had a terrific team and we thought we were the better team. It seemed like everything went your way. Balls that we hit that should have been home runs stayed in the park, and balls the Mets hit found holes in the infield and outfield."

"I don't think we took the Mets lightly," said Earl Weaver. "You guys just played great baseball. And, things that happened in that series might not happen in a 162-game season. In those five games the Mets played as good as any team could play. You guys played terrific. On the other side, we had a great season and won 109 games. Even though we lost to the Mets, it was a good year. We came back and won 108 the next year and won the world championship. Sorry, I have to go. I have a tee time in twenty minutes." (Retirement's tough.)

"I knew the Mets had a good team," said Mike Cuellar. When they beat us in Game Two I knew it was going to be tough. When we lost Game Three I said to myself, 'We better do something different.' It looked like everyone on the Mets was playing together and we started to become overanxious."

The Orioles' loss in the World Series also had negative effects on some people outside baseball. "Just like the Colts' loss, the Orioles' loss hurt us too," said former Baltimore mayor, Thomas D'Alessandro. I remember the catch Ron Swoboda made that broke the Orioles' back. That was the turning point in the World Series. And, he's from Baltimore, too!"

Hollywood writer/director Barry Levinson, a Baltimore native, recalled, "The thing that stood out in my mind was that in a short series sometimes things go wrong, and that's exactly what happened. Great catches by the Mets, umpires' decisions, everything went wrong for my team. When Swoboda made that catch, I just said, 'What! Swoboda making that play; I don't care if he is from Baltimore!'" After more reflection, Levinson added, "Coming from Baltimore we despised New York teams. For both Baltimore teams to lose in 1969 (Colts and Orioles), especially as they were both looked upon as the best in their sport, was devastating. I constantly find myself saying, what if?"

One person who was very happy the Mets won the World Series had just returned home from a place where he didn't want to be. "In April of 1969 I was in Vietnam," said Ned Foote. "I was a corporal in the Marine Corps and a big Mets fan. My life changed that April when I was out on patrol and stepped on a land mine. I ended up losing my foot and was sent to St. Albans Naval Hospital in Queens at the end of May. I was in the hospital for over a year, but only at St. Albans until September. I was then sent to a VA Hospital in Albany, New York. I can't tell you how much listening to the Mets that year helped me. Listening to the games made me feel good. It took my mind off my problems, and I just felt better about things. There wasn't much else to make me feel good. When the Mets won the World Series there were a bunch of us around a TV. A lot of New Yorkers were there and a lot of nurses. Everyone was pulling for the Mets."

One of the New York Jets was at Shea Stadium to see us win. "I was right behind home plate when you guys won it," remembered defensive tackle John Elliott. "The people running onto the field, it was crazy. We won the Super Bowl as underdogs and you were underdogs, too. The Jets and Mets represented working-class people more than the elite in New York. I remember the Jets had a lot of guys from Texas on our team and the Mets had Texans, too. That made me feel good."

Even Ron Santo got caught up in the Met victory. I asked him if he watched the World Series in 1969. "Believe it or not, Glenn Beckert and I took our wives to Las Vegas to the old Flamingo Hotel. We're sitting at a blackjack table and this big curtain opens and it's the World Series. It was the last thing we wanted to watch. Everybody in Vegas was pulling for the Mets. When you lost the first game, I remember Frank Robinson getting interviewed. He said, 'How did the Mets ever get here?' And, I looked at Beckert and we both said, 'He shouldn't have said that.'"

Ferguson Jenkins also followed the World Series in 1969. "I watched all of the games and quite honestly thought the Mets had the best pitching," said Fergie, who should certainly know. "Also, I always thought with Tommie Agee, Cleon Jones, and guys like you and others, that if you scored some runs you could win it all. You guys had timely hitting, great defense, plus that great pitching. That's how you win, particularly in a short series."

Back in our clubhouse the party was still going on. There was a rumor going around that Donn Clendenon had been selected as the World Series MVP. Donn did indeed have a terrific series. Pearl Bailey, who had been a Mets fan for a long time and a very good friend of Mrs. Payson, came in. She sang the National Anthem before the game and also had some conversation with Jerry Koosman. "I was out in the bullpen waiting to warm up for the fifth game of the World Series," said Koos. "And Pearl was getting ready to march out onto the field with the color guard for the National Anthem. She said to me, 'Koos, just relax, you're going to win the game. I see the number eight, but I don't know what it means, but just know you're going to win.' We won the game 5–3 to win the World Series."

When Ms. Bailey came into the clubhouse after the game, the first person she looked for was Koosman. When she found him she planted a big kiss on him. Some of us thought it looked pretty passionate. Koosman had this to say, "When I saw her, I said you were right and then gave her a big kiss. The passionate part has been blown way out of proportion."

Joan Hodges remembered a conversation with Gil. "After we won the World Series, I went in to Gil's office and kissed him and congratulated him. His first words to me were, 'I was able to bring a championship back to the greatest fans in the world.' When he first took the job to manage the Mets he was apprehensive about it because he didn't know if he could give the fans back what they had given him for so many years." Mrs. Hodges added, "Gil was extremely proud of everyone on the team. We used to have discussions about all the different characters. He did realize that everyone had their own personality, but he also wanted all the players to understand that when they put that uniform on and walked out on to the field, they were under his charge and he expected certain things from them. The trade-off was that he cared for all of them."

After the clubhouse party I went out to dinner with my family and some friends. The city was in an unbelievably festive mood. There was confetti all over the streets. People were dancing on the sidewalks. It was like New Year's Eve except the celebration started early in the afternoon. Car horns blasted all evening. Every bar and restaurant had a victory celebration. The restaurant we went to was abuzz when I walked into the place. I'm sure that's how it was for every member of the team when they went out that night.

So many things were about to happen for all of us. It started when the whole team appeared on the Ed Sullivan Show the next Sunday. The following day, Monday, was declared "Mets Day" in New York City. Part of the day would be a parade up Broadway in lower Manhattan. It would turn out to be the biggest parade in New York City history.

The Sanitation Department was already cringing at the thought of the post-parade clean up. They had a taste of Met hysteria on the previous Thursday when fans celebrated in the streets right after the last game of the World Series. The motorcade was scheduled to start from Battery Park at the lower tip of Manhattan, then to proceed all the way up Broadway to Bryant Park behind the main library at 42nd Street. It turned out to be the most incredible ride anyone would ever want to take. Banners were everywhere and tons of confetti showered from office windows. Tens of thousands lined the streets to pay tribute to their heroes. And it wasn't just the main guys on the team. The people were paying tribute to our manager and every player and coach who was part of the most incredible sports turnaround ever. Yes, the Jets had done something no one thought they could do. But they were never considered "lovable losers" like the Mets. An experience like the parade lasts a lifetime. The city belonged to us. All the problems on the outside, and there were many, were forgotten for a while. Yes, we made people believe again.

At Bryant Park there was another ceremony with more speeches and more adulation. "Parades are tremendous for civic pride," said former New York City mayor Rudy Giuliani. "They give the city a focal point, a thing to rally around and a thing to celebrate that says, 'New York.' They give people a sense of hope. When people see the unexpected happening in sports they think, 'Well, maybe it can happen to me too if a team like the Mets can win.'"

Soon after, Donn Clendenon received a 1970 Dodge Challenger for being named MVP of the World Series and Little Al Weis got a new car, too. "I was given a car as a gift by Volkswagen. My nickname was 'Mighty Might,' and Volkswagen also had a car called 'Mighty Might.' They felt that I should have something because of what I did in the World Series."

All sorts of things were starting to happen. Seven of us went to Las Vegas to appear in a show: Seaver, Koosman, Clendenon, Jones, Agee, Kranepool, and myself. We did two shows a night, dinner and midnight. We were on stage with comedian Phil Foster. After a few jokes and funny lines we sang "Impossible Dream," and we sang it badly. They had to put professional singers behind the curtain to make us sound better. We rehearsed for three days before we started the two-week engagement. We each made $10,000 for the two weeks, about half of our average baseball earnings. Imagine being in Las Vegas, at Caesar's Palace, and our names in headlines and on the big billboard out front for seventeen days. We were on top of the world. I still kid Clendenon about him being paged all the time in the hotel. I always thought he was paging himself just to hear his name. I asked Cleon why he couldn't learn the words to "Impossible Dream" after two weeks, and he said, "I learned the song. I just couldn't sing."

On his time in Las Vegas, Jerry Koosman said, "It was a blast. The only problem was I was out of my realm in Las Vegas. But, we were stars wherever we went out there." When I asked Jerry about all the pages for Clendenon he said, "I heard your name a lot, too."

Kenny Boswell, Wayne Garrett, and Rod Gaspar appeared on *The Dating Game* television show. When the girl picked Gaspar and came around the screen to meet him, she must have been in shock and wanted to have another pick. On the other hand, think of how Boswell and Garrett must have felt losing out to P.P. Rod and his "date" won a trip to Europe. "She happened to pick me and I had nothing better to do so we went to Switzerland," said Rod. "She was cute, but nothing happened. We had three rooms, but the chaperone moved in with the girl to protect her. I guess they didn't want any hanky-panky. That kind of ticked me off."

On October 29, 1969, Tom Seaver was given the Cy Young Award for the National League. A month or so later, he would be edged out for National League MVP by Willie McCovey of the San Francisco Giants.

Sometime during the winter it was announced that a full share coming to the Mets for winning the World Series were a little over $18,000 per man. It was more than some of us made the whole season. The following season, at the first home game, the players would receive world championship rings.

That winter would be non-stop action for those of us who stayed in the New York area: appearances, speaking engagements, banquets. New York was more in love with the Mets than ever before.

Many players, fans, writers, and others reflected on that miracle year. "Your team unified the city," remarked Maury Allen. "Everyone became a baseball fan. Everyone got caught up. Plus, your victory ended the drought of missing the Dodgers and Giants. People could finally stand up and say, 'I'm a Mets fan,' and say it with a lot of joy and a lot of pride."

"I grew up in New York and the Mets were my team," said Spike Lee. "Cleon Jones was my favorite. In 1969, I ran on the field three times. And I had the turf for two or three years and then my mother made me throw it out."

"I had a chance to see the Mets when they first came into the league, and they really struggled," said Ernie Banks. "Then they finally put it all together. I knew they were going to be a good team because of their pitching. They were the 'Amazin' Mets.'"

"It was great for the city and great for the fans," said Yogi. "I would like to have another one!"

Joe Namath told me, "I followed the Mets in '69. You were earning respect. Like us, it was heart and persistence, the desire and courage to keep going."

"I know the fans were in love with us," Ken Boswell confided to me. "Not much in my life was more special than being on that team. Great memories, great friends, and great times in the city. By the way don't you owe me money for some room service charges that year?"

"For me it was everything grand," Al Weis said. "I was originally born and raised in New York. Playing in the World Series, and playing exceptionally well, was definitely gratifying. All my relatives were at the games so that was special. Everything that transpired after the World Series was great. Those are memories I will never forget."

"It was the most satisfying year of my career," said Don Cardwell. "Everybody contributed, and being a pitcher on that staff was terrific. I think it made all of us better. I live in Clemens, North Carolina, and people still talk to me about the 1969 Mets, about my feelings, and how I felt playing in the World Series. And everyone wants to see my championship ring."

"Our accomplishment was special, something that doesn't happen every day," said Ed Charles. "It was like we had an angel from heaven looking over us that year. We transcended victory for the underdog and belief in any possibility. We came from nowhere to be on top of the baseball world. When something like that happens it's once in a lifetime. People will always connect with that accomplishment. But, the good thing to remember is it wasn't just for us, it was for the people of New York."

Diane Gagliostro, a die-hard Met fan, remembers vividly, "I was born and still live in Flushing, which is the home of the 'Magical Mets' and Shea Stadium. I have been a Met fan all of my life. In 1969 I was eleven years old and can remember screaming and jumping for joy. The memory of that year and the feeling of victory when we won the World Series is something I will never forget. It was indeed a magical time. The memory will stay with me forever. Let's Go Mets!"

Mary O'Brien, another Met fan who started her love for the team back in 1969, recalled, "I was in seventh grade at Mary Queen of Heaven School in Brooklyn. The Dominican nuns we had were major Met fans.

The last game of the World Series we were in the hallway of the third floor of the school, and Sister Madeline and Sister Maureen set up a TV for all the seventh graders. Classes were postponed for the afternoon so we could watch the game. My mom, also a major Met fan, would watch or listen to all of the games. One of the best memories I have is coming home from school and she would be in the basement ironing and listening to the game. Without fail, every time I would come in, Cleon Jones would be up at bat and always end up with a hit."

Former governor Mario Cuomo said, "The Mets were a bunch of really good players who were not perceived as great. They weren't a dynasty by any means. They were underdogs who were winning. And when they won, all those immigrants and sons and daughters of immigrants, and the poor people following the team won, because you were the underdog."

Donn Clendenon put it simply: "So many crowds, so many memories. Great for New York. It's never out of my mind."

Pete Flynn reminisced, "It was unbelievable. The Mets winning the World Series is the greatest thing I have ever seen in my lifetime of sports. It was great for everybody in New York. The players still remember and come by to see me."

"Winning the World Series really affected my life," said Wayne Garrett. "You know you have accomplished what you dreamt of as a kid. No one can ever take that away from you. It wouldn't have mattered if I never played another game in the big leagues."

"It was a dream year," said Rod Gaspar. "It was an incredibly fun year. Just a wonderful time. I think about all the great guys we had on the team. We're still as close now as in 1969."

"I remember losing the first game of the year in 1969 to Montreal which was an expansion team that year," said Jerry Grote. One important thing I remember is that Gil Hodges and Rube Walker had enough confidence in me that they never told me what to call and never signaled to me for a pitchout. That was great! I also think about how Rube really put that pitching staff together. He nourished it."

"It was something you cannot put into words," Joan Hodges said. "I was a big baseball fan to begin with, but when your husband and his team are going through all that, it is very exciting."

"My first thought is that we all come from a world in which playing and winning a World Series was always going to happen to someone else," said Tom Seaver. There is a real explosion in your mind when all of a sudden it is happening to you, and you can be a world champion. This was something that was always a dream for all of us; from the time we were playing youth baseball. And, all of a sudden it is right there in front of us." Tom added, "To me one of the most important things about that team was every time a player went to the plate or fielded a ball it was important because we could win. Every aspect of the game, every individual play, was important. Every game seemed close and every at bat was important. Every pitch was important. That was the gist of that team. Everybody contributed. We were the personification of the impossible underdog that wins. It was the impossible dream in New York, in the middle of the war, with a franchise that was not supposed to win. What's better than that?"

"I will never forget the ticker tape parade after we won," Ron Swoboda said. "Every face that watched us had a smile on it. We reached so many people in such a wonderful way back then. That is the most gratifying thing. People still tell me how priceless that time was to them and what we meant to them."

"It was a great year for us and Met fans," said Cleon Jones. "The thing that really stands out in my mind is that there were a lot of things going on in outside the world. We were able to bring the city together."

"We caught the world by surprise," remarked Ed Kranepool. "We were the underdog, the guy in the street who had been struggling all year and having problems. That was a rallying cry behind everybody. Everyone was a Mets fan, even Yankee fans in October of 1969. We were the down and dirty guy, the hard luck guy for all those years. We were 'Basement Bertha.' We attracted the world. We were everyone's idea of going from rags to riches. We went from the outhouse to the penthouse."

"It made my life complete," commented J. C. Martin. "It was the ultimate goal as a baseball player to play on that Cinderella team and win the World Series. I'm living in Advance, North Carolina, where most of these people are Atlanta Braves fans. But they know about the 1969 Mets and want me to talk about it all the time. They love to look at my championship ring. That's as good as it gets."

Ron Taylor recalled, "They called us the Miracle Mets, but I really didn't like that term because I thought we had a very good ball club. The fact that we were so much a part of New York City that year was amazing. There were so many people who were into our team that they couldn't bear to miss a pitch. And, you know what? It was proven that crime was down in New York City when the playoffs and World Series were being played."

Not all the memories were good. Jim Palmer said, "In retrospect, if we would have won the 1969 World Series, we would have been considered one of the great teams in baseball history. As it turned out, when we had the great teams of '69, '70, and '71, we only won one World Series. And that's the way we have been judged." Jim also remembered, "We were at a sports dinner in Pennsylvania one night over the winter of 1969 and also invited was Shag Crawford, the umpire who was behind the plate when Weaver was thrown out of the game in the World Series and involved in the J. C. Martin baserunning play. Eddie Watt, the relief pitcher, was with me. They made an announcement that Shag Crawford couldn't make the dinner because of a death in his family. So, Eddie Watt got up to speak and said, 'We are really sorry we couldn't see Shag Crawford tonight. Apparently, a death in the family means one of the Mets died.'"

Palmer finished off his conversation with me by relating, "I remember Tom Seaver a few years ago telling me, 'Jim, it's been a long time. You've got to get over it.' Last year I came to New York by train for a dinner. When I arrived at Penn Station there was a big picture of the 1969 Mets. Then, I went to lunch and I ran into Tug McGraw. And, on top of that, my coat check number was 41 (Seaver's number). I just can't get away from reminders of 1969."

"It was a team where everyone contributed," recalled Bobby Pfeil about the 1969 club. "Gil Hodges has to get a lot of credit for that because he made everybody feel like they belonged. Everybody played, even if you were a fringe player like myself. I got a chance to play a couple times a week and got some at bats. That is the definition of a good team. My World Series ring always reminds me of my perseverance and how, if you are honest and work hard, things will go your way."

"We shared the stadium and we had a lot of friends on that Met team. Those will always be special times for all of us," said Gerry Philbin.

Kerry Schacht was a sergeant in the United States Army in 1969. "1969 was not one of my better years in life. I was serving with the 101st Airborne Division in Vietnam and I was happy when the Jets won the Super Bowl but I kept thinking about where I was at the time. When the Mets got into the playoffs and made it to the World Series my first reaction was being upset that I wouldn't be able to go to any games. The day before the first game of the World Series I got orders to go out on patrol. Ten days later when I got back I went to the USO in Saigon and saw films of the Met victory. I was so excited and I thought about my friends who I imagined were having the times of their lives celebrating. I have to say

God works in a funny way. I've been home from Vietnam for many years now, but when I think of the 1969 Mets it still brings a smile to my face. Their win put reassurance back in my life that things happen for a reason and now when I go to a ball game I appreciate it more than I did. I have come to realize that if you give it your best you'll obtain positive results. The 1969 Mets did just that for me."

"I was twelve years old and a big Met fan," said TV star Ray Romano. Back in 1969, I got wrapped up like everybody with what was happening to the Mets. I got hooked on their magic. I was on the field after you won the division. I took some grass and the next day I went to school and showed the grass in my class." Ray also talked about his TV show, *Everybody Loves Raymond*, when I and a few of the '69 Mets made guest appearances. "We had an episode where my brother has the dog named "Shamsky" and we come up with this idea of visiting the '69 Mets at the Hall of Fame. How can it get better than to meet the '69 Mets on my TV show?" Ray finished by saying, "The 1969 Mets were a classic underdog story. It was a tremendous bonding between the players and the city that made it special."

With all the fans like Spike Lee and Ray Romano snatching a piece of turf as a souvenir, it was a tough but enjoyable job for the groundskeepers to keep up the field after the Jets' championship game and the Mets' division, pennant, and world championship celebrations. Pete Flynn recently voiced a final and quite understandable thought, "I'm just glad the 1969–70 Knicks didn't play at Shea."

Phil Rosenthal, the creator and executive producer of *Everybody Loves Raymond* was another big 1969 Met fan. "If you lived in New York City like I did, that's all anybody talked about. The 1969 Mets were everything to all my friends and me. We lived, breathed, and ate the Mets. From the Mets, I developed a kind of hope and possibility in underdogs. We all looked to the Mets as a positive example of how it can be done." When I asked Phil why he picked my name for the dog in the show he said, "Ray portrays a sportswriter and your name came to mind because you were one of my favorite '69 Mets. Forgive me, but Shamsky sounds like a good name for a dog." And Phil added one more thought. "You guys did something so wonderful. You were the ultimate underdog team. You touched a lot of people. Rarely has there been anything like that. Art, you're fortunate, you got to live it."

Drew and Tracy Nieporent, famous New York City restaurateurs, recalled their feeling at the end of the first game of the series. "Well, Shamsky screwed up in the ninth inning and we thought the bubble might have burst. But, when the Mets won the next game we were happy because we thought they could play with the Orioles." Their elation after the series was shared by many. "It was unbelievable. The clubhouse celebration is a classic. When the Mets won, it was one of the greatest moments in sports history. The whole country, except for Baltimore, was for the Mets. It was unbelievable."

Mary Dattner, who today works at Credit Suisse/First Boston, has been a die-hard Met fan since the age of eleven. She was a thirteen-year-old high school freshman when the Mets won the World Series in 1969. She has vivid recollections of that time. "I remember being in school and all the kids and the teachers had radios throughout the series. We would listen to the game in and outside of school. It was so great to root for the underdogs. My favorite Met player of all time was Cleon Jones. I just loved him; he was the best player ever. I remember thinking that he should have been named the MVP of the World Series, but indeed it was Donn Clendenon who, well let's just say did have a great series. But to this day I am the biggest Met fan ever. To be a Mets fan back then in 1969 was just so great! I can't describe it. I still have that same thrill when I think about it. I was also a big Joe Namath fan then as well, and what a year it was to be a Mets fan as well as a Jets fan. Just great!"

"It was my freshman year at college in Houston and I actually sold beer in the Astrodome," remembered actor Robert Wuhl. "That year I really got into baseball. You never thought the Mets could beat Baltimore because they had such a good team. When the Mets lost the first game of the series I thought maybe their bubble is bursting. But, I was wrong. Everything went right for the Mets. That team and that World Series will never be forgotten."

Never forgotten is exactly right. Amazing, unbelievable, incredible, memorable, and remarkable are just a few of the words to describe the 1969 Mets. History will show that a team that was a 100-1 long shot at the beginning of the season became the toast of the sports world seven months later. But history will also show that the 1969 Mets were not just a World Series winner, but also, more important, a team that belonged to a city and its people. I have always said that the 1969 New York Mets probably weren't the greatest baseball team to win a World Series, but they certainly were one of the most memorable.

All of our fans embraced the team back then and still do. To this day the team is as popular as ever. Along with the New York Jets in 1969, the

1969 Mets turned New York City around. These two teams uplifted the city from the depths of despair. But the two teams were only two thirds of *The Magnificent Seasons*. There was another New York City team starting its quest for a championship. It wasn't going to be easy following the first two, but this team had the right mix of players and a coach to handle that kind of pressure. When the Mets' world championship season was officially over on October 16, 1969, the New York Knicks had completed the first two games of their regular season and won them both. The magnificent seasons were about to continue.

POLITICS AND SPORTS: THE METS MAKE A MAYOR

On the first Tuesday in November, Mayor John Lindsay was re-elected as mayor of New York City. That win could certainly be characterized as a monumental turnaround for someone who had lost the primary two months earlier. David Garth described John Lindsay's political situation early in 1969 when the Mets went to spring training: "As always, John was fighting for survival. We never had an easy time in the years he was mayor. But, after the Jet win, John became a little bit of a symbol of the city getting off the mat. Even though he was not a sports fan and didn't really know the rules in any sports, including tennis which he played badly, he figured out to start playing off the success of the city's sports teams."

All those strikes were particularly difficult for the mayor's image with the people. Garth explained, "The unions tried to pick up the momentum they had lost over the years. Political activists took the lead in the strikes. That's when I developed the now famous slogan for the mayor's campaign, 'It's the second hardest job in America.'"

"With the Mets, he happened to be in the right place at the right time," added Garth. "That picture of him getting doused with champagne after your victory was priceless. I don't think he would have won reelection if he did not have the Met victory in the World Series. We put out some ads that said, 'If the Mets can do it, New York City can do it.' We played off the Mets' victory to help Lindsay. Along with the Jets' victory, it could be the greatest emotional moment in New York City history."

"The Mets' win was an enormous help to a beleaguered mayor," said Jeff Greenfield. "All of us on Lindsay's staff understood the Mets were a big deal for the city, a really big deal because it was, in many ways, a really tough time. I joined John Lindsay's staff the day the teachers' strike began in September 1968. One of the things to remember is that in addition to the country having gone through all the turmoil since the beginning of 1968, tensions in New York City were constantly at a high point."

"I think it probably helped the Mayor," said David Halberstam. "The Mets' victory stayed with people longer. It was such a complete surprise."

"I don't think there was any doubt about us helping him," said Tom Seaver. "Coming in the clubhouse, being in the middle of the celebrations, getting doused with champagne, was the best thing in the world for him."

"I guess you could say that I was part of Lindsay's election team," recalled Rod Gaspar. "That picture of me dousing him with champagne must have got him a lot of votes. We got him reelected."

"Sure," said Robert Lipsyte regarding John Lindsay. "He walked into the clubhouse and it looked like he was one of the players. It turned out to be great timing for him."

PART IV

THE KNICKS

13. The New York Knickerbockers

"My years with the Knicks were not the most appealing years for the fans."
—Richie Guerin

The oldest franchise of the three champions in the magnificent seasons is the New York Knickerbockers, who came into existence on June 6, 1946. A group of businessmen decided to form a professional basketball league and named it the Basketball Association of America. Eventually, the league evolved into what is now known as the National Basketball Association.

The Knicks were one of eleven franchises split into two divisions. The Eastern Division teams were made up of the New York Knicks, Boston Celtics, Philadelphia Warriors, Providence Steamrollers, Washington Capitols, and Toronto Huskies. The Western Division included the Pittsburgh Ironmen, Chicago Stags, Detroit Falcons, St. Louis Bombers, and Cleveland Rebels.

Ned Irish, a former sportswriter, was hired as team president, and his relationship with Madison Square Garden and the Knicks would last over forty years, and include the two Knick championship years of 1969–70 and 1972–73. Irish could be classified as somewhat of an innovator as he built up interest in college basketball as well as professional. Sam Goldaper, a former sportswriter for the *New York Times* recalled, "There was a rumor that Irish was covering a college basketball game between Manhattan and City College and had to climb through a window in the tiny Manhattan gym to see the game. He ripped his pants and decided he wanted to bring college basketball to bigger arenas. That's when he decided to go to work for Madison Square Garden."

When Irish needed a nickname for his new team in the Basketball Association of America the word "Knickerbockers" became an easy choice. It referred to the first Dutch settlers who founded New Amsterdam, which later became New York. Knickerbockers were a style of pants worn by the early settlers that were rolled up to below the knee and the word Knickerbocker became sort of an informal name for a person living in the city.

The colors the new professional basketball team chose were the official colors of New York City, orange, blue, and white. The first logo showed the figure of Father Knickerbocker, a caricature of a man wearing a wig, tricorne hat, knicker pants, and buckled shoes dribbling a basketball. That logo remained until the 1965–66 season when the Knicks changed to a basketball logo with the blocked letters of KNICKS above the ball. That logo stayed through the 1991–92 season, when the current design was created.

In 1946, the Basketball Association of America had their inaugural season. The Knicks played most of their home games at the 69th Street Armory because Madison Square Garden had too many other events. The Madison Square Garden the early Knicks called home was actually Madison Square Garden III. Located at 49th Street and Eighth Avenue, and known as the "Old Garden," it was built in 1925. The very first Garden was actually built on 26th Street and Madison Avenue in 1874. Garden II was constructed on the same site of Garden I in 1890. This Garden closed in May of 1925 and so the "Old Garden," Garden III, was born. The Old Garden became world renowned for major events including circuses, rodeos, political conventions, and sporting events.

The Knicks played their first game at the "Old Garden" on November 11, 1946. It remained their home for twenty-two years. They played their last game in that arena on February 10, 1968.

On November 1, 1946, the Knicks opened their first season with a game in Toronto. Although they lost their first game, they won ten out of their first twelve games. The coach that first year was Neil Cohalan, a former Manhattan College coach. Players on that team included Ossie Schectman, Leo Gottlieb, Stan Stutz, Jake Weber, and Ralph Kaplowitz. The team finished that first season with a record of 33–27.

The following season Joe Lapchick replaced Neil Cohalan as coach. Lapchick was able to lead the Knicks to eight consecutive playoff appearances. Before the 1949–50 season, the Basketball Association of America merged with the National Basketball League, forming the National Basketball Association. The NBA took six teams from the National Basketball League and the eleven from the Basketball Association of America and formed three divisions. The Knicks remained in the Eastern Division.

In the 1950–51 season, the Knicks decided to break the color barrier in professional basketball and became one of the first teams to have an African-American player, "Sweetwater" Clifton. Their record during that season was a respectable 36–30. In the playoffs they beat Boston and Syracuse and met Rochester in the best of seven for the championship. It was an exciting series as Rochester won the first three games and the Knicks came back to win the next three. In the final Rochester won 79–75 in a game that was close all the way to the end.

Carl Braun was the Knicks' best player but because of military duty missed the 1950–51 season. Braun, who was out of Princeton, averaged 13.5 points per game over thirteen seasons. When he retired he held the record for most points scored as a Knick with 10,449. That record would last until the era of Willis Reed, Walt Frazier, and later Patrick Ewing.

The Knicks didn't have a shortage of stars at this time. Along with Braun, Harry "The Horse" Gallatin and Dick McGuire became Knick stars. Gallatin was a terrific rebounder and once played in 610 consecutive games, a club record. "I limped through a lot of games. I just loved to play," Gallatin told me in an interview. During the 1953–54 season, Gallatin led the NBA in rebounding, averaging 15.3 rebounds a game. In one game against the Fort Wayne Pistons that season he pulled down 33 rebounds, setting a franchise record later tied by Willis Reed in 1971. "We didn't have tall teams back then," recalled Gallatin. "That's why they drafted me. I was six foot six inches. The game I got thirty-three rebounds turned out to be a game when everything went right for me. As far as my nickname, "The Horse," Gallatin said, "shyness was not a feature of mine. I liked to mix it up a little bit."

Dick McGuire, who played eight seasons with the Knicks, from 1949 through 1957, was a terrific guard, leading the team in assists for six of those years. After his playing and coaching days, McGuire remained with the Knicks as a scout and later director of scouting services. Both he and Harry Gallatin are enshrined in the Basketball Hall of Fame.

The Knicks lost to Rochester in the NBA finals in the 1950–51 season, but returned to the championship series the next season against the Minneapolis Lakers. Like the season before, the finals went seven games. Again, the Knicks lost as the Lakers won the NBA championship.

The next season, 1952–53, the Knicks once again made it to the NBA finals. But, again, the results were the same. The Lakers, behind the legendary George Mikan, won the championship in five games.

Before the start of the 1954–55 NBA season the owners decided to install a 24-second shot clock to speed up the games. In the past, teams had been just holding on to the ball, especially if they were undersized compared to their opponents. It was also boring basketball to watch and as a result attendance was showing a decline.

The rest of the fifties saw the Knicks play mediocre and sometimes respectable, but not championship caliber basketball. From the 1959–60 season through the 1965–66 season, the team failed to make the playoffs. Of course, this led to frequent head coaching changes made by management. Coaches for the Knicks in that period included Vince Boryla, Fuzzy Levane, Carl Braun, Eddie Donovan, and Dick McGuire. All these coaching changes contributed to the Knicks putting together only one winning season from 1955–56 through 1967–68. Perhaps the Knick teams of the early to mid-sixties were taking some cues from the Mets at the time.

One of the bright spots of the team during that period was the play of Richie Guerin. Guerin, who came out of Iona College, turned into a great pro player. A perennial All-Star in his eight-year career with the Knicks, Guerin scored 10,392 points and averaged 20.1 points per game. Those totals put him in the team's all-time top five in both categories. In 1959 Guerin became the first Knick to score fifty points in a game when he put in 57 points against Syracuse. Not only was he a top scorer, he was known as a good passer as well. On December 12, 1958, he passed out 21 assists against the St. Louis Hawks, a franchise record. "My years with the Knicks were not the most appealing years for the fans," said Guerin. "When I was there we only made the playoffs one year. For me personally, it was very frustrating. Coaching changes and a lot of different players made the situation difficult."

Dick McGuire, later Knicks coach and now a scout with the team, described the early years with the Knicks. "I just enjoyed playing. The fans were into professional basketball, but we didn't have great teams. Asked why the team had so much difficulty till the late sixties he said, "It was mainly because we didn't get lucky in the draft."

The problem wasn't the Knicks scoring points; it was their opponents scoring more. Defense never seemed to be their strong suit. For example, in the 1959–60 season the Knicks averaged 117.3 points per game. However, their opponents averaged 119.6 points. A pretty good reason they finished with a record of 27–48 for that season.

While the Knicks were still playing at the "Old Garden," plans for a new Madison Square Garden, Garden IV, to be built above Pennsylvania Station, at 33rd Street between Seventh and Eighth Avenues, were announced in November of 1960. Actual groundbreaking took place in October of 1963 and the new arena officially opened on February 11, 1968.

While a new Garden was in the planning stages this period produced mediocre Knick seasons, the worst being 1960–61. That year the team only won twenty-one games. And, defense was still a major problem. On November 15, 1960, the Lakers' Elgin Baylor scored 71 points against them. And, on Christmas Day the same year, the Knicks were a terrific "present" for Syracuse when they suffered their worst beating in franchise history, 162–100.

The following season, 1961–62, the team didn't fare much better. Although their record improved, they still only won twenty-nine games. Richie Guerin, however, averaged over 29 points a game. That mark would remain number one for twenty-three years until a great scorer by the name of Bernard King broke it in 1984–85. Guerin's 2,303 total points for the year set a franchise record that lasted thirty years until Patrick Ewing surpassed it in 1989–90.

That same 1961–62 season saw another game and record the Knicks aren't very proud of. On March 2, 1962, they played the Philadelphia Warriors in Hershey, Pennsylvania. Not only did the Knicks get humiliated in the game by a score of 169–147, but the Warriors' Wilt Chamberlain scored 100 points, the best single-game scoring performance in NBA history. The Knicks did have three players score over 30 points each that game, but it didn't matter. It was another embarrassing mark for the team.

I recently asked Guerin what he remembers about New York City basketball fans during this period. "The fans back then knew the game of basketball as good, if not better, than now. New York City college basketball in those times was terrific. There was great exposure for basketball in the city. On Tuesday nights there was an NBA doubleheader so the fans got to see four NBA teams."

If the fans came out to see the Knicks in 1962–63 and 1963–64 they had to be disappointed because those were two more bad years. In 1962–63 the Knicks only won twenty-one games while losing fifty-nine, and in the 1963–64 season they only improved by one game. While these two years were truly bad seasons, things started to change for the better when the Knicks drafted Willis Reed out of Grambling for the 1964–65 season.

Reed showed his value immediately. In his rookie year, Willis ranked seventh in the NBA scoring with an average of 19.5 points per game and fifth in rebounding with an average of 14.7 a game. The Knicks also showed some other young players on the rise as Jim Barnes and Howard Komives, along with Reed, were selected to the NBA All-Rookie team. The season also saw Reed as the first New York Knick named NBA Rookie of the Year. The Knicks still only won thirty-one games that season and lost forty-nine, but a glimmer of hope began to shine for the future.

In 1965, Eddie Donovan was appointed general manager of the team. The Knicks' chief scout Red Holzman, who had been with the organization since 1959, was his assistant and Dick McGuire was the coach. The glimmer of hope became short-lived as the 1965–66 season turned to a huge disappointment when the team finished with a record of 30–50. The Knicks, however, did make a trade with Los Angeles for a player who would not only help them right away, but in the future. Dick Barnett, a good shooting guard and accomplished defensive player would make his mark on the championship team.

In the 1966–67 season the Knicks improved to 36–45 and finally made the playoffs for the first time since 1959. However, they lost to the Boston Celtics in the division semifinal. One bright spot again was Willis Reed, who won honors by being selected on the All-NBA second team.

Midway through the 1967–68 season, Red Holzman replaced McGuire as coach. At the time of the change the Knicks had a losing record of 15–22. After Holzman took over, the team immediately began playing better. Under Red, the team finished the rest of the season 28–17 and ended up with a record of 43–39, their first winning season since 1958–59. The Knicks also developed a core of fine young players that included Walt Frazier and Phil Jackson. Both Willis Reed and Dick Barnett played in the league's All-Star game that season and Frazier and Jackson received honors on the NBA All-Rookie Team. Also, the Knicks were able to play at the "new" Garden above Penn Station after February 11, 1968.

Entering the 1968–69 season Red Holzman and the Knicks' front office realized a few moves here and there would move them into contention for the playoffs. The season did turn out to be successful as they won fifty-four games and finished in third place in the Eastern Division behind the Philadelphia 76ers and the Baltimore Bullets. However, their fortunes really started to change on December 19, 1968 during the season. That's the day the Knicks made a trade that changed their future. They traded Walt Bellamy and Howard Komives to the Detroit Pistons for forward Dave DeBusschere. DeBusschere, who had also pitched in the major leagues for the Chicago White Sox, was an important ingredient the Knicks needed. He was a hard-nosed, tough competitor who came to play every game. The Knicks put together separate winning streaks of ten and eleven games after the DeBusschere trade.

As a result of their new look and winning ways, the Knicks began to gather fan support. The team had fourteen sellouts at home during the season at the Garden in 1968–69. The Knicks' style of play and the make-up of the team was bringing on high expectations from the fans. After Holzman became coach the Knicks developed a special affinity for defense. Red made it clear that all his players had to play defense and it showed in the win-loss results. In the 1968–69 season, the Knicks allowed a league low 105.2 points per game. Defense now became their trademark. Willis Reed set a franchise record of 1,191 rebounds, averaging 14.5 per game. On offense, the team had a core of dependable scorers and Walt Frazier ended up third in the NBA behind Oscar Robertson and Lenny Wilkens in assists with 7.9 per game. In the playoffs, the Knicks swept a powerful Baltimore Bullets team, but lost to the Boston Celtics in six games in the division finals. The stage was set for the 1969–70 season.

14. The Sweet Season

"Defense was our team's key."
—Cazzie Russell

T he previous season became the spark that ignited the New York Knicks and their fans for the 1969–70 season. The Knicks knew they could compete with any team in their division. Beating a very good Bullets team in the playoffs reinforced their confidence. "The success we accomplished in 1969–70 didn't start in 1969," said Willis Reed. "It started in at the beginning of the 1968–69 season and continued until we finished that season in Boston. Clyde Frazier pulled a groin muscle and we got beat in that last series. When that series was over everyone in the locker room felt like next year could be a special year for us. We came into practice the next season in great shape and ready to go. I was not surprised by our fast start."

To say the New York Knicks got off to a fast start in the 1969–70 season would be a gross understatement. With the World Series still being played in October, the Knicks won their first two games of the season. Perhaps they were taking a cue from the Mets. The team won their first five games of the season before losing in San Francisco on October 23rd.

Back in New York, basketball fans awakened to the talent-laden Knicks. The team did indeed possess outstanding players. The starting five included Willis Reed at center, Dave DeBusschere and Bill Bradley at forward, and Walt Frazier and Dick Barnett at guard. It was a perfect blend of scoring, defense, and smarts. Coming off the bench the Knicks lost very little with players like Cazzie Russell, Nate Bowman, Bill Hosket, Don May, Mike Riordan, Dave Stallworth, and Johnny Warren, the only rookie on the club. Phil Jackson spent the whole season on the disabled list and did not play, but kept busy with other pursuits with the team. Cazzie Russell would eventually call the Knick subs "The Minutemen" to give them their own identity.

The Knicks loss in San Francisco turned out to be just a small blip. From October 24th until November 29th, the Knicks never felt defeat. They won eighteen games in a row to bring their season's record to 23–1. It was truly an incredible start.

While the Knicks were in the middle of this remarkable run, things were not going so great outside. On November 13th and 15th between 250,000 and 500,000 protesters staged peaceful anti-war demonstrations in Washington, D.C. A week later, for the first time, the country was shown explicit photographs of dead villagers from the My Lai massacre. As if this wasn't enough, on November 10th, bombs exploded at the RCA Building, Chase Manhattan Bank, and the GM Building. These followed a string of bombings of government buildings stretching back to July.

While the world was in turmoil, the Knicks were developing into a terrific cohesive unit, and they gained insight on themselves as a team, their coach, and his philosophy about what it took to win.

I was fortunate to interview Dave DeBusschere before he passed away in March of 2002. Dave and I knew each other when we played baseball against each other in the minor leagues. He was a solid pitcher and tough competitor. On the mound he looked gigantic. When he let go of the ball it looked like he was stepping right on top of you. It wasn't easy for the opposition. Even though he was major league material, Dave's choice of professional basketball over baseball certainly paid off. In discussing the start for the Knicks in 1969–70 Dave said, "We knew we were a good team. You don't win that many games in a row in the NBA unless the team is good. The summer before gave us an opportunity to reflect on losing in the playoffs to Boston in the spring of 1969. During the early part of the season the team played incredibly well and we knew as a team what it took to be successful. We knew because Coach Holzman instilled in us the importance of teamwork and defense."

"The great start of the 1969–70 season gave proof we were good basketball players and a good team," related Willis Reed. "I always talk about the one major aspect of that team most people don't understand. When Red Holzman became coach he showed us a different perspective for the team than his predecessors. Red became involved in the drafting and the trading for every player on the Knicks. When he became coach he understood the personalities of the players and the qualities each brought to the table. He took that and utilized it to the maximum. He was liberal on what he would let us do on offense, but very demanding on how we played defense. When we went to practice he started us on defense and ended practice working on defense. He knew the team could play offensively. He used to say, 'I don't care what you run on offense, but the trade-off is you are going to do what I want you to do on defense.' When he called a time-out we talked about adjustments we needed to do on defense, and only as we were getting ready to walk back on the court he would say, 'What are you guys going to run on offense?'"

Cazzie Russell said, "Defense was our team's key. If you can sell that to your team and have your players take pride in their defense then you are a good coach. Coach Holzman did that."

"His timeouts started out always about defense," recalled Phil Jackson on Holzman's style of coaching. "When he was through talking about defense he would ask the players, 'What do you want to run? What do you think will work?'"

Walt "Clyde" Frazier was thankful for Holzman's mania for defense. "The reason I got a chance to play was my defensive prowess. When Red took over, team defense was the first thing he implemented. He emphasized picking up guys from baseline to baseline. Defense and team play were the two most important things. The greatness of Coach Holzman was that he got us to buy into that philosophy."

"Obviously, our team was good," said Bill Bradley, "but, more than that, Coach Holzman knew what he wanted. I think he was a very good leader of our team at that time. He made it clear what he wanted and insisted on that. Basically, he wanted you to help your teammate on defense and see the ball. On offense, he wanted you to hit the open man. He was amenable to guys coming to the bench and saying, 'Let's try this.' Defense was the key. On offense, sometimes we could do what we wanted, but it had to be in a team way. The team had twenty-five or thirty plays, and we suggested different ones. Coach Holzman would say, 'That sounds good.' He never said don't do that play. He gave us flexibility to do and call what we wanted, but freelancing is something we never did."

On a lighter note, Gail and Charlie Papelian, Red's daughter and son-in-law, recalled a time in the early sixties when Red was asked to coach a summer league team in Puerto Rico. "Red was asked by the owner of the Ponce team in Puerto Rico to come down and coach their team. The players and fans there wanted to know who this guy from New York was. The owners said, 'He was a great coach and a former great player, a prominent person from New York. You'll see.' The first game Red coached his team was blown out and the fans went wild. They threw things on the court and were very upset. The fans said he couldn't coach. The owner tried to calm the fans and asked why do you think he can't coach after one game? The fans all said Red couldn't coach because he didn't carry a clipboard in the huddle. It just goes back to the fact that Red always felt that his players were prepared enough and smart enough to play the game."

On November 29, 1969, with an eighteen-game winning streak and a season's record of 23–1, the Knicks lost to the Detroit Pistons at home in the Garden. At the time the eighteen-game winning streak was an NBA record, but since broken. However, the winning streak is still a Knicks' franchise record.

The next three games in the first week of December 1969 turned into victories for the team. On December 9th, their record was now 26–2. The Knicks lost their next game to Cincinnati and the next three out of four to bring their season's record to 27–6. "Those losses just made us work a harder," said Mike Riordan. The Knicks won the next six out of eight games and their season's record stood at an incredible 33–8 at the midway point.

It was obvious to many this Knick team was not only made up of exceptionally talented individuals, but even better team players. They were also men of individual capacity and style on and off the court.

"There were some characters on the team," said broadcaster Marv Albert. "Clyde, because of the way he dressed. Phil Jackson, Bradley, and Dick Barnett were the intellectuals, always debating something. Danny Whelan, the trainer, was a character. He and Red liked to smoke cigars. As far as Phil Jackson, I always thought he would end up being the art or movie critic for the *Village Voice*."

"I covered the team a lot that season," said *New York Times* sportswriter Ira Berkow. "They were a fun bunch. One time Cazzie Russell bought a new car. The team was playing in Philadelphia. Cazzie decided to drive his new car there to try it out and not go on the team bus. Holzman didn't like that. He had a rule that everyone traveled together. When Cazzie arrived in the locker room the team was already there. Red said to him, 'It's a hundred dollar fine if you don't travel with the team.' Cazzie said, 'I know, but I wanted to try out my new car.' Red then said, 'How much were the tolls on the way down?' Cazzie, thinking that Red was going to give him money for the tolls said, 'I think it came to about seven dollars.' Red said, 'Okay, the fine will only be ninety-three dollars. I'll take off the tolls.' "

"Dick Barnett had a unique perspective on life," said Mike Riordan. "He knew a lot about certain things and a little about a lot of things. You know he's Dr. Barnett now. I remember one time during that season one of the bench players needed some extra tickets and Red helped out the player. We were getting big crowds and famous people came to the games. It was starting to be important to be seen at our games. Right before the game a security guy came in to our locker room and said, 'Red, we've got a problem with those tickets you left in the Knicks' section. They're being scalped.' "

"I think Dick Barnett was a character," said Cazzie Russell. "He was always giving me a book to read. He would give me a book and say, 'This is for your perusal.' And our trainer, Danny Whelan, was also a character. Once when we were on a plane, and he was having breakfast, I saw him put a lot of Tabasco sauce on his eggs. I said, 'What are you doing? He said, 'Caz, don't knock it until you try it.' I've been using Tabasco sauce ever since."

Phil Jackson told me about his experiences with the trainer and coach, "Red and Danny Whelan got me into smoking cigars. Actually Danny taught me the technique of smoking cigars. He made me believe there was a finesse to it. When I was hurt and unable to play I used to be the last guy in the locker room and went out with Danny and Red to the court. Red would always remind Danny to have the bottle of Johnnie Walker Red available after the game."

When I asked about how he got his nickname "Clyde," Walt Frazier related, "I bought this hat in Baltimore. It was just before the movie *Bonnie and Clyde* came out. I wore it and guys made fun of me and I became self-conscious. It was a little ahead of its time. Later I wore it to a game and came into the locker room. Danny Whelan yelled out, 'Look at

Clyde,' and everyone laughed. It just stuck with me. I thought it was cool. It was a good moniker and my teammates like it."

"Yes, I gave Clyde his nickname," Danny Whelan told me a few weeks before he passed away. "I also gave him his other nickname, 'Don Juan.' " I asked Danny who his favorite player was. "When you're winning you like them all. When you're losing you'd like to put them in a room, throw in a match, and burn them all up. But I'll tell you, when Willis said something everyone listened," Danny said. I asked him if he was surprised at Phil Jackson's success as a coach. Danny replied, "Holy shit."

Even though Phil Jackson's belief in the Zen philosophy officially started in 1971, Phil said it began earlier. "I took religion as a major in college. I went back to college in the summer when I started playing professional basketball. I wasn't making a lot of money and began working for my master's degree in psychology. During that time I was looking for various forms of meditation and spiritual growth."

On trying to interview Red for television, Marv Albert said, "Red would always tell me to talk to the players. He wanted to deflect questions to them. Why not? He had a great group of players. When I finally did get him on television, he always asked me, 'How did I do?' I would rate him. It usually was around a four, maybe a six. A couple of times he got an eight and was pleased."

Gail Papelian, Red Holzman's daughter, recently remembered how her father would complain about frequently being stopped by security at Madison Square Garden. "He would tell us that sometimes he walked out of the locker room toward the court and security asked him for identification. He didn't complain. He just said, 'Maybe I don't look like a coach.' " Gail also recalled, "My dad always had the same disposition after the games. He was the same whether the team won or lost. Once in a while my mom would ask him something about the game on the drive home. I think he turned on his selective hearing at that point."

At the midpoint of the 1969–70 season two things were evident about the New York Knicks. First, the club had established themselves as one of the elite teams in the NBA. Second, Red Holzman was an exceptional leader with a talent for developing relationships with his players based on mutual respect and shared values.

"Red had a good relationship with all the players," said Dick Barnett. "He trusted the veterans on the team. He understood we knew the lay of the land."

"He was a prince," said Danny Whelan. "He was nervous all the time. The cigars relaxed him."

Willis Reed recalled, "In those days we didn't have a lot of people besides the players, a coach, and one trainer. I was captain and if Red heard of a problem with someone he asked me what was wrong. I would usually just reply, I don't know. Maybe, you better talk to him. I was sort of a conduit."

Richie Guerin, who coached the Atlanta Hawks in 1969–70, had this to say about Holzman. "Red was respectful to the players and gained respect by the way he treated them. He let them play and didn't over coach." Sportswriter Ira Berkow offered an example of how Red Holzman dealt with people. "In Madison Square Garden they had an executive dining room and Red invited me to come with him," recalled Berkow. "The waiter came over and said, 'Hello Coach. What will you have today?' Red said, 'Let me ask you something. Is your soup hot today?' How many times have you ever asked that at a restaurant? 'Of course, Coach,' said the waiter. Then Red said, 'Okay, I'll have a bowl of soup.' The soup came out piping hot. Apparently, the soup wasn't hot the last time. Red didn't want to offend the waiter, but he wanted to make it a positive. That's how he coached, in that indirect kind of way. That was Red Holzman. He was wonderful."

This kind of leadership combined with the players' skills, discipline, and unselfish behavior proved unbeatable. By mid-season, with their great start at the beginning of the campaign, the Knicks never lost command of first place in the Eastern Division. The Milwaukee Bucks, however, with a record of 27–14, were only six games behind in the standings. The Baltimore Bullets were in third place at the halfway mark with a record of 25–15.

The second half of the 1969–70 season started on a down note as the Knicks lost to the Boston Celtics, their archrivals, at home 111–104. New Yorkers weren't too happy about other events either. Subway and bus fares went from 20 to 30 cents, their single biggest hike in the city's history. The nation also received some more bad news; the death toll for Americans in Vietnam had reached 40,000.

Through all this disquieting news the Knicks kept their focus. They went on the road and won the next six of eight games to bring their season's record to 39–11.

On January 24, 1970, the Knicks came back home to beat San Diego at the Garden. That game started an eight-game winning streak lasting until February 4th when they lost to the Hawks in Atlanta. That loss did not turn into a losing streak as the Knicks proceeded to win ten out of their next thirteen games.

The final ten games of the regular season saw the team win only three games, they even lost the last four games in a row at the end, but that proved inconsequential as the Knicks coasted to the Eastern Division title. The final Eastern Division standings for the regular season showed the Knicks with a record of 60–22, followed by the Bucks who came on strong at the end to finish at 56–26, four games behind New York. The Bullets remained in third place with a record of 50–32.

During the final few weeks of the NBA regular season, New York City experienced a few days that shook the country. On March 6, 1970, three members of the Weathermen faction of Students for a Democratic Society died in an explosion on West 18th Street. The house they lived in was used to make bombs. They had been planning to blow up the Columbia University library. On March 11th, explosions rocked the corporate headquarters of IBM, Mobil Oil, and GTE; another explosion killed two black radicals in an East Fifth Street tenement. As far as national bad news, on March 17th the United States Army charged fourteen officers with suppressing information related to the My Lai massacre. And to top it all off, the nation was in the midst of a postal strike. President Nixon would eventually call up the Army Reserve to handle the mail until the strike was settled. These events and the ongoing Vietnam War coverage paled the usual excitement generated by the impending NBA playoffs.

When the regular season ended on March 22nd the Knicks had four days to prepare for the playoffs in this worrisome atmosphere. In the Eastern Division Semifinals the Knicks would face the tough Baltimore Bullets. It was a best-of-seven series that had every other game at home for the Knicks. The good news was they had home court advantage.

RED HOLZMAN—PLAYERS ON THEIR COACH

"Coach Holzman was a person I trusted," said Dave DeBusschere. "We respected each other partly because we both loved the game and knew what it took to be successful. The other part was he handled situations as good as any coach who ever coached me."

Willis Reed had a close rapport with Red: "My relationship with Red was terrific, Red kept things low key. He never got excited about things, especially during bad times. That's where I thought he was especially good. We'd lose and he would just say, 'There were a couple of bad calls, a few missed shots, and a few bad plays.' That was it and he walked away.

Mike Riordan recalled, "Coach Holzman knew how to handle the sixth man, and the eleventh or twelfth man, as well as the starters. I respected him because everyone was part of the team. He knew how to handle that part of the game." Mike also said, "He was a disciplinarian, he had full control of the team, but let us create on our own at times. Red basically concentrated on the defensive end of things, substitutions, and motivating. While he gave us some flexibility, he was a no-nonsense coach who didn't tolerate anything that wasn't going to be good for the team."

"My relationship with Red was good and interesting," recalled Cazzie Russell. "He was tough when he first took over. He got me a couple of times. He was a tough disciplinarian. But he recommended me to be drafted by the Knicks. I always wanted more playing time."

"I would classify my relationship with Coach Holzman as respectful, excellent, and mellowing over time," said Bill Bradley. "He definitely was a leader."

Phil Jackson confessed, "Red had a great deal of influence on me. I was an observer in 1969–70. I watched and learned at the same time. His techniques of managing people, more than anything else, influenced me. Red wasn't a strategist. He never put Xs and Os on paper. He probably used salt and pepper shakers more. When I won the Coach of the Year Award with Chicago it was called the Red Auerbach Award. But I call it the Red Holzman Award because Red taught me almost everything I know about coaching."

Dick Barnett said, "Coach Holzman preached defense. He would let us try certain things on offense, but when it came to defense he was a stickler who understood how important it was. And he was able to make us believe that importance, the mark of a great coach."

"My relationship with Coach Holzman was excellent," said Clyde Frazier. "He was a player's coach. He allowed the players to have an impact in what we were doing if we were winning. If we were losing he could be a terror. He was hard, but he was fair. That's why he got the most out of his players."

15. The Bruising Bullets

"It was the most exciting basketball series I ever saw."
—Ira Berkow

The Bullets had an outstanding team. At center they had a talented bruiser in Wes Unseld. At forward two outstanding scorers in Gus Johnson and Jack Marin. And at guard, the fabulous Earl "The Pearl" Monroe and highly regarded Kevin Loughery. Loughery was still having problems from a collision he had with Lew Alcindor (who later took the name Kareem Abdul-Jabbar) in a game the previous month where he broke three ribs and incurred a punctured lung. His playing time would be split with Fred Carter.

The Knicks and the Bullets were matched up almost perfectly. The year before the Knicks had swept the Bullets in the playoffs in four games, so the Bullets were looking for revenge.

Because of the nationwide postal strike, military reserve units were called to active duty to fill in. Mike Riordan and Cazzie Russell were in reserve units and called up. They both missed team workouts the day before the first game, and everyone was concerned they might miss the opening game or worse. As it turned out both made it for the whole series.

Due to the injury that sidelined him for the season, Phil Jackson found some unusual part-time work. "I was interested in photography when I came out of college and came to New York," said Phil. "When I was injured and couldn't play I found a spot on the court to take pictures and made friends with George Kalinsky, the official Garden photographer. "I got a whole new insight seeing things through a lens," recalled Phil.

The opening game in the semi-finals turned out to be a classic. It was back and forth throughout the game and at the end of regulation the game was tied 102–102. Battle lines were drawn and both teams put up a tremendous fight. The game went into two overtimes. In the first overtime period both teams scored eight points. Twice in the first overtime Clyde Frazier was able to make steals that led to points to keep the Knicks in the game. In the second overtime the game was again a seesaw contest. With thirty-three seconds left the score was tied 117–117. The Knicks got the ball to Walt Frazier, who made a nifty pass to Willis Reed, who took it in for a basket. The Bullets still had time to come back. Earl Monroe took a shot and missed, but Wes Unseld was able to get the ball back and with time running out took a last-ditch shot that missed too. In an incredible double-overtime the Knicks won the first game of the series 120–117.

Willis Reed led the Knicks by scoring 30 points and pulling down 21 rebounds while playing fifty-four minutes. For the Bullets, Earl the Pearl put in 39 points and Wes Unseld scored 15 points. Unseld also pulled down an incredible 31 rebounds. It was a fantastic start to the playoff series. That day Red Holzman told the New York *Daily News*, "It was a great game. I wish I could have seen it. I mean as a fan."

The second game was played the next day, March 27th in Baltimore. Trailing by six points after three quarters, the Knicks got unexpected help when Mike Riordan came off the bench and scored 11 of his game total 13 points in the final period. With Mike's clutch shooting the Knicks came out on top 106–99. What made this win impressive was the way the team was able to stay in the game after the starters struggled in the first half. Reed was again the high scorer for the Knicks with 27. Good defensive play held Earl Monroe to 19, although Gus Johnson was able to throw in 28. Once again, Wes Unseld was a terror off the boards pulling down 21 rebounds. Although, the Knicks won this game in regulation to go up two games in the series, it certainly wasn't easy.

The third game of the best-of-seven series was played back in Madison Square Garden on March 29th. The Knicks led at halftime, but the second half was all Bullets. The Knicks, feeling confident, blew their chance to go three games up by letting the Bullets score 127 points to their 113. It wasn't so much being outscored; the Knicks were simply out-muscled. Wes Unseld pulled down 34 rebounds. The whole Knick team had only 30. Still, the Knicks were up by one game in the series going into the fourth game.

The next game of the series in Baltimore turned into more disappointment for the Knicks. What confidence they had when they were two games up disappeared as the Bullets stormed back to tie the series at two games apiece by winning handily 102–92. It was all Earl the Pearl and Wes Unseld as the Bullets gained the momentum for the series. Monroe pumped in 34 points and Unseld pulled down another 24 rebounds. He now had 110 rebounds for the first four games. Defense carried the Bullets in this game as they limited the Knicks to 38 percent shooting. In an interview after the game, Clyde Frazier said, "We're a bit dented, but undaunted."

The fifth game saw the Knicks bounce back at Madison Square Garden. In one of his greatest games, Willis Reed scored 36 points and grabbed 36 rebounds to lead the Knicks to a 101–80 win. He outplayed Wes Unseld, and the rest of his teammates chipped in to give the Knicks a 3–2 lead in the series. The Bullets were only 7 points behind the Knicks going into the fourth quarter, but the Knicks defense was at its best holding the Bullets to 11 points in the last quarter. Clyde Frazier also had a strong game as he held Monroe to 18 points, scored 16, and took down 16 rebounds.

It was now Game Six and the Bullets had to win back at home or face elimination. In this back-and-forth series, the Bullets prevailed 96–87. It was a case of too much Earl Monroe and Gus Johnson as they scored a combined 60 points: Johnson 31 and Monroe 29. With Wes Unseld pulling down another 24 boards the Bullets out rebounded the Knicks 64–50. The Knicks' defense held up, but the culprit that contributed to the loss was poor shooting. The Knicks' 87 points marked their lowest point total of the season. The closeness of this series and the even match-ups of the two teams gave the fans of both teams thrills and heart-stopping chills. The only good thing about having to play the Bullets in a seventh game was the venue. The game would be played at Madison Square Garden in front of the home fans, hopefully, a great advantage.

The last game in the playoffs of any sport can be a flip of the coin.

Anything can happen. In the Garden packed with over 19,000 fanatical fans, the Knicks needed to prove they could handle the wear and tear of a grueling seven-game series and still have enough left to move to the Division Finals.

It turned out to be not even close. The Knicks came to play and took command almost immediately. Dick Barnett and Dave DeBusschere each scored 28 points and Cazzie Russell came off the bench to put in 18 to lead the team to a 127–114 victory in this extremely hard fought seven-game series. Willis Reed scored 14 points with 14 rebounds and Clyde Frazier put in 15 points, but more importantly helped hold down Earl Monroe in the crucial fourth quarter, even though the Pearl scored 32 points for the game. The Knicks had escaped the Bullets, but it was a very physical and emotional seven games.

"It was the most exciting basketball series I ever saw," commented sportswriter Ira Berkow. "They were not only great games but physically tough."

"I was emotionally and physically drained," said Dave DeBusschere. "I bounced off Wes Unseld so many times it took my body a while to get over the soreness."

Earl Monroe concurred, "It was a very closely contested series. We realized the teams were mirror images of each other in terms of guards, centers, and forwards. We both were very much alike." When asked about being matched up against Clyde Frazier, Monroe said, "Back then, it wasn't so much point guard and shooting guard. We were all guards. There were occasions when Clyde and I were matched up, but also occasions when Dick Barnett and I were matched up. The Knicks had this little thing they used to run with me when they would try to get the ball out of my hands. I always knew when that was coming. They had a special play. When I went to a certain area they would converge on me and try to make me give up the ball. As far as the series against the Knicks, no one game stands out, but it was classic basketball I know the fans enjoyed."

"After we beat the Bullets in four straight the year before, we knew they would be looking for us in the playoffs in 69–70," said Willis Reed. "That series was as tough as any we ever played. It went back and forth for seven games. The Bullets had great players. Wes Unseld and I battled every game."

"There were perfect matchups," recalled Mike Riordan. "I remembered when Unseld out rebounded our whole team in one game. That was some performance. Then, Willis came right back at him the next game."

"The thing about the Bullet series I remember," said Phil Jackson, "was that we were able to overcome difficult situations. There were great matchups. The Bullets were built like us, and it was proven by the way the series went back and forth."

Clyde Frazier remarked recently, "Even when we won, we lost. We got battered mentally and physically for seven games. That series actually prepared us for the pressure in the next two series. The Bullets were very physical and had a running team. It was very demanding. Once we defeated the Bullets we gained confidence in our ability to get to the finals."

"Matchups told the story about the Bullets series," said Bill Bradley. "From a pure basketball standpoint it was perfect. We had good games and bad games, but we prevailed."

The day the Knicks were winding up their playoff series against the Bullets in New York, the city's police department announced that all inspections of police units would take place indoors because of the danger of sniper attacks on policemen. Besides the country, New York City was also in a war.

The next test for the Knicks would come five days later on April 11th, in the Eastern Division finals, against a very good team with a great young rookie player who, ironically, grew up in New York City.

16. Battling the Bucks

"I need another beer . . . this is a special occasion."
—Walt Frazier

The Milwaukee Bucks came off the regular season winning fifty-six games and finishing only four games behind the Knicks in the Eastern Division. In their semifinal series they defeated Philadelphia in five games. Ably coached by Larry Costello, the Bucks posed a different problem for the Knicks than the Bullets. Whereas Wes Unseld for the Bullets was a dominating rebounder, Lew Alcindor could rebound, score, and play defense. The Bucks, however, lacked the physicality of the Bullets. Besides Alcindor, the starters were Bob Dandridge and Greg Smith at forward, and Flynn Robinson and Jon McGlocklin at guard. Both Dandridge and Smith, like Alcindor, were first-year pros.

While the starters lacked experience, Alcindor more than made up for that with his extraordinary talent. The former New York City phenom and UCLA All-American had a huge height advantage over Willis Reed, who was listed at 6' 10", but was shorter than that. Alcindor was listed at 7' 1" and most people believed he was taller. Even though he was a rookie, he was a tremendous force. As far as bench players, the Bucks' top three consisted of Guy Rodgers, Fred Crawford, and Len Chappell. The Knicks had a better bench. The Bucks finished their semifinal series on April 3rd, so they had a slight edge on the Knicks of three extra days to rest.

This playoff series had a different format than the first round. The teams would play at Madison Square Garden for the first two games and then move to Milwaukee for the next two. If needed, the fifth game would take place in New York, the sixth in Milwaukee, and the seventh game in Madison Square Garden.

Over in the Western Division semifinals the vaunted Los Angeles Lakers showed their skill by coming back from a 3–1 deficit to defeat the Phoenix Suns. They were getting ready to play the Atlanta Hawks in the best-of-seven Western Division final.

The opening game of the Knicks-Bucks series took place April 11th in front of the usual 19,500 fans at Madison Square Garden. The inexperienced Bucks proved no match for the Knicks, losing 110–102. Alcindor scored 35 points, but 15 of the 35 came in the fourth quarter after the Knicks built a double-digit lead. Willis Reed was up to the task, scoring 24 and pulling down 12 rebounds. Clyde Frazier only scored 6, but teammates Bradley, DeBusschere, and Barnett contributed a total of 53 points. The Knicks bench again proved strong as Cazzie Russell played eighteen minutes and scored 18 points. After the game Frazier told the *Daily News*, "Today it all worked. I think they became frustrated after a while. They played like a rookie team should. They made a lot of bad passes." Alcindor, on the other hand, told a reporter, "I don't think I played as well as I could have. I'm not worried about it."

The second game of the series was played two nights later at the Garden. This game turned out to be much more difficult for the Knicks than the first. With Alcindor scoring 38 points, the Bucks kept the battle close from the start. The Knicks led after one quarter 35–31, but the Bucks went in at halftime with a 66–63 lead. In the second half, the lead kept changing back and forth until the very end of the game. Although Alcindor played a great game, he missed two vital free throws in the last minute as the Knicks squeaked by 112–111. Reed also had a great game as he scored 36 points and grabbed 19 rebounds. Clyde Frazier displayed star power scoring a triple-double: 10 points, 14 assists, and 12 rebounds. The Knicks were now up 2–0 in the series with the next two games scheduled for Milwaukee.

John McGlocklin, now a Bucks broadcaster, recalled, "I think going into that series we were the underdog. The Knicks were a seasoned, veteran team that knew what it took to win. They were probably the most intelligent basketball team I've ever seen, and they functioned so well. They were the essence of a team. Plus, they had home-court advantage. We were still a fledgling expansion team with a rookie as its star player. The Knicks' defense was very good and they created problems for Flynn Robinson and myself. It was Alcindor's first year and he was great, but he didn't have the experience."

The third game of the series, however, turned out to be all Bucks, and all Lew Alcindor, as they won 101–96. The Knicks had to play catch-up the entire game as he dominated throughout. Even though the 33 points scored were Alcindor's lowest point total of the series so far, he was spectacular in every other facet of the game. With 31 rebounds, he only had ten less than the whole Knicks team. Willis Reed, who scored 21 and pulled down only 10 rebounds, couldn't contain Alcindor. Bucks' coach Larry Costello addressed the media after the game, "It was a superb performance for Lew. It was the best game he's played as a pro."

Game Four was played two days later in Milwaukee. The Bucks were riding high off of their third-game win and the Knicks had to contain Lew Alcindor. He did score 38 points, but this time he only grabbed 9 rebounds. But the rest of his teammates were held down as the Knicks posted a 117–105 victory to go up 3–1 in the series. The Knicks got their usual help from the bench as Cazzie Russell once again came up big. Cazzie put in 18 points in 26 minutes of play to help the team run away with the win. Even though they were down by twenty at halftime, the Bucks' persistence paid off as they made a game of it in the third period. But once again the Knicks bench demonstrated its value. All season the Knicks proved to everyone how balanced a team they had become.

"The fourth game was the turning point of the series in my estimation," said Jon McGlocklin recently. "When we lost that game at home I realized going back to New York and trying to win there was going to be very difficult."

While the Knicks still had to win one more game against the Milwaukee Bucks to gain the Eastern Division crown and get to the NBA finals, the Los Angeles Lakers swept the Atlanta Hawks in four games in the Western Division finals. The great Lakers star, Jerry West, scored 39 points in the last game against Atlanta. It was the Lakers' seventh victory in a row, an NBA playoff record. They now could rest as the Knicks and Bucks battled it out.

Game Five of the series returned to the Garden on April 20th. It was

bedlam at the Garden as a standing-room-only crowd sensed a trip to the
NBA finals. If you got to the Garden a few minutes late, the game was
pretty much over right after the tip-off. The Knicks came out flying as
Dick Barnett hit his first five shots and scored 16 points in the first quarter. The Knicks led by 13 points after only five minutes and by as much as
24 two minutes into the second quarter. At halftime the score was 69–45.
In the second half, it was more Knicks as they outscored the Bucks by
twelve points in the half. The final score was 132–96, a humiliating defeat
for the Bucks, but an impressive victory for the Knicks. Alcindor scored
27 points, but was outplayed by Willis Reed, who scored 32 and dominated the middle. In the second half of the game the Garden fans started
to chant "Good-bye, Lew." Jon McGlocklin remembered that, after the
game, "I was in the locker room and Howard Cosell walked up to me. I
had never met him before. He said to me, 'Jon, I want to apologize for the
New York fans chanting against Lew.' To this day I don't know why he did
that."

After the game, Red Holzman commented to reporters, "It was the
best offensive showing we've had in a long time. We moved the ball and
got it to the right guy most of the time." Willis Reed said, "It was the best
game we've played in the playoffs. The way we played should give us momentum for Los Angeles." The Knicks would need that momentum
against the Los Angeles Lakers with their three superstars.

The Knicks locker room had a "quiet" celebration, as the players
knew there was a huge job ahead. Most of the drinking was of the beer nature, not champagne. Clyde Frazier confessed to reporters, "I need another beer because I spilled most of mine. This is a special occasion. The
next one will be even more special. Then we'll have champagne." The
Knicks would have four days to get ready for the mighty Los Angeles Lakers. It would be their first appearance in the NBA finals in seventeen years.

17. Knicks vs. Lakers—The Perfect Finals

"I went this far. I'm going to finish it."
—Willis Reed

T he Lakers were on a roll, having won seven playoff games in a row and were well rested. The Knicks were coming off one of their best games of the playoffs and seemed to have the players to compensate for the great Jerry West, Wilt Chamberlain (who was being bothered by knee problems), and the aging, but still great, Elgin Baylor. West was the one player the Knicks felt was unstoppable. He was clearly one of the very best players in the game. The Knicks would have to find a way to slow him down and at the same time, keep Wilt and Baylor at bay. The other starting players for the Lakers were Keith Erickson and Dick Garrett. Garrett was a shooting guard who came out of the same school as Clyde Frazier, Southern Illinois University.

Jerry West played tough against the Knicks over the course of the regular season, averaging 34.3 points a game, even better than his league-leading 31.2. Clyde Frazier would be the guy to initially guard West. Early in the week before the series began, West was also voted the NBA's top defensive player by the coaches. Clyde remarked to the *Daily News* before the series started, "If I'm going to sacrifice offense, I might as well do it on West." Willis would have to defend Wilt, and DeBusschere would be on Baylor. That left Bill Bradley to guard Keith Erickson. The Lakers' top three players on the bench consisted of Mel Counts, Happy Hairston, and Johnny Egan. Once again, the Knicks had the better of that matchup. The finals promised to be memorable.

Knicks and Lakers players recently recalled their thoughts before that famous clash began. "We thought we could beat them," said Willis Reed. "I felt like it was our year, and we were playing very well. I had just come off playing Alcindor. Wilt didn't bother me, particularly because I knew he had recently come back from knee surgery."

"I was thinking it was the best accumulation of players in the world," Phil Jackson said. "They had three future Hall of Famers, and we had great players, too. But, the Lakers had scorers. In practice we talked about exploiting their off guard Dick Garrett."

Clyde Frazier noted, "We knew it was going to be a formidable task. We hoped we could remain healthy. Plus, we did have the home court advantage which could work in our favor."

"It was a pro basketball fan's dream," stated Bill Bradley. "Two outstanding teams with great players in a championship setting. A perfect situation."

Elgin Baylor reflected, "I was injured a lot during the regular season and missed twenty-eight games that year. I was hoping to stay healthy. I knew the series was going to be difficult. That year the Knicks had a terrific team. They were well-coached, played very good and sound basketball, and had excellent players."

"Before the series started, my whole thought process was on winning," confessed Jerry West. "I like to think I have been blessed by a crazy inner desire to win. The frustration of losing to Boston so many times had taken me to the point in my life where I just didn't know if we were ever going to win. The only thing I cared about was trying to win a championship."

Recently, I asked Jon McGlocklin if he thought the Knicks could beat the Lakers. "I thought it was a great matchup going in. You not only had great individual names, but also had two great teams. I did believe then that the Knicks were the team of destiny, and a better unified team than the Lakers."

There was also an interesting side note to the series. Still-injured Phil Jackson was now an official part-time photographer. "I actually sent pictures of the championship series to the *New York Times*," said Phil. "I even got paid."

Game One was played in front of another packed house at Madison Square Garden on April 24th. The National Basketball Association could not have asked for a better situation for its championship series; outstanding players with two great teams from the two biggest markets in sports. A marketer's dream.

The game started out looking like a rout by the Knicks. After the first quarter they led by ten, and at the half by eleven. But, the story of the game was the second half. After Jerry West scored 16 points in the third period, Red Holzman called on Dick Barnett to take over for Clyde Frazier who was in foul trouble. That move became a key factor in the game. Barnett was able to hold West to one point for an eight-minute span. That lull helped the Knicks come back and outscore the Lakers by 15 points in the fourth quarter and win the game 124–112. Once again, Cazzie Russell came off the bench to score valuable points to help the Knicks' cause. West scored 33 in the game while Elgin Baylor scored 21. Wilt put in 17 and pulled down 24 rebounds. For the Knicks, Reed was outstanding with 37 points and 16 rebounds. Dave DeBusschere had 19 points and 16 rebounds. The Knick bench did its usual stellar job. Along with Barnett and Cazzie's heroics, Mike Riordan played 25 minutes and scored 19 points. The first game of the championship series was a classic Knicks' team effort.

The only thing bad that came out of the first game was a bruised shoulder Willis Reed suffered in a second-quarter collision with the Lakers' Happy Hairston. The day after the game Willis was feeling the stiffness in his shoulder, and the Knicks were concerned he might not be able to play in the second game. For the Knicks he was a key man. They needed Willis to hit from the outside to bring Wilt out from under the basket. Lakers' coach Joe Mullaney wanted Wilt to challenge Willis up to fifteen feet, but Wilt barely moved away from the basket. Wilt didn't do that in the first game, and if Willis was not playing then Wilt would have no reason to come out.

It turned out Willis was able to play in the second game and he contributed 29 points and 15 rebounds. It was a very close game all the way, and with seconds left in the game the Lakers were up by two. With the Garden crowd hoping for a score, the Knicks came down court with the ball. With time running out Reed got the ball and put up the shot to tie the game, but Wilt blocked it and the Lakers held on to win 105–103.

Jerry West and Wilt Chamberlain led the Lakers to this important road victory at the Garden to even the series at one game apiece. West scored a game high 34 points, 17 in each half, while Chamberlain scored 19 and grabbed 24 rebounds. Not only was West able to get both Frazier and Barnett in foul trouble, but he also hit two free throws with forty-six seconds left in the game for the winning margin. It was a game of missed opportunities for the Knicks, and for the Lakers it was a game where two of their stars rose to the occasion. The split of the first two games showed that this was going to be a hard-fought championship series.

During this exciting time the underbelly of New York was showing again, giving the fans more than the championship to contemplate. The *New York Times* ran a story about police corruption. A policeman named Frank Serpico had come forward detailing graft, narcotics, and gambling on the New York City police force. Mayor Lindsay appointed Whitman Knapp, a Wall Street lawyer, to head a commission to investigate. When the investigation was over, no high-ranking officers were indicted, only beat cops. One of the most famous incidents in New York City police history eventually became the basis for a best-selling book and a hit movie starring Al Pacino. It appeared as if the Knicks would just have to work even harder to capture the city's attention and take the fans beyond the carnage, strife, and corruption they were witnessing almost daily.

Two nights after the Knicks' loss, the third game was played in Los Angeles. The Lakers gained confidence with their win in New York, so the Knicks needed to come up big to regain theirs. This game turned out to be one of the most memorable ever played in NBA playoff history.

The battle started off poorly for the Knicks. At halftime they trailed the Lakers by 14 points. Fighting back with everything they had the New Yorkers managed to tie the score at 96–96 with 1:18 left in the game. Dick Barnett, who put in 13 of his game total 18 points in the fourth quarter to keep the Knicks in the game, hit a jumper with eighteen seconds to go to give the Knicks a 100–99 lead. With thirteen seconds on the clock Wilt Chamberlain was fouled. He made one of his two free throws to tie the score. Then, with three seconds left in regulation Dave DeBusschere hit a jump shot. The Knicks were now ahead by two. The Lakers had no time-outs left, and, if they were lucky, one last shot might be possible. The Lakers in-bounded the ball to Jerry West. He dribbled twice and heaved a shot sixty feet away from the basket. Incredibly, the ball went in to send the game into overtime. The Los Angeles crowd went berserk while the

Knicks were stunned. They could have lost their composure, but they didn't.

The Lakers scored first in overtime on a Chamberlain basket. The Knicks countered with a Willis Reed score. A couple of Dave DeBusschere hoops around an Elgin Baylor free throw gave the Knicks the lead at 108–105. The Lakers tied the score at 108–108, but Willis Reed hit a crucial foul shot to give the Knicks the lead. Dick Barnett then hit a jump shot for the final basket to seal the victory 111–108. It was an incredible win for the Knicks to put them up 2–1 in the series. For the Lakers Jerry West was again the leader, scoring 34 points and making that incredible shot to force overtime. Wilt was held to 21 points, but pulled down 26 rebounds. On the Knicks' side, Willis was superb again, scoring 38 points and grabbing 17 rebounds. Besides Barnett's heroics, DeBusschere added 21 points and 15 rebounds, and Clyde scored 19 with 11 rebounds.

"I remember I was so tired," Jerry West told me. "I played almost every minute of every game because we didn't have much depth on that Laker team. By the grace of God that shot went in. I often think about the rules today. If they were the same rules back then [it would have been a three point basket] we would have won the game. I believe if we won Game Three we would have won the series in six games."

The win in the third game provided the Knicks with the fortitude and mental strength they needed. Reflecting on West's last second shot in regulation, Mike Riordan told the *Daily News*, "If there's any justice they're not going to win on something like that. It happens once in a thousand times. It was probably done for the TV ratings." Even though the Knicks were up 2–1 in the series, a lot of work still had to be done.

Jerry West also told me, "I was so tired and in the overtime my play was horrible. Of course, I always blamed myself when we lost. It was another bitter disappointment."

The day after the game it was reported that West was suffering from a badly bruised left thumb. There was a possibility he might not play in Game Four. Since West was a right-handed shooter that seemed remote.

The concern about Jerry's ability to play was unfounded as he started the next night in Los Angeles. Not only did he play, he was fantastic. In another overtime game, West scored 37 points and handed out 18 assists in leading the Lakers. The game went back and forth as the Knicks were up by as many as 9 in the first period and the Lakers were ahead by as many as 11 in the third. With forty-seven seconds left in regulation, Bill

Bradley hit a shot to give the Knicks the lead. West then tied the game at 97–97. Clyde Frazier made two free throws at the thirty-five second mark and with twenty-five seconds left Elgin Baylor hit two free throws to tie the game again. With a chance to win the game, the Knicks called a time-out with nine seconds remaining in regulation. John Tresvant, who hadn't played at all in the series, was now in the game for the Lakers and he batted the ball away from Willis Reed on the in-bound pass. Again, the Knicks in-bounded, this time successfully to Frazier. Clyde wasn't able to get off a clear shot so the teams went into overtime for the second straight game.

Back and forth baskets kept the overtime close. With 3:30 left, West made the basket that put the Lakers ahead for good. Little-used Tresvant stole the ball from Reed, was successful on a couple of foul shots, and made a great pass to West for a bucket. The battle ended with the Lakers on top 121–115.

All three Laker stars contributed to the win as Elgin Baylor put in 30 points and Wilt Chamberlain had 18 along with 25 rebounds. Although it was the Lakers' stars at their best, it was John Tresvant, who coach Joe Mullaney wisely substituted, that helped tie the series at two apiece. "We needed some rebounding strength," said Mullaney to a reporter. "I never expected the other bonus things."

Dick Barnett's 29 points led the Knicks, while Willis was held to 23. Game Five would be back in New York at the Garden. This championship series was living up to all the expectations.

The day before Game Five both Willis Reed and Elgin Baylor did not practice, and it was possible both might miss the important game. Willis only missed one game all year, but sore knees bothered him frequently. This time it was the right knee that was most troublesome. Going against Wes Unseld, Lew Alcindor, and now Wilt Chamberlain in the playoffs, didn't help the situation. But Willis, who was honored as the Most Valuable Player in the NBA, was proving he deserved the award. Team physician Dr. James Parkes, a noted orthopedist who would also become the Mets' team doctor, recommended Willis work out before the game, and if needed, take a cortisone shot. Baylor, who was hampered by groin pulls the last few years, was also limping before the game. The Lakers' team physician had recommended rest and treatment. Unfortunately, time to rest was not much of an option.

Madison Square Garden was its usual packed, frenetic place as Game Five began. Both Elgin Baylor and Willis Reed showed their determination and were in the starting line-ups. The Lakers jumped out to an early lead, ahead by as much as 10 points nearing the end of the first quarter. Bad news came early for the Knicks as Reed left the game with another injury, this time a seriously bruised hip with less than four minutes remaining in the quarter.

Willis suffered the injury driving to the basket, and he fell and grabbed his hip in pain. He was taken into the Knicks' locker room and given a shot of Novocain. He did not return to action. "After scoring seven points in the quarter," recalled Willis, "I got the ball high out on the perimeter and started to drive toward the basket. My thigh and hip muscles gave way on my right leg and I went down." "When Willis went down in Game Five I was very concerned," said Clyde Frazier. "But, we showed the world what we could do with adversity."

When Willis left the game the Knicks trailed by 10 points, and at halftime the Lakers led 53–40. But, the Knicks stormed back in the third quarter. The defense started to pressure the Lakers and caused 19 second-half turnovers of the 30 they committed in the game. Everyone helped out guarding Chamberlain, but mostly it was Dave DeBusschere who got the job of trying to contain "The Stilt." With help coming from all over, Wilt only scored 4 of his 22 points in the second half. Jerry West was held to 20 points for the game. The Knick bench again proved its potency as Cazzie pumped in 20 points and Dave Stallworth 12 to counter the loss of Willis. In the fourth quarter the Knicks held the Lakers to an unbelievable 10 points while scoring 32 to win the game. It was truly a credit to all of Reed's teammates that they were able to cover the loss of their captain and defeat the Lakers 107–100, and go up 3–2 in the series. "It showed what kind of team we had," said Willis. Bill Bradley told me that game was one of his best memories of the season. "The team went in at halftime and came up with a whole new offense. We went out and executed in the second half and won." It was indeed a magnificent victory. But, the question remained: What about Willis for Game Six, or Seven if necessary?

"It was a very disappointing loss for us in Game Five," recalled Jerry West. "I thought we had an enormous advantage with Reed out. We didn't take advantage of the opportunity. Everyone thought we were great, but I felt we didn't have the best of teams that year. We didn't deserve to win that game with our performance, especially after Reed went out. Over the years I learned that experience allows teams to overcome adversity and the Knicks certainly did that. The credit should really be to the Knicks in that game. They played so selflessly and as a result were difficult to matchup against because of the way we played as a team."

The Knicks-Lakers battle drew a lot of media attention, but another tragic event shocked the country. At the same time as the Knicks' dramatic victory in Game Five, shocking news was flashing over the land. Four students at Kent State University in Ohio were killed and eight wounded by National Guardsmen during a campus demonstration protesting U.S. incursion into Cambodia. Television reports and photos of the dead students traumatized the nation.

When the Knicks returned to Los Angeles amid this unsettling situation, they faced a tough decision regarding Willis Reed. There was a day off for travel but he was limping and Dr. Parkes told the media, "If the game was tonight, there is no way he could play." Coach Holzman said, "I'm not going to listen to Willis. I know him. He'll say he wants to play. As far as I'm concerned, it's entirely up to the doctor. I'm not going to take any chances with him. His future is too great." There were no broken bones in the hip, as X rays proved, but there was a strain of two muscles that ran from the pelvis across the hip to the knees. Willis was given oral medication along with ultrasound and massage therapy. There was also the possibility of another cortisone shot before the game depending on how Willis felt. The fact the Knicks were up 3–2 gave Red Holzman the confidence he could hold Reed back and give him some added days rest if needed. It would come down to a game-time decision.

Game Six was played in Los Angeles on May 6th. The decision not to play Reed came three hours before game time. Willis had been given a shot, oral enzymes, massage therapy, ultrasound, and alternating hot and cold baths for the injury. After all this, Dr. Parkes ruled out any chance for him to play. "He has pain, and he just can't make the moves necessary for him to play," Dr. Parkes told reporters. Coach Holzman simply told the media, "If there's any gamble I won't take it."

Without Willis, Game Six turned into a rout for the Lakers. The game got out of hand in the first quarter as the Lakers rolled to a 20-point lead at the end of one. At halftime the Lakers still led by 20. The strong Knicks bench couldn't help, even though Cazzie Russell came off the bench to score 23 points. Unable to achieve what they had in the previous game in New York, the Knicks couldn't stop Wilt Chamberlain. With Willis in street clothes sitting on the bench, the desperate Lakers got a fantastic performance out of Wilt who knocked down 45 points and grabbed 27 rebounds. West contributed 33 points as the Lakers ran away with the game by the score of 135–113. It simply was a case where the Knicks, without the presence of Willis Reed in the middle, couldn't contend. The good news was that Game Seven would be played back in New York at the Garden. The bad news was that as of that moment no one knew if the captain, Willis Reed, was going to be able to play.

On the day off between games all eyes were on Dr. James Parkes. He was the one person who had some control over Reed's medical situation, and he was somewhat optimistic Willis could play. "It's 50–50 that Willis will play Game Seven," Dr. Parkes told reporters. But even if he did play, how effective could he be?

"I was worried," Dave DeBusschere told me. "Willis meant so much to our team. I had a little luck earlier in the series trying to stop Wilt. But I didn't want to try and do it again."

Jerry West told a group of reporters, "If Wilt goes to the hoop like that again, there's no way we can lose." When I asked Jerry about that quote he said, "I didn't think there was anyone on the Knicks who could compete with Wilt if he played Game Seven like he played Game Six. Even Reed couldn't compete with him. He was too big and too strong. Looking back, I realize that we had two rookies starting. The one position I thought we had an enormous advantage against the Knicks was at center. But, Wilt would have to play like he did in Game Six."

"Chamberlain destroyed us in Game Six," recalled Clyde Frazier. "I didn't know who was going to guard him. It didn't look good. To be honest, I think our confidence wasn't too great for Game Seven."

Once again, the Knicks were faced with a Game Seven situation. This time, though, it was for the championship. When it comes down to one game, in the seventh game of a best-of-seven series for a championship, anything can happen. You can only hope your best players get an opportunity to play. For the New York Knicks, that was going to be determined at game time.

"It looked like we were dead," Knick trainer Danny Whelan told me. "I knew Willis was going to play no matter what. He told me, 'I went this far. I'm going to finish it. I might not do much, but I'm gonna try.' We had a day and a half to figure it out. I ate with him at four o'clock in the afternoon of the seventh game, and we just didn't know."

Willis remembered the day vividly. "I knew I was going to play. I just didn't know how well I was going to play. I spent nearly the whole day with our trainer, Danny Whelan, and went out on the court early in the afternoon and shot around a little. Danny gave me more treatments, and he and I ate together."

The Garden crowd didn't know what to expect. They were there to see a possible championship, and yet their captain, Willis Reed, might not play. If he didn't, the Lakers had a great opportunity.

"Willis said he was going to play," recalled Phil Jackson. "So, we all anticipated him playing. Emotionally or spiritually he was going to try and help us. He was walking around pretty stiff before the game."

Right before game time as last-minute, pregame warm-ups were taking place, Willis was in the Knicks' locker room with Danny Whelan and Dr. Parkes getting some last-minute treatment. Phil Jackson was there also. "Dr. Parkes asked me how I felt," recalled Willis. "I said I'm going to give it a go. Reluctantly, I let Dr. Parkes inject me with a cortisone shot that seemed to take forever. When he finished, I just said, 'Let's go.' "

"I went into the locker room for a minute before the game and came back out before Willis," said Cazzie Russell. "I came back out on the court and, of course, there was speculation on whether Willis might or might not play. The fans saw this guy [me] emerge from the tunnel and the applause and ovation started to pick up. When I got closer the fans realized it was me and not Willis and the applause stopped as if to say, 'Caz, we're glad to see you, but you're not Willis. You're not who we're looking for.' "

The game was even held up for a few minutes to see if Willis could make it out. Both teams were winding up their pregame drills. The fans were nervous and expectant. Slowly, from the tunnel near the Knicks' locker room, out came Willis.

"When I came onto the court I was thinking about the last game when Wilt scored all those points. We're in a real predicament, I thought," recalled Willis. "All of a sudden the Garden erupted and the fans went crazy. I got this incredible ovation. I was taken by surprise. The crowd was unbelievable."

"The drama of Willis coming onto the floor was amazing," recalled Bill Bradley. "It was an electric moment because we truly didn't think he was going to play. Then he came out, and the crowd took the roof off the Garden."

That moment when Willis walked onto the Garden floor for Game Seven has become an iconic moment. The sight of him walking in with a limp is one of the most historic events in New York sports history. Over the years it has represented an image of the enduring quality of both Willis Reed and the New York Knicks.

"I remember doing a pregame interview with Willis before the game and he told me he was going to play," said broadcaster Marv Albert. "When he came out onto the floor, the crowd went crazy. It's interesting that Willis's comeback is now part of sports terminology. When a guy gets hurt in any sport and comes back you hear people say, 'He's pulling a Willis Reed.' When he came out onto the floor it became one of the milestone moments in NBA history."

"I was in the locker room with Willis before he came out," said Phil Jackson. I took pictures of him getting a shot of cortisone. I walked right out behind him and couldn't believe the crowd reaction. Everyone seemed mesmerized by it."

It wasn't only the crowd that was mesmerized. "I know it psyched the Lakers out," said Clyde Frazier. "They stopped what they were doing and watched; Chamberlain, West, and Baylor. They turned around and were watching Reed. I said to myself, 'We got these guys.' I could see in their eyes they were like dazed for that moment. Right then it gave me a lot of confidence. The crowd was incredible. It lifted all of us."

"It was crazy," said Knick trainer Danny Whelan. "People were crying. I couldn't write that script."

"The seventh game was very dramatic," said Elgin Baylor. "When Willis came out with all the cheering and everything else, it was dramatic. I think it gave the Knicks an emotional lift—just his presence. He was their team leader, 'The Captain.' At the time, I'm sure the Knicks didn't know how much he could contribute. But, by being there he gave the Knicks inspiration."

"When Willis came out the crowd went berserk," said Cazzie Russell. "DeBusschere turned to me and said, 'Caz, look down at the other end.' It was West, Baylor, and Chamberlain looking at Willis. DeBusschere said, 'We got them.'"

On the other hand, Jerry West told me, "I was happy when Willis came out for Game Seven." I thought it was great because we got a guy against us who can't even move. It should have been four on five. I never paid much attention to crowds. I think you always know in New York the crowds are loud, particularly if they have a good team. I guess emotionally, Reed did what they wanted him to do."

Even with all this incredible excitement, a seventh game still had to be played, although no one knew how much Willis would be able to contribute. More important, could the Knicks stop Chamberlain?

With the Garden crowd on its feet at the start of the game Willis, noticeably limping, promptly hit his first two shots in the first minute and a half. With that impetus the Knicks took off. "When he hit his first two shots it was bedlam," recalled Marv Albert. Bill Bradley shared his recollection of that moment, "The drama of him coming on the floor and hitting his first two shots was amazing. It was an electric moment because we truly didn't think he was going to play."

"Once he started playing and ran down the floor you could see he wasn't very mobile, but he hit his first two shots and that really gave the Knicks a big lift," said Elgin Baylor. "However, don't forget what Frazier did that last game."

Reed did play twenty-seven minutes and only scored on those first two shots. He took pain medication and another cortisone shot at halftime, but thankfully wasn't needed that much. It was his inspiration that led the Knicks to a one-sided victory over the Lakers by the score of 113–99. The Knicks were simply unstoppable. They led by 14 at the end of the first period and were up 69–42 at the half. Even though Willis became the inspiration for the final game victory, it was an incredible performance by Clyde Frazier that led the Knicks to their first NBA Championship. Clyde scored 36 points and dished 19 assists in this remarkable game.

The Knicks were able to hold Jerry West to 28 points, but more important, Wilt Chamberlain, who had destroyed them in Game Six with 45 points, was held to just 21 by Dave DeBusschere and others. It was simply a magnificent team victory.

The Garden crowd had witnessed a trademark game from the Knicks: offense, outstanding defense, and contributions from everyone.

This time in the locker room there was champagne as the Knicks celebrated the franchise's first championship. Just as it was for their predecessors, the Jets and the Mets, the celebration was sweet. "The Jets and the Mets put a lot of pressure on us," said Clyde Frazier. "We had to keep up."

Reed was shortly announced as series MVP to go along with his All-Star MVP and NBA League MVP honors. Well deserved honors for a true warrior.

Coach Holzman, who would eventually be named NBA Coach of the Year, on talking about Reed to the media said, "Just his presence on the court made a big contribution."

In the visitor's locker room Lakers' coach Joe Mullaney was gracious. "The Knicks played very, very tough defense against us. They played so aggressively we never got a chance to run our offense. They forced us into turnovers and they forced us into hurried shots."

Wilt, too, was gracious in defeat. "They were great," he said after the game. "The Knicks did everything right. They played great defense and caused us to falter." Asked if the Lakers should have done things different in the game, Wilt replied, "Whatever could have been done is impossible to do now that the game is over. It's foolish to talk about it."

Back in the Knicks' locker room, as the celebration continued, Clyde Frazier was telling reporters he thought he didn't get the recognition he deserved. "At the time I told the press I was pissed," Clyde told me. "Momentum can only carry you so far. Willis inspired us, but it was the play of others and myself who carried us. At the time I thought I should have been MVP of the series. But, I was young and trying to make my niche in my third year in the league. I was trying to get up there with West and Robertson. That's why I spoke out. I never took it against Willis because I had too much respect for him. It was the media hype that played it up. Still, today people tell me, 'I didn't know you had that kind of incredible game.'"

When I asked Phil Jackson about Frazier's heroics in Game Seven, Phil said, "I think it was an ultimate moment that vaulted Frazier into the limelight. He had an incredible game."

Jerry West had this insightful comment: "Somebody always has to play exceptional for a team to win in that situation. The two teams were so different. We depended on a couple of people to score points for us. The Knicks didn't. They could have had anyone lead them that game. In my mind it was one of the most disappointing games in my career in terms of not winning because you get to the point when you've been there so much and it just doesn't happen. It was great for the city of New York. It was great for basketball. It's great when you had good teams in the big cities like New York, Chicago, and Los Angeles. It created more interest in the league."

On May 8, 1970, the New York Knicks became the third New York City professional sports team to win a world championship in the short span of sixteen months. After twenty-four years of existence the Knicks finally won their first franchise championship. The city went wild for the Knicks just like they did for the Jets and the Mets. Three miracles in such a short period of time, truly remarkable. New York City, America's largest city, with all of its problems, basked in the brightness from these phenomenal teams during an incredibly dark period in the history of our country.

On the same day the New York Knicks were winning their first NBA championship, about two miles south in lower Manhattan, 500 construction workers stormed City Hall and forced the raising of the American flag, which Mayor Lindsay had ordered flown at half-mast due to the killings at Kent State. The hard hats then attacked a peaceful anti-war protest at Pace College. More than sixty protestors and bystanders were injured as many police just stood by and watched.

A few days after the Knicks victory, the NBA held an expansion draft. The Knicks lost three reserves from their championship team, Don May, John Warren, and Bill Hosket.

On Tuesday May 12th, Willis Reed received a Dodge Charger for being selected as the MVP of the championship series. With his usual modesty Willis told reporters, "This is really the icing on the cake for me. Last April, when we were eliminated by the Celtics we got together after the game and said, 'We could do it this year.' We went into training camp with that idea in mind, that we could win the title. One of the most inspiring moments in my life was when I got hurt in Game Five in the championship series and was in the locker room listening to the game and my teammates beat Los Angeles."

Although, there would be no parade for the Knicks, Friday, May 15th was declared New York Knicks Day in New York City. Mayor John Lindsay feted the team at Gracie Mansion. Some people speculated that since he was now reelected, he didn't need to gain publicity by giving the Knicks a big parade.

At the Gracie Mansion ceremony, Willis Reed spoke to the crowd and said, "We're glad to be part of a winning family; the Jets, the Mets, and the Knicks." Mayor Lindsay spoke briefly hoping the New York Rangers might make the city a "100 percent city of champions" the following year. He also gave out special certificates to members of the team. When informed that three members of the Knicks had been "lost in the draft." He assumed it meant the military draft and said, "Uncle Sam has got them now."

Some additional thoughts about the championship series and that season came from the players, notable fans, and other astute observers:

"On reflection, I probably have a better perspective now than when we were playing," commented Dick Barnett. "It was a very intelligent team; it had people who knew how to play and had an appreciation for each other's talents. All of us knew how to maximize the assets of the team, and also to disguise the liabilities of each player. So, we had a unique combination of youth and maturity and a coach who really knew how to work with the players."

"We were a blue-collar team that fans loved to watch play," said Dave DeBusschere. "We played basic, fundamentally sound, hard-nosed basketball. New York fans enjoyed that."

"The opportunity to play on that championship Knick team was a real blessing for me," said Cazzie Russell. "The things I learned about teamwork and unselfishness helped me not only as a coach, but as a person."

"We were a sharing community," said Phil Jackson. "It got that way simply by DeBusschere coming to the team and Willis stepping into the center slot. The solidification behind Reed as the captain sort of made everything fall into place. We had a lot of guys who could do a lot of different things. Everyone on the team could handle and pass the ball. And Red's motto was, 'Hit the open man and see the ball on defense.' People bought into it."

"I was very disappointed when we lost to the Knicks," recalled Elgin Baylor. If you are a competitor, anytime you lose, particularly if it is a championship, it is very disappointing."

"I was a big fan of the Knicks in 1969–70," Rudy Giuliani told me recently. "The Knicks were a great team to watch because of their style of play."

"We didn't play a lot different than the great Celtic teams," said Bill Bradley. "I do think we played as a unit; we were unselfish and we moved the ball. There would always be three or four passes before a shot. You don't see that now. Everyone on our team had the courage to take the last shot. It created a kind of dynamic. I also believe that at that time the composition of the team, racially, ethnically, and by geographic background, created an interest in the people of the city who were thirsting for basketball success after never having won a championship."

Former New York governor Mario Cuomo said, "The Knicks were another chapter of sports greatness for the city back then. Reed coming onto the floor was an emotional moment. He is thought of as a heroic figure. The heroic moment is what gives the heroic memory."

"The Knicks kept alive the spirit of what the Jets and Mets had started," said David Garth. "John Lindsay was able to capitalize on all of them, but it was still tough times."

"I would call the Knicks of that time an aficionados team," said David Halberstam. "The sweetness in which they played; that team was memorable the way the ball moved."

"Watching that 1969–70 team is when I got really interested in the Knicks," said Spike Lee. "Frazier was my favorite. Just thinking about that time, it was amazing when all three New York teams won championships."

"I wasn't that big of a basketball fan," said director Barry Levinson. "But when the Knicks beat the Bullets in the playoffs that year I said, oh no, another loss to a New York team. I finally got over all the Baltimore losses except when I watch *Classic Sports* on television. When they have Super Bowl III on, I keep rooting for the Colts to pull it out."

One of the most interesting aspects of that championship Knicks team was the later success of the players after their playing days were over. Here are some of their thoughts and perspectives on that subject.

"I'm not surprised at the success of my teammates," said Dick Barnett. "Guys were very focused and understood the transition from playing can be very traumatic. They were prepared for it emotionally and psychologically. I consider myself very lucky to have played professional basketball and lived my dream. It was a hell of a life to live, to live your dream. Every moment, whether it was the championship or just playing a game during the season, fit into my parameters of that dream. The championship was great, but so was the first game I played. One of the best athletic experiences for me has been the lifelong relationships I have developed. The guys on the Knick championship team were great and all of it has been very rewarding."

"When I think back to that season," Dave DeBusschere said to me, "I just think about that championship. How it was our goal. We had a storybook year like the Jets and the Mets. It was a difficult time in our country and the city. All the teams brought the city alive. When I think about that I just tell myself I was lucky to be part of it. I knew my teammates would all succeed in whatever they did. We had a team of character."

"Our team was smart and that carried over to private life," said Mike Riordan. "I knew many of my teammates would go on to big things." When asked about Bill Bradley going into politics, Riordan said, "He was very calculating and always on track. It was very unusual for a sports figure at that time. He had this long-term vision of what he was going to do in his life. He would always take a lot of books with him on road trips. I would ask him, 'What's the topic this trip?' Basketball was something he was doing at that time, but he had his eyes on something else."

"I never thought Phil Jackson would turn out to be a solid coach like he is," commented Cazzie Russell. "But all of us had good education and good leadership."

Phil said, "I'm not surprised at any of my teammates. Twelve years after we won the championship we were celebrating Bill Bradley's jersey being raised in Madison Square Garden. Selma Holzman [Red's wife] said to me then, 'People forget the type of character that team had.' It was more than the players' abilities; it was the character they brought to the game."

"The success of the players on that Knick team outside of basketball is easy to explain," said Clyde Frazier. "It is the exquisite character of the players. We all came from different walks of life, but in meeting some of the parents of my teammates I realized that a lot of us were raised similar. They raised us to be team oriented, to blend in with other people, and to be giving. Even Dick Barnett, who was a shooter when he came to the Knicks, conformed to our style and the rules. And Coach Holzman had everything to do with it. He demanded teamwork and defense. If you didn't adhere to his philosophy you weren't going to play. We were ready for life after basketball when that happened."

"We had an extraordinary group of human beings," said Bill Bradley. "We came together and realized that individually we could not accomplish as much unless we worked together. So, we gave ourselves to each other and to the team. That's how we won. That created a real bond. The true character of the players is demonstrated by what happened to everyone when their playing days were over."

When asked about the success Phil Jackson is having as a coach in the NBA, Bradley had this to say. "At the time I didn't think of Phil as a coach. But in retrospect, he possessed all the attributes of a great coach. He was analytical about the game. He had a strong work ethic. He was unselfish and he treated each teammate as an individual. And, he loved the game. Put those things together and you have the characteristics of his coaching style. Even when he was hurt in the championship season he watched and learned from Coach Holzman."

Gail and Charlie Papelian, Red Holzman's daughter and son-in-law told me, "One of things that we're most proud of about Red is that all of his players on the 1969–70 championship team have gone on to successful careers. Red gave them confidence as players. He allowed them to have input on the court, and he always gave them credit for the team's success. He believed the players came first. It's a tribute to him that his players have gone on to be successful in whatever they have done after basketball."

"In people's minds the Knicks were proof positive that class and racial integration could work," said Robert Lipsyte. "Here you had Dave De-Busschere, a lunch pail guy, Bill Bradley, a banker's son who went to Princeton, and three black players who were very different in their own ways. The Knicks were seen as this perfect construct of what America could be like."

Mike Francesa, radio talk show host with station WFAN in New York City, had this analysis: "The Knicks were the quintessential New York City team. They not only had great teamwork, but also played with a level of sophistication that New York likes. It was a like a great jazz combo. They were a classic team because they were so smart. You must realize what a good Coach Holzman was, and the extension of Holzman is Phil Jackson. That team was enormously talented, however guys subjugated their egos. Every guy was different yet they played together as a team. That team is a team for the ages in New York because basketball is the city's game."

"Living in New York City at that time when the Knicks won the NBA championship after the Jets and Mets won championships, seemed like the center of the universe," said television producer Phil Rosenthal. "Back then, it seemed like New York always won."

Restauranteurs Drew and Tracy Nieporent, teenagers at the time, shared these Knick memories. "We both were thinking the Knicks could win. When they got DeBusschere, that's when they started to become very good. When the Knicks won we both thought that we might not ever lose again. We were proud to be New Yorkers and the three teams made us much more proud."

"Even though the Cubs didn't win in 1969, it was a gratifying year because we were so close," said Ron Santo. "But when the Knicks won after the Jets and Mets, I said, 'God lived in New York back then.'"

"The Knicks were a continuation of the magic carpet ride," said actor Robert Wuhl. "It was a big carpet because the Jets, Mets, and Knicks were all on it."

KNICKS OPPONENTS GIVE THEIR OPINION

The Knicks faced remarkably good teams in the 1970 NBA play-offs and finals to capture the championship. These talented adversaries include many of the best to ever play the game. Here is what a few of the most notable felt about their foes in those important games:

Los Angeles Laker great, Elgin Baylor, had this to say about what is often considered one of the best NBA championship series ever played. "It might have seemed like we were the favorites, but if you understand basketball and know the kind of team the Knicks had, it wasn't that big of an underdog's victory. The passing, the teamwork, the coaching, and their unselfishness are what led to their championship."

Earl "The Pearl" Monroe played for the tough Baltimore Bullets team against the Knicks that season. The Knicks and Bullets were dogged rivals all year, as witnessed by the great playoff series in 1970. Earl explained the Knicks' magic this way: "You knew the Knicks connected with their fans in the Garden that year. The Knicks played as a team. It was how basketball should be played."

"They really were the essence of a team," said Jon McGlocklin, a key member of the 1969–70 Milwaukee Bucks playoff squad and now broadcaster for the team. "They were always on the same page mentally, and the way they shared the ball they were just a wonderful basketball team. It was their time. You could tell that collectively they were a very good defensive team. And because they were smart, Coach Holzman let them have flexibility on offense."

Jerry West of the Lakers, remains one of the best players in the history of the NBA. A man of great insight and analytical acumen for the game, he had these in-depth observations: "Sometimes things happen for a reason and you don't understand it. Chemistry is a credible thing. You have certain teams that seem to find that kind of magical moment even in the locker room. They might not be the best team on paper, but yet there's something inside and they develop this attitude that we're going to win at any cost. Some teams can do that. It's almost a magical thing. When you watched a team really in sync like the Knicks in 1969–70, you saw a team that that was one of the smartest teams I ever played against. I always said I would have fit nicely on that team. You admired the way they played together. It didn't make any difference who scored on that team. They could win a defensive game or offensive game. They could win a slowed-down game or fast-paced game. It was a tribute to the players who were flexible and versatile enough to do things like that."

Asked to comment on the fact that Red Holzman was a stickler for defense, yet allowed his players to have a say in the offense, Jerry told me, "Players who are really good are flexible and adaptable. If you can find special people or players with that magical quality, that's great. It's a trust factor. The Knicks had enough smart players to do that, and the Lakers didn't. It was like one mind out there with the Knicks. I believe certain teams are preordained to win. No matter what you do those teams have the resilience and special quality that allows them to do something a little bit different and a little bit better than their opponents. Invariably, those are the ones who win the championships. That was the 1969–70 Knicks."

PART V

WHEN THE PEOPLE NEEDED
THEM MOST

18. When the People Needed Them Most

"It was good for the people."
—Yogi Berra

The impact of the exploits and success of these three teams on the people of New York City, and even the nation, was unprecedented—and much needed. People of appropriate ages who lived through that time understand the fear and trepidation evidenced in their daily lives if they were, or had loved ones in, the armed forces. The daily and vivid reports of war permeated our existence. Life was also trying for those principled individuals engaged in efforts to bring about true racial and civil equality in our country. Whether one believed what the United States was pursuing in Southeast Asia was a good and worthwhile cause or an unpopular folly, the ever-present emotions involved were true and conflicted at the same time. With so much serious upheaval on a daily basis, everyone was in need of something to uplift his or her spirit and outlook. The teams and players who created *The Magnificent Seasons* did just that. Not only for New Yorkers, but also for many citizens of our country, and as we have seen, for the men and women serving our nation. These unlikely guys, underdogs and overcomers of adversity as they were, made people believe again in the American Spirit. Here then are some thoughts worth our consideration:

Before he passed away Dave DeBusschere told me, "People always say how much they rooted for us and how everything in the city and country was screwed up; it was bittersweet times because of what was happening outside our realm."

Yogi Berra, as only he could, said a lot in a few words. "It was good for the people."

"We were in a world and a city that was troubled," said Phil Jackson. "I think we were able to help people through difficult times. I think all three teams did that."

Al Weis said he still hears this loud and clear: "Vietnam War veterans I meet often tell me we made them feel a little bit better during the play-offs and World Series. It was a tough time for everybody, but we made people feel better about their lives for a brief period of time, and that makes me happy."

George Sauer said, "Winning the Super Bowl was a great achievement. I ended up leaving football a few years later. I felt I had accomplished everything that I had to do. Looking back at the times I think we did help people forget about their problems for a short period of time."

David Garth, well-known political strategist, had these thoughts: "All three teams were symbols of getting up off the mat. The teams were great examples of underdogs winning. In an incredibly bad time for New Yorkers, those teams did more for the city than anyone or anything else."

"It was probably the greatest boost any city could get," said Bill Gallo, New York *Daily News* cartoonist-journalist. "This came at a time when New York needed something like these teams. It made us think there was something great in New York, and the greatness was in sports. You forgot momentarily about Vietnam, the crime, and rotten politics. New York had something to be proud of."

Sportswriter Maury Allen said, "The three championships couldn't have come at a better time for New York City. All the teams gave lifts to a city that needed help."

"I think there were so many things happening back then. Our team had a positive influence on many people because of the way we played, and to some extent we also were underdogs," said St. John's University professor Dr. Dick Barnett.

"All three teams were called miracles," recalled Ira Berkow. "It seemed like only in New York do these kinds of miracles happen. It was a tremendous boost to the city in bad times."

Mike Riordan commented, "All three championship teams were able to help people during bad times. I still hear that all the time."

"It makes me feel good that we gave people a chance to let go of some of their frustrations in their personal lives," said Ken Boswell. "It had to be the same with the Jets and Knicks fans."

"When you realize that you had the power to ease some of the dilemmas that people faced in their daily lives, it makes you feel good," commented Emerson Boozer. It's a great feeling to hear those sentiments."

Bill Bradley agreed, "We took people out of their daily lives in an inspirational sense. They saw what we accomplished together and felt they could accomplish this, too. I think that was an important lesson. Also, people really loved what they saw. It was good entertainment."

Ed Charles remembered, "Back then there was a lot of polarization going on. All the championship teams helped people get though that a little easier."

"It's fair to say the Jets, Mets, and Knicks at that time uplifted the city," said CNN senior analyst Jeff Greenfield. They were all something the city of New York needed."

Former governor Mario Cuomo, a big sports fan and an attorney fighting the public's battle at the time had this to say: "The Jets, Mets, and Knicks won't be remembered solely on what they accomplished on the field. Their importance goes beyond that. It's what they did for New York City that everyone remembers."

"The three teams united the city in a way that is almost unexplainable," said Rudy Giuliani. "They not only got their fans involved, but also other people who got interested. It carried over to the way people felt about themselves. All three teams lifted the spirit of the city when there was almost no spirit at all."

"We made people believe," said former Jet Dave Herman. "Then the Mets and Knicks continued that. All of a sudden there were believers again."

"A lot of bad things were happening back then," recalled Ed Kranepool. "There were a lot of distractions, and I get people telling me all the time how we helped them get through some bad times."

Donn Clendenon stated, "Many Americans were dying in the jungles of Vietnam. It was not good times in the city either. I believe the Mets helped people a lot."

"People looked at all three teams as underdogs," said Pete Lammons. "Anytime the underdog comes up and wins, it changes the whole picture. It made people, especially in New York City, feel good."

"People in the city did come together around the Jets, Mets, and Knicks in that period," said Robert Lipsyte. "Those teams became very powerful in the city at that time. It was a way for people to communicate who were afraid to talk to each other about anything else."

"There was turmoil everywhere," Joe Namath remembered. "It was all around you. That political era added to the lack of confidence in the honesty all people were dealing with, and the social and racial problems happening at that time. The fact that three New York City teams won championships was a huge bright spot. Everyone needed something to brighten their lives and all of our teams helped."

"All three championship teams were a light for a city and country that was dark," said Ron Taylor. "We made people feel better about their lives for a short period of time back then."

Rod Gaspar remembered, "We were all focused as ballplayers in baseball. But, unless you were totally caught up in your own world you knew that there were a lot of problems out there. I know we brought people together."

Ken Boswell had similar thoughts; "While it was fun playing in New York for the Mets then, I was aware of the problems in the city and the country. I knew the same person that was excited about the Mets was the same person who probably had a lot of problems going on in his life."

"Those Jets, Mets, and Knicks championships will always be measured in the context of the times," said actor Robert Wuhl. "Back then people needed distractions. The city was in disarray and broke. When the three teams won championships, it overshadowed a lot of the problems."

It is indeed true, the Jets, Mets, and Knicks of those magnificent seasons helped New York City get through perilous times. This had a big influence on how the three teams developed legacies over the years that continue to grow. Years from now when other championship teams are forgotten, the Jets, Mets, and Knicks of 1969–70 will be ever present in the memories of sports fans.

19. A Living Legacy

"It was a special time, special moments, and special people."
—Bill Bradley

I t is not difficult to look back at these three teams and realize the impact
their championships had not only on the players and coaches and everyone who followed them, but also on the public at large. Nor is it difficult
to understand why the three teams are still cherished today. Their legacies
have, in fact, grown stronger. These surrogate heroes provided excitement
and joy to many down-hearted people all over the country during those
difficult war-torn and strife-filled times. They also brought a sense of
pride and accomplishment to New Yorkers everywhere who were desperate to find light in a period of darkness.

The life of every player, coach, and manager of the Jets, Mets, and
Knicks of 1969–70 changed from the moment their team won the championship. Decades later New Yorkers, and indeed many people all over
this great land, have never forgotten what these teams did for their morale
and belief in the will of the underdog. The following sentiments are only
representative of the thousands of such words I heard over the years from
those who never forgot the Super Bowl III champion New York Jets, 1969

world champion New York Mets, and 1969–70 NBA champion New York Knicks.

"It's almost fable now because of the history of the teams before they won," said Marv Albert. "All first-time winners and, of course, it was important in the context of what was going on around us. When you look back now you appreciate it and recognize how unbelievable it was. To have three championship teams in that same period was incredible for the city. Their significance has become legendary."

Dick Barnett gave his perceptions: "People have long memories. Sports are more transitory now. There was a different feeling about teams back then and those memories have been passed on to generations."

"There was magic, particularly with the stars of those teams," said sportswriter Ira Berkow. "First of all, all three teams came out of nowhere. And, the aura of the stars Frazier, Seaver, and Namath, everyone was likeable. It was like the movies. Everyone wanted heroes and in these three teams they got them. Back then there was an element of good nature, charm, professionalism, and great athletic ability. A legend has developed with these teams. I don't think the aura will change, especially for the Knicks. Five guys running around in their underwear playing intelligent basketball. The teams had outstanding coaches and a manager you could relate to."

"What a great time for sports in New York City," said Willis Reed. "I was a big Jets and Mets fan, too. We were all first-time winners and people will remember that. The world and the city were crazy, but sports in New York were special. Over the years those championships have taken on so much meaning."

Sportswriter Maury Allen explained, "It's a mystical story. It was three downtrodden teams and there was mysticism about them. Part of it was the underdog syndrome and part was that the teams all had colorful figures. The chemistry of the teams was phenomenal. And, I think all three teams had a sense about playing in New York City. Those seasons put a stamp on New York City sports. In simple terms, the three teams have become legends."

"The Jets have never won another Super Bowl," said sportswriter Dave Anderson. "The Mets will always be the 'Miracle Mets.' The Knicks will forever be the consummate team. Their legacies are stamped in people's minds and will continue to grow for years to come."

"I don't know what legacy means," said Yogi. "But, the 1969 Mets will be talked about forever. Yeah, and the other two teams, too."

"When I come back to New York a lot of people still want to talk about that year," said Ken Boswell. "Most people don't remember who won the World Series five years ago. But people all over the world remember who won in 1969. I wish I could go back and shake every hand that I shook that year. I wish I could go back and meet every girl I met that year. Great memories and a wonderful time of my life."

"1969–70 was so special," said Emerson Boozer. "I doubt there will ever be another time such as that where three teams from the same city win championships. It was a special time for New York City sports fans. I always run into guys from the '69 Mets and the '69–70 Knicks and we always talk about it. Together, the players from those teams have a special bond and people can feel that."

"All of us on the three teams are still enjoying the benefits from that season," said Ed Charles. "Whether it be appearances, meeting new people, or just reminiscing about it, there are great benefits. I never realized at the time the effect our team had on the fans and the city. I do now. All these years later people are still talking about us, the Jets, and the Knicks."

"For me, my life sort of went full circle back then," said Donn Clendenon. "Where I was at the start of 1969 and then where I was at the end was an incredible journey. What our team accomplished will never be forgotten. You can talk about all the great teams in the history of the game, and you can be sure that the 1969 Mets will be right there. Not just about our ability, but by where we came from and how we brought the country and the city of New York to some unbelievable highs. Those memories are just passed on."

"Each of these team's legacy lives on because it was won against all odds," said John Schmitt. "That's America. The three teams exemplified the willingness to pay the price to play together as a team. All of us were little guys in the bar who succeeded. The seasons were magical, and people will always remember those times."

"There was so much going on in the world and most of it negative," said Cleon Jones. "And here comes this young ball club in New York City. It would have to be New York City with its media for all this to happen and become such big news all over the world. Even for the people in the service in Vietnam it was something they could look forward to everyday, knowing what we did. It did a lot for the city and country. It's the same for the Jets and Knicks. And, because of what we did, the legacy of my friend Tommie Agee lives forever."

"One of the reasons for the teams' legacies is that it happened for the first time for the three teams," said John Dockery. "And, it all happened in a short period of time. So much of it was unexpected. It just lifted the city, and people have remembered that. A lot has to do with the players who made up the teams. I think all of the players from each team are intertwined with each other." Then Dockery added, "It's more of a surrealistic memory than anything else. I remember standing on the sidelines as the Super Bowl was winding down thinking that here I was from the Ivy League and this was the Super Bowl. It made me part of history. I meet grown men in their fifties and sixties who still go back to that moment, recall where they were when it happened, and become kids again. When people see my Super Bowl ring they want to hear everything about that game."

Ron Taylor had a poignant firsthand experience, "I made a trip over to military hospitals in Okinawa and Guam and Japan in 1968 at the end of the season. I just remember going through a lot of hospitals and wards and saw a lot of burn victims and amputees. It made quite an impression. I became quite emotionally involved with the war. Also, Tug McGraw and I went over to Vietnam in the winter of 1969 after we won the World Series. We traveled with one of those USO tours and went into fire support bases. We talked to the guys and they were telling us that when the Mets won the World Series they all fired their weapons in the air. The 1969 Mets helped them in some way get through an awful time. Do you think they will ever forget that?"

Wayne Garrett said, "In the Mets' case, it was seeing us come from the bottom to the top. Plus, there was a lot of strife going on and we made people feel good, and they have passed that on to generations. All three team's championships gave hope to everyone. That lasts forever with people."

"The Jets, Mets, and Knicks back then made a shaky city less shaky," said David Garth. "One can't measure the impact those championships had on the morale of the city. Yes, the Mets win did help John Lindsay get reelected. But, everyone didn't vote for John Lindsay. I have to believe that these three teams did make everyone feel better about their lives during that period."

"We were a 100-1 shot at the beginning of the season," said Rod Gaspar. "The world loves an underdog. The three teams were all underdogs. You think people are going to forget that? As a matter of fact, all these years later people still ask me about my prediction on the 1969 World Series."

Jeff Greenfield gave some good insights, "Memorable sports events have an enduring quality. Certainly, the Jets and the Mets are more than just Super Bowl and World Series winners because of the character of Joe Namath, and the Mets going from last to first. The Knicks seemed to be more than just a team. With their mix of talented players, who all had dynamic personalities, and a terrific coach, they have become legend over time. Independently, any of the three stories would be pretty powerful in a community. If you put them all together within a space of less than a year and a half that's pretty good stuff. Add that to a city that felt itself under siege and you have a long lasting story."

"Being part of one of the three teams makes me very proud," said Dave Herman. "I still live in the New York area. I am so proud to have played for the Jets and Weeb Ewbank. To be part of that era where three teams won championships one right after the other is incredible. I have a great deal of pride for what our team accomplished. I can only imagine that players from the other two teams have the same feeling. We did it for New York. There's only one New York, and for it to happen the way it did was amazing. I don't think it will ever happen again."

"We were all underdogs," remarked Winston Hill. "People remember that and they remember how we won. Put together our victories and the times, and you have legacies."

Joan Hodges has a unique view of what happened then and the effects now. "As far as the Mets are concerned, the players all liked each other and the fans felt that they were a part of the team," said Mrs. Hodges. "It was a family and people felt that. Plus, the times were bad and the Mets made people believe again in things. The '69 Mets will always be part of history. Every player, coach and, of course Gil, will be remembered forever."

"The '69 Mets' win was a huge part of people's lives," said Ralph Kiner. "And, so were the Jets and Knicks. People have passed that on to their children and grandchildren. Sports have always been a common thread. That period of time in sports was what a New York fan dreams about. It was heaven."

"When we won right after the Jets and Mets it was so special," said Mike Riordan. "I thought if I was a sports fan back then, it was the best period in New York sports ever. Over the years, more and more people talk about that period. They remember those wonderful teams."

Cazzie Russell had this to say: "There were so many bad things going on back then." "The fact that all three teams won sort of buffered some of the stuff that was going on. As I put things into perspective, it makes it all more special. I feel very blessed to be part of history and part of the 1969–70 New York Knicks."

"There is a definitive legacy to all three teams," said Phil Jackson. "New York people are extremely loyal. They savor their children and these three teams were lost children. These teams were all miracles. They won by inspiration and by the support of their fans."

Clyde Frazier has a philosophical take on it. "For all the teams it was their first championship. There is nothing like the first in anything. First love, first child, it lingers on. Look at the players on these three teams and see how they gained so much respect from the fans over the years. And all of us have given back to the fans and the kids. We all have set good examples. Also, the era with all the turmoil and all three teams helped people forget about their troubles for a little while. People just don't forget that. It's been passed on over the ages."

Bill Bradley commented about the impact of the three teams and especially the quality of the fans: "It was first championships for all three teams," said Bill. "It was a special time, special moments, and special people. All three teams have their legacy. In the Knicks case, we played a distinctive way and the Garden crowd was astute to basketball. The fans would applaud the pass that led to the basket and not simply the dunk. The teams took people out of their daily lives in an inspirational way and they saw what we could accomplish. They felt that they could accomplish things because they saw what we did together. I think also people loved what they saw. It was good entertainment. It was something they realized they might not see again for a while. I think people remember the virtuosity itself on the court and that is unforgettable."

Andy Esposito, assistant editor of *Mets Inside Pitch* had this to say about the legacy. "Ask any American about the course of events in 1969 and three moments always stand out: Apollo 11 landing on the Moon, Woodstock, and the Miracle Mets. And what the Mets, Jets, and Knicks were able to accomplish for the city of New York that year is immeasurable, resonating to this day, a magical convergence of celestial entities arriving at the same championship destination.

"As a teenager growing up in Flushing, near Shea Stadium, it was my pleasure to witness some of these events unfolding firsthand. As the city battled civil unrest, mixed emotions regarding a faraway war, and a troubled economy, the ultimate underdogs won hearts and games and saved our sanity.

"There was something extra special about that band of brothers playing baseball, a bond which holds firm even now. It has also been my pleasure to witness that kinship, and of all the championship aggregations these eyes have observed after nearly twenty-five years of covering baseball, it is apparent that one of the reasons the 1969 Mets were able to overcome not only their opponents but a legacy of losing is their undying devotion to each other and to their manager, Gil Hodges.

"On a personal note, it has also been my pleasure to enjoy the company of these great athletes in their post-baseball careers. They were then, and still remain, the embodiment of a team."

"Fans today love the 1969 Mets," said Ed Kranepool. "From adults to kids, everyone related to the 'lovable losers.' Everyone related to being down and here was a group of guys who had been down for so long, but got up to rule the world. Everyone felt like they were part of it. They related to us then and still do today. It is something that will live on with everybody. The following of the '69 Mets have now is as big as it was in 1969. The legacy of the team is that people will forever remember every player's name on that team."

Jerry Koosman agrees, "Fans in New York City were starving for a team when the Mets came into existence. Along we came, sort of clowns for seven years, and overnight we turned an expansion club to world champions. It was significant that it came at a time in our country's history that was horrible. Because of that, the legacy of our team will be passed on forever."

"I think it's the fans," said Pete Lammons. "They remember. It's part of New York culture. The three teams will be remembered as long as people talk about sports."

"Things have changed in so many ways," commented Robert Lipsyte in giving an in-depth analysis. "To many people those three teams seem to be the last good years, so there is a special sense about those three teams. From a media point of view, I don't think the industry has ever had the kind of access to athletes they had then. Also, the kind of people you had on those teams only made them easy to talk to and people sensed that. Writers like myself will always go back to those times when the athletes not only made history in their sport, but made our lives easier because we were able to talk to them on a human level. There were so many factors. I don't think that in history so much has ever come together quite so well: the need of a country, the need of a city, the nostalgia of individuals, and the fact that all the teams had very attractive people in every way. There was a sense of collectivity. Free agency hadn't started yet. Why are there fantasy leagues now? Back in those days the Jets, Mets, and Knicks were the fantasy."

"In those years I was working as a sports reporter at Channel 2 in New York," said Sal Marciano. "With the darkness in the world and the city, to think that three New York City teams could all win championships for the first time within a short period of time really took over our metropolis. It was a source of pride. The Jets were second sister in town to the Giants. The Mets were second sister to the Yankees. And, the Knicks took basketball from a gymnasium game at the Garden where only guys went, and made it entertainment because of the make-up of the team and the way they played. I think most of all the three teams' popularity and success made them cross over the line from sports to entertainment. They made new fans in all three sports. They got women involved. If you saw Pearl Bailey at a Mets game you knew something was going on."

"People wanted good things to happen back then," said Don Maynard. "We can look back and smile because of all that happened then. New York fans remember. They never forget. We made history."

"Winning is always great," commented Joe Namath. "But, it takes people to win. Everyone on the three teams stepped up. Collectively it was incredible. Any underdog out there in the world has to appreciate what happened that year when they see someone from the back of the pack pull it off. We were all underdogs and people will never forget."

"I think because it happened in New York has added to the legacy," said Bobby Pfeil. "Those teams exemplified New York City. People remembered that and passed it on."

"We were all underdogs," said George Sauer. "I think those three championships were good for the people who followed the underdogs. All three teams gave people confidence to try something and say, 'You know, I can do it.'"

Tom Seaver explained his insights: "The fact that people are still writing and talking about the teams are indications of how they are perceived. No matter what else we did as individuals before and after, the fact remains that those of us who were part of those three teams are linked together in the memories of people who were there. The legacy of each team has been passed on to others by them."

"Not only have I remained friends with my teammates from the Super Bowl Jets," related Matt Snell, "but I have become friends with players from the 1969 Mets and the 1969–70 Knicks. We are all special, having been part of an incredible run of championships. One wasn't more important than the other. Each had its own importance. But, the truth of the matter is, it is part of New York City history; it has become folklore, and everyone I meet still wants to talk about it."

"Ours was one of the biggest upsets in sports history," said Mike Stromberg. "And, so was the Mets. The Knicks were underdogs, too. It was a one of a kind period in sports, and it happened in New York City. It was all like a fairy tale. It will still be a fairy tale years from now."

Ron Swoboda stated, "It was a period in New York City sports when everything seemed possible, and it happened. Three champions with their own legacy and yet, that time really is just one big legacy."

"We should be very proud of what we did," said Ron Taylor. "The fact that it has remained a historical Super Bowl, a historical World Series, and a historical NBA championship is important to us all. We take pride in having made it that way."

"It amazes me that I still get fan mail and to see the turnouts that come to see the '69 Mets at certain events is incredible," said Al Weis. "It's gratifying. I don't think we will ever be forgotten because we had such a great team. I figure Al Weis's name will be around a long time."

Mike Francesa gave an astute thumbnail analysis of each teams unique characteristics. "First of all, the Mets win was so unlikely. It created underdog heroes. People didn't realize how good the platoons were and how well they worked. I think the Mets proved if they could win, anything is possible. The 1969 Mets are one of the great Cinderella stories of all time. The Jet win is remembered because it is one of the two most important games ever played in the NFL. The first was the Giant/Colt game in 1958, which ushered in the modern pro football and TV eras. The second was the Jet Super Bowl win that gave the AFL a strong hand in the merger of the two leagues, and at the same time created the first real cultural crossover star in Joe Namath. And, the Knicks, because they were great talents able to mesh into one unit, are regarded and respected as one of the great teams in the history of the league. New York really liked the way that team played, the way the team went about its business. They had a sophistication, unselfishness, teamwork, and intelligence that the city was very proud of."

Cartoonist/journalist Bill Gallo wrapped it up nicely. "Those three season were collectively unforgettable. The events transcended sports.

There were people who never saw a football game, a baseball game, or a basketball game who followed those teams. You can't forget an era like that. Those seasons in sports are one of the most unforgettable seasons in history. Like the '27 Yankees, those three teams will be around forever."

Afterword

The word "legacy" is described in the dictionary as, "something handed down from the past, a heritage or tradition." To me, it simply means 1969–70. While I can't speak for any other player who was part of those magnificent seasons, I can only relate my story as I have experienced it. Life is about ups and downs, hoping your dreams come true. I can honestly say my dream came true. As a young boy growing up, my life was basically two things, following the St. Louis Cardinals or playing baseball with my friends. The dreams I had as a child were simple, play baseball as long as I was able to do it. To get an opportunity to play professional baseball was the result of all the days I practiced and played with my friends.

When I made it to the major leagues, I thought that it was the greatest thing that could ever happen to me. But, the fates were still with me when I was lucky enough to be part of a wonderful and incredible experience playing on the 1969 World Champion New York Mets. This wasn't just an ordinary team and it certainly wasn't an ordinary group of players.

The friendships I made on that team will be with me the rest of my life. In a strange way, 1968 was an important year for all of us on the Mets. Not only because we became friends, but because we learned that losing was not going to be acceptable. We knew what we had to do. The losing part of it was not fun, but in retrospect we became a closer-knit group. Humility always makes success that much sweeter. When we won the World Series the next year in 1969, all of us appreciated it more. We had lost together, but more importantly we won together. Considering the Mets' history, the way we won, the timing of it, our World Series victory can never be measured in simple terms. History might say that the 1969 Mets weren't the greatest team to win a World Series, but in many people's minds, we certainly are the most memorable.

One of the most gratifying aspects about the 1969 Mets is that while we had great players, in reality everyone on that team was important. As the years have gone by, even if the stories have been embellished a little bit, fans who meet us whenever we are together want to talk to every member of that team. Everyone on that team has become a household name. People have passed the story about the 1969 Mets on to other generations. It was a team where everyone, every player, every coach, and the manager, contributed to the success of the group. I truly believe that is the legacy of the 1969 Mets.

For the Jets and Knicks, I tried to give a realistic perspective of their importance to New York and to sports fans. All the players I spoke with on both teams have the same sense of achievement, camaraderie, and understanding of what they accomplished for themselves, their fans, and New York City.

As the years have gone by, other New York teams have won championships and, no doubt, others will also do so in the future. But most likely, there will never be another period of time when three professional teams from one city each win for the first time in their franchise's history, one right after another, and do so in a time where their city and country are faced with the enormous trials and tribulations of that era. No doubt, the legacies of the three teams will continue to endure forever because of the players, the teams, the settings, and the fans. Very simply, the 1969–70 Jets, Mets, and Knicks championships will always be remembered as The Magnificent Seasons.

FANS REMEMBER THE LEGACY

Fans are the reason any professional sports team exists. Not a very profound statement, but often taken for granted. The three New York championship teams had some of the most loyal, fanatical, best-educated, and loving fans you can find anywhere. Here are some of the thoughts about the remarkable legacies left by these clubs:

"The city was not feeling good about itself, and the country was not feeling very good about itself either," said Rudy Giuliani. So, you ended up with three teams carrying the name New York that at least in the case of the Jets and Mets, did the impossible. The Knicks did, too, but to a lesser degree. Their wins had a profound effect on the city. The fact that they were all first-time winners made it more appealing. It was miracles happening. Those teams gave the city a sense of pride and inevitability that things were looking up in my own life."

"The Jets, Mets, and Knicks back then were a dream come true," said Ray Romano. "Especially, the Mets. When someone mentions the New York Mets, I start thinking about 1969."

"Those magnificent seasons are some of the great moments in sports history," said Phil Rosenthal. "And, sports endure for people much more than movies or TV shows. People will always identify with their heroes from those teams. It goes beyond entertainment and becomes a metaphor for life, achievement, and the true potential of human beings. That's why those teams endure and have legacies."

David Halberstam added the following: "All the teams were a high. Within darkness, there was a light. The teams did allow people to feel a little bit better about themselves and about the city. All three are memorable and that will always last."

Andy Parton, vice president of marketing for Chase Bank, had these comments about the three teams: "As a kid those were the greatest seasons you could have because almost every team I followed won. It was a great time to be a sports fan growing up in Brooklyn. The customers of my bank turned into children when they meet the players from these teams. We're in a relationship business and building relationships is a long-term process. Every time we have done something related to sports using former players from those teams to entertain clients you see people's eyes light up, and they turn into children. When people are around players from those three teams they come back to a simpler time. It was a magical ride for everybody."

"It was New York City and the make-up of the teams," said Robert Wuhl. "The Jets had Broadway Joe, and with the Mets it was just a fantasy story because they were the 'lovable losers.' The Knicks were sheer professionalism. It was the way they played basketball. They played so smart. It's the myth of Willis Reed limping back onto the court, and Clyde Frazier, who was so stylish. It was great for a New York City sports fan. It was nirvana for New York. That will always be remembered."

Mario Cuomo had some thoughtful analysis of the impact these three teams created: "What the three teams did can't be measured. It's the American tale. You could never say it too much or remind yourself too often. The little people, the immigrants, and the poor built this country and all three of the teams represent that. It was reassuring about a lot of simple truths that are simply virtuous. The three teams epitomized operating against the odds. If you keep trying, if you keep pushing, it is possible you will win and win gloriously. What the three teams did was give people undeniable evidence of this. That's what it was. People would just say, 'If it could happen to them, why can't it happen to me?' All of this has memorability. It's part of the history of New York."

Former marketing director at Manufacturers Hanover Bank Charles McCabe said, "New York had been starved for winning teams and all three came together in that period. It was a fun time for sports in New York and people remember that. It was a very negative time and these victories were an oasis of happiness people could focus on. The players on those teams were, and are, a lot more approachable than today's athletes. Years from now people will feel the same about those teams."

Drew and Tracy Nieporent, famed New York City restaurateurs, were respectively sixteen and fourteen years old in 1969, and by then steeped in New York sports. "We went to the Jets games when they were the Titans. We went to the Knicks games when we could afford them. In 1962 we adopted the Mets and have every program from their history." When asked about what these three teams gave to the fans, here is what they concluded: "They were all underdogs that rose up and won against great odds. It is the character of all the players who made up those teams. They were people with great personalities. No one was making big money back then, and they had a greater appreciation of what they had accomplished. Fans related to all the teams. The players were more accessible and interacted much better than today's athletes. People remember and pass that on. Those three teams are teams for all generations."

Name Index